W9-BAJ-806

# NEED TWO

Published by St. Simons Press
P.O. Box 24378
St. Simons Island, Ga. 31522

Huckaby, Darrell
Need  Two
Copyright  1995
All Rights Reserved
Printed in the United States of America
September, 1995

First Edition

ISBN  0-9647867-3-7

# NEED TWO

Darrell Huckaby

# Author's Note

This is a novel. The characters and events depicted in this book are fictional. Any similarities between actual people or real life events are completely coincidental—or wishful thinking. Some people may think they recognize bits and pieces of themselves in this book, but again I say, this book is a work of fiction. Except, of course, for the part where we beat Notre Dame for the National Championship. That was real.

The two boys whose stories are told in this book are regular guys. Their thinking is not politically correct. They talk ugly at times, and think about girls, and one of them drinks too much. In short, they are a whole lot like most twenty-one year old Southern males. There are self-righteous and sanctimonious people among us, with poor memories, who would be quick to condemn these guys, and yours truly. But don't. They turn out all right. One of them even makes a preacher.

And if you simply must throw stones, please remember who should toss the first one.

*For Stump*

# Chapter One

December 27, 1980

Whit Johnson was asleep. He knew he was asleep and wanted desperately to stay asleep, because he was having the ultimate dream; the one all red-blooded male college students drift off to sleep hoping they'll dream. And as long as Whit Johnson could remain asleep, he had a chance to see what he could never hope to see in the real world. In his dream, Gladys Gibson was about to remove her wonderfully tight sweater to reveal that with which she'd been so generously endowed by her Creator. The persistent ringing of a telephone threatened to bring Whit back to consciousness before he got to see the twin treasures he'd spent so much time fantasizing about over the past four years. He could sense more than hear it. His subconscious mind struggled valiantly to remain asleep. At the very moment of truth, the telephone won out and chased his dream away, bringing him to the edge of wakefulness and leaving him in the exact same emotional and physical state all other encounters with Gladys Gibson had left him—frustrated.

"Damn," Whit muttered through his reverie, as he knocked over two half-filled glasses of water, one of which had green scum floating on top, and a clock radio, before successfully lifting the telephone receiver out of its cradle, finally silencing the hateful noise that had disrupted his most pleasant dream of the past two months. He held the receiver in his hand without speaking as he gazed at the green numbers on the disheveled clock radio, waiting for his eyes to focus well enough to read them.

1:45. A.M.

Whit took a quick inventory of the health status of his immediate family. There were no heart conditions that he knew of; nobody with any terminal illnesses that might have been thoughtless enough to kick the bucket while he was on the verge of scoring with Gladys Gibson. None of his family would have been out on the highway at this time of night to have been involved in a wreck. So it had to be Andrew Hawkins.

"Hold on Andrew, I got to take a whiz." Whit finally uttered those words into the mouthpiece of the phone and started for the bathroom without listening for a reply.

"Damn, Andrew!" were the next words out of his mouth. Whit had successfully navigated the pitch black bedroom, across an assorted array of dirty and semi-dirty underwear, socks, T-shirts, and sweat pants, in search of the bathroom door, when his left thigh slammed painfully against the sharp corner of his oak veneer dresser. He continued to swear under his breath as he limped into the bathroom, rubbing his newly bruised leg. As he began to drain his body, he couldn't resist the urge to lift up the Venetian blind above the small bathroom window, just above his toilet, and peer through the darkness at the trailer next door, thirty feet away.

"Well, I'll be damned," Whit thought aloud, having used his favorite curse word three times in the space of ninety seconds, a new record. The living room lights were still on in Mrs. Harrison's trailer next door, and Bobby Jacobs's pickup was parked outside.

Mrs. Harrison was the wife of the local funeral director. That is, she was soon to be his ex-wife. About two months earlier she had deemed it necessary to file for divorce from her husband. Late one evening, she had happened into the back room of the Rest Assured Funeral Parlor and found her husband, his secretary, two deacons from the Baptist church, and two women she didn't know cavorting around naked in the coffin room. Thankfully, there were no customers involved. Mrs. Harrison had moved out of the Funeral Parlor and into the River's Edge Mobile Home Community that same week and taken the double wide right next to Whit's.

She had been especially neighborly to Whit, who remembered her as his counselor during his Baptist training union days. During the recent Christmas season she had brought him fruitcake, sugar cookies, pumpkin pies, mulled cider, or some other treat almost every evening, as soon as he came home from his job at the hardware store. Ever since she had filed for divorce, she made Whit very uncomfortable. She dressed, smelled, and acted more like a sex-starved teenager than a forty-two year old lady who had taught Whit what scriptures he knew and made him feel guilty by warning him every Sunday and Wednesday night, throughout high school, against the evils of the flesh, thinking lustful thoughts, and spilling God's sacred seed through acts of self-abuse.

About a week earlier, five or six days before Christmas, Mrs. Harrison had called Whit on the phone at about 10:30 at night, right in the middle of the Kentucky-LSU basketball game. She said she was worried because she smelled gas and wanted Whit to come over and check for a leak. He had slid a pair of jeans over his gym shorts, put on his sneakers, and gone over.

Mrs. Harrison met him at the door, more out of than in a silky, black lace negligee. Her face was made up with heavy mascara, thick eyeliner, and bright red lipstick. The only light in her trailer came from two dozen glowing candles, placed strategically around the living room. *"Stairway to Heaven"* was playing on the stereo, and the whole placed reeked of

Boone's Farm Apple Wine. She threw herself into Whit's arms, shouted, "Make me scream, sweet boy," pulled his head down to hers with her right hand, squeezed a big handful of his rear end with her left, and rammed her tongue straight down his throat.

Whit was so startled that he bit her tongue. Hard.

She screamed.

Whit ran out of her trailer and back into his as fast as he could.

He called her on the phone and told her that he wasn't real good with gas, but that his friend, Bobby Jacobs, had worked for Napier Appliance ever since the two were in tenth grade together. Mrs. Harrison was very eager to get Bobby's number and his truck had been parked outside her trailer every evening since, but was always gone by 11:15. Bobby's wife, Jennifer, got home from her job on the second shift at the nursing home at 11:30.

Having taken care of nature's call, Whit let go of the blinds and wallowed back through the cluttered room to his bed and the telephone, which was still lying on the floor, with Whit Johnson's best friend and constant companion, Andrew Hawkins, presumably on the other end.

"What do you want, Andrew? It's nearly two o'clock in the morning. Are you in jail again?"

It was indeed Andrew Hawkins on the other end of the line.

"Naw, man. I ain't in jail. I ain't even drunk," was the offended reply.

Whit knew that last part was a lie.

"Andrew," he reasoned, "I was born at night, but it wasn't last night. Of course you're drunk."

"Well, I ain't real drunk," he argued. "You've seen me drunker."

"Well, if you're not in jail, what do you want? It's the middle of the night, and I've got to go to work tomorrow."

"Whit," pleaded Andrew, with desperation in his voice. "I can't stand it. We've got to go!"

"Go where, Andrew? For God's sake, it's 2 A.M."

"Go where? Go where? To New Orleans, Louisiana, you fool! To the by damn Sugar Bowl; where else? The Georgia Bulldogs are playing Notre Damn Dame for the National Championship of the whole United States of America in college football, and we're sitting here in Leesdale, Georgia." Andrew was on a roll now. Jack Daniel was pushing him along and telling him what to say, and he got louder and louder and more and more excited with every syllable.

"Listen, Andrew." Whit couldn't believe they were having this conversation in the middle of the night. "I've been telling you since the Auburn game, I can't go to New Orleans for the Sugar Bowl, and neither can you. For one thing, we ain't got tickets. For another, neither of us has a car that would make the trip. I have to work at the hardware store all week, and I don't even have money to go back to school this quarter. I'll be doing good to be back in by spring so I can graduate at the end of the summer. And you know your daddy won't give you a dime, not after you dropped out of school the way you did, and haven't even bothered to get a job because you think it might interfere with your drinking and carousing."

"Think about it, Whit!" He hadn't heard a single word. "New Orleans, Louisiana—Bourbon Street—Flaming Hurricanes—strippers—drunk coeds—and Herschel Walker and the Georgia Bulldogs playing Notre Dame for the right to say 'We're number one' for a whole year. Hell, Whit. We've got to go. We don't have a choice. We'll never be able to live with ourselves if we're not in the Superdome on New Year's Day."

"We'll see the game on television," Whit rebutted. "I don't drink, remember, so Flaming Hurricanes don't interest me. We can see strippers in Atlanta. Peachtree street is crawling with them. And all those coeds will be back in Athens next week, and they'll be just as drunk, and they still won't give us the time of day. Face it, Andrew. We just can't go. Now leave me alone and let me get some sleep."

"But you don't understand, Whit." Andrew's voice was quieter, and more serious. "I just saw a replay of an interview a national news guy did with some of those Catholic boys that play for Notre Dame. They said that this game was going to be the North's way of life against the South's. They said that Georgia hadn't played anybody, and that Southern football was overrated, and that the Southeastern Conference players were a bunch of pansies who were too stupid to get in real schools. One guy said that they would whip Georgia worse than Sherman had. He said he doubted any Georgia students would have enough guts to even go to the game, and that all Georgia fans really ought to just go on up to Appomattox instead of New Orleans, because we would be ready to surrender again by halftime."

Whit Johnson sat silently, staring into the dark without looking at or seeing anything, holding the telephone receiver loosely in his hand, his mind digesting the insults heaped upon his heritage by those damnyankee Notre Dame football players. Finally, Whit took a deep breath and spoke into the receiver. "Meet me for lunch tomorrow at the cafe, Andrew. We're going to New Orleans. We just got to figure out how."

Andrew Hawkins took a long sip from his glass of Jack Daniel's and Coca-Cola and grinned into the darkness of the upstairs bedroom of his parents' large and pretentious home.

"Hot damn," he thought, as he softly hung up his phone. "We're going to New Orleans!"

Whit decided to make one more trip to the john. By now his eyes had grown more accustomed to the darkness, and he escaped further injury along the way.

"Oh, hell," he thought, as he saw headlights turn into the narrow space between his trailer and the love nest next door. He saw Jennifer Jacobs, still in her nursing uniform, get out of her '72 Ford Torino and run up the steps of Mrs. Harrison's trailer, two at a time.

Before she could even knock, the door was thrown open, and there stood Bobby and Mrs. Harrison, arm in arm. Bobby was without a shirt or shoes, and was wearing only a pair of plaid pajama bottoms. Mrs. Harrison wore the matching top, completely open down the front, and nothing else.

Whit stood transfixed at the bathroom window, awaiting the fireworks. To his utter amazement, Mrs. Harrison threw herself into Jennifer Jacobs's arms, reached out with her right hand and pulled Jennifer's head down to her own, reached around with her left hand and squeezed a big handful of Jennifer's rear end, and stuck her tongue halfway down Jennifer's throat. Bobby pulled them both into the trailer and shut the door behind them.

Whit backed away from the window, and slowly let go of the blinds. He could only shake his head in disbelief at what he had seen and mutter to himself, "These are strange times we're living in."

Then he crawled back under the covers of his bed and began to toss and turn, trying to figure out a way to get to New Orleans and do his part, whatever that may be, to help his beloved Georgia Bulldogs achieve victory over the dastardly Yankee invaders from South Bend, Indiana.

"Me and Andrew are going to New Orleans, and it's going to be us against them," were his last thoughts before drifting off to sleep. Ugly Irish football players replaced Gladys Gibson in his dreams for what was left of the night.

It would be years before Whit Johnson found out that Andrew Hawkins had invented the whole story, and that there had been no televised interview with any Notre Dame football players.

# Chapter Two

"Is that my tip, boys?"

Whit Johnson and Andrew Hawkins turned their heads in unison at the sound of the familiar voice. Both knew from years of experience to turn their eyes to table level first for the most advantageous view of the long, golden legs that belonged to the owner of that voice. The two friends' eyes simultaneously traversed the familiar path, first resting on two wonderfully firm thighs for as long as they dared, and then following right on up to the hem of the tight white uniform skirt, lingering for a moment on the shapely hips, then briefly taking in the ample bosom, which threatened to pop buttons off the uniform blouse at any time, and finally, into the bright, brown eyes of the speaker, Bonnie Faith Dimsdale.

Bonnie Faith was smiling good naturedly, smacking, as always, on Juicy Fruit gum. Her face was painstakingly made up and her bleached blonde hair was its normal, tangled mess on the top of her head. She gave her undivided attention to the two young men seated in the corner booth at the Town Square Diner, known to everyone in town as simply, the cafe. Since it was Saturday, the lunch crowd was slim, which afforded Bonnie Faith a chance to visit longer than usual with two of her favorite regulars. Having totaled up the amount of their check, she tossed it on the table, put her pencil back in its customary resting place, behind her right ear, and leaned forward, propping herself on the table with both hands and crossing one foot behind the other. This maneuver caused her widely celebrated derriere to jut out at a most delightful angle. Bonnie Faith was able to provide the two lucky customers with an excellent view of her lovely breasts, which were straining against the lacy, white cotton fabric of the bra she intentionally bought a full size too small, and at the same time give all the other men who were lunch time regulars a chance to enjoy the breathtaking view of her marvelous legs and perfect bottom.

Bonnie Faith stared pointedly and with curiosity at the small pile of bills that was spread out on the red checkered table cloth, among the salt and pepper shakers, ketchup, Tobasco, and salad dressing bottles, packages of sugar, and dirty lunch dishes.

"In your dreams, Bonnie Faith." The speaker was Whit, who had finally forced his gaze upward from the waitress's cleavage and into her sparkling eyes. He grinned at her, and she matched his grin with one of her own. Although Whit had always considered himself painfully average in the looks department, and was in fact, very self conscious about the small pot belly he had begun to develop, Bonnie Faith had always thought he was "cute."

"Shoot fire, Bonnie Faith," broke in Andrew. "You ain't never gonna get a tip like that—not even as tight and short as you wear your uniforms."

"Oh, hush up, booger breath." Bonnie Faith stood up, turned, pulled her pencil from behind her ear, and tapped Andrew playfully on the forehead, all in one graceful movement.

Everyone thought Andrew was good looking. He was tall and lean with a naturally dark complexion and mischievous brown eyes that actually glistened. He would have made a great pirate, and had curly dark hair which he always wore a bit longer than fashion dictated, and a dark mustache. Andrew's mustache was his greatest source of pride. It had appeared above his lip while he was in the seventh grade, and he had cultivated it ever since. It had cost him a spot on the high school basketball team, and several mothers refused to allow their daughters to date such a physically "mature" individual. It had been a long-standing source of conflict between him and his father, but no matter what the cost, his mustache had always remained a part of him.

As for Bonnie Faith, she had been fueling the lustful fires of the patrons of the Town Square Diner for for nearly ten years—ever since she first took on a waitressing job at the age of fifteen. She was a town treasure, and all of the men that frequented the diner knew that with Bonnie Faith, the policy was "look at as much as you can see, and flirt all you want, but don't even think of touching." Otherwise, you might have to answer to her husband, Wayne, who was a former all-state linebacker, former Marine, and current 6'4", 285 pound, sawmill foreman at Walker Brothers lumber yard. Everyone in town agreed that Wayne Dimsdale was much a man, and not even Bonnie Faith's charms, which were considerable, would be worth crossing him.

"No kiddin', fellas. What y'all doin' with all that money piled up on the table?" Bonnie Faith's curiosity had been aroused.

Whit and Andrew looked at one another, each waiting for the other to speak.

Finally, Whit shrugged and ruefully shook his head before answering. "Bonnie Faith, that dinky little pile of bills represents the total assets of the two sorry individuals sitting here in this corner booth."

"Well, so what?" was Bonnie Faith's casual reply. "You boys don't need much money. Your mamas will feed you if you get hungry. You're both young and good lookin', and you both got your health. Just count your blessings and be happy with what you have, like I am."

This time Andrew spoke up. "You don't understand, Bonnie Faith.

Me and Whit need to get some more money up. Lot's more. We got to get to New Orleans by next Thursday so we can watch Georgia play Notre Dame in the Sugar Bowl. We might need as much as five-hundred dollars a piece, and right now all we have is forty-seven bucks between us."

"Five hundred dollars a piece!" Bonnie Faith was obviously startled. "That's nearly a thousand dollars."

"Close to it," Whit agreed.

"Right there at it," Andrew added.

Even with the generous tips Bonnie Faith picked up from the male patrons of the cafe, a thousand dollars was serious cash. "Why in the world y'all gonna need that kind of money, just to go see a football game?"

Whit had appointed himself accountant for this undertaking, and he began to read figures to Bonnie Faith from a paper dinner napkin. "Well, it's over a thousand miles there and back, and with gas being about a dollar and a quarter a gallon these days, we'll need  a hundred and fifty dollars just for gas."

"I'm taking my break, Regina," Bonnie Faith shouted to the young black girl who had just walked into the dining room from the kitchen. Catch my tables, would you honey?" Bonnie Faith was taking off her apron as she spoke and slid into the booth beside Whit and took the napkin turned ledger from his hand to study this high finance for herself. Then a thought hit her.

"Who's car y'all goin' in?  Whit, you know that old '68 Buick your daddy left you won't make it that far. You do good to make the seventy-five mile round trip to Athens and back in it every day." Then she smiled across the table at Andrew.

"Andrew," she teased. "Has your daddy done broke down and forgave you for totaling his Cadillac on Thanksgiving night?" She knew she would hit a nerve.

"Dammit, Bonnie Faith," Andrew sputtered. "A deer ran out in front of me. That's why I ran off the road. It could have happened to anybody."

"Oh, right, Andrew," was the skeptical reply. "And I'll just bet it was the same deer that caused you to run off the road three days earlier and total your Cutlass. I'll bet there's a killer deer out there somewhere, and he's got it in for Andrew Hawkins. He hides at the edge of the woods, just waiting for you to come down the old lake road at 3 A.M., drunk as a skunk, so he can jump out in front of you and watch you wreck."

Whit was rolling with laughter, enjoying this tongue in cheek tirade against his irresponsible friend to the fullest.

"Well for your information, Miss Smart Ass of 1980, we're going in my sister's car, so there."

"Terri Lynn Hawkins is going to let you drive her practically brand new Camaro to New Orleans, Louisiana? I'll believe that when I see it!"

"Well, you just be waiting by the highway about day after tomorrow, because we'll be heading out in it, just as sure as maple sugar's sweet."

"What did you promise her?" Bonnie Faith was suspicious. She knew Terri Lynn Hawkins too well to believe she would trust her fast and loose brother with her precious car.

"I didn't promise her anything. I just found these." Andrew held up a sheaf of invoices with McEver's Pharmacy's logo across the top.

"Those look like prescription bills to me," Bonnie Faith replied.

"They are. Six months' worth. My dad thinks he's been paying for asthma medication for his poor little baby girl. But I got a little lucky. I found out that he's really been paying for these all the time."

He reached into his jacket pocket and pulled out a round, pink container with a clear plastic dial on the front.

Bonnie Faith Dimsdale couldn't believe her eyes.

"You mean that sweet little girl has been on the pill? You could knock me over with a feather. I thought she was the leading candidate to be the last living virgin in Leesdale."

"Well, to tell you the truth, so did I," Andrew readily agreed. "But I was digging through her purse this morning, trying to find some money to -er - uh - you know - borrow - and lucky me - I found these, along with copies of the pharmacy bills. I think Mama and old Mr. McEver are in on it. She swore they were 'just in case,' you know, 'better safe than sorry,' but she sure didn't want Daddy to find out. Getting her car was easy. If she had any money left after all that Christmas shopping she did, I could have gotten it, too."

"Well, I'll be." Bonnie Faith couldn't bring herself to believe it. "Who do you think she's doing it with? I never knew her to go out with the same boy more than once or twice. Everyone just figured her for a Miss Goody Two Shoes. We all figured that after a date or two, guys would get fresh and try something and she'd just drop them because of it."

Whit remained untypically silent during this entire discourse, nibbling at the cold french fries that were left on his plate, and hoping that neither of his companions noticed the slow blush that was turning his ears a bright red.

"I don't know who the guy is who's responsible for Miss Goody Two Shoes going on the pill, but I know I'm driving her fancy red car to New Orleans." Andrew was in his element, thrilled at getting something over on his little sister, whom part of him dearly loved and another part of him deeply resented.

Whit saw an opportunity for a welcomed change in the conversation and went for it. "Not unless we find a money tree somewhere," he interrupted. "We still have this one little problem. If we don't get some money from somewhere, fast, we'll be watching Georgia play on television, like I've been saying all along."

"Well, shoot y'all. My daddy says you can see the game better on the TV, anyway. And Wayne hates Georgia. Ever since they promised him a scholarship and then gave it to that colored boy from Valdosta instead of him, he's pulled for Alabama. He couldn't bring hisself to be for Georgia Tech, no matter how mad he was at the Bulldog coaches. Wayne said that they just had too many pimply faced nerds at that school."

Whit and Andrew exchanged amused glances and winked at one another across the table. They both knew that Wayne Dimsdale had been an outstanding high school athlete who could do anything with a football, except autograph it. They had heard about all the letters Wayne had gotten from large schools, but weren't sure who had read them to him. They were also aware that you could get into the Marine Corps with a score of 500 on the SAT, but not college.

"Bonnie Faith, it's not just seeing the game that matters to me and Andrew. It's being in New Orleans to show our support for our school, and our state—shoot, for the whole South." Whit had taken it upon himself to try and explain the complexity of the situation and help Bonnie Faith understand why it was so important that he and Andrew be in New Orleans on New Year's Day. "Notre Dame represents the North; they've won the national championship lots of times. Why in 1961, they went for a tie against Michigan State and the Yankee press still voted them number one, ahead of Alabama, even though Bear Bryant's boys had a perfect record."

"All them folks from the North will be down in New Orleans, parading up and down Bourbon Street, looking down there noses at us—calling us ignorant crackers—laughing at the way we talk. Shoot, we could talk proper English if we wanted to, but some of our buddies would just think we were putting on airs."

Andrew broke in, "Yeah, Bonnie Faith. We got to be there to stand cheek to jaw with those Northerners and stand up for the state of Georgia and the South. It's way more than a game. It's our way of life against theirs."

Bonnie Faith's eyes danced and she waved her hand and laughed at them both. "Oh, you boys are so crazy. Whit here may really believe all that stuff about the South and the North. After all, everybody in town knows about his great grandpa, and how he got his leg shot off at First Bull Run and then fought on a stump and got killed in Pickett's charge at Gettysburg. But, shoot Andrew, you just want to party and you think the farther from home you get, the better chance you'll have of getting laid."

Andrew was genuinely offended. "Now you see here. I'll admit I take a drink now and then, and I do like to party, and I don't cull much in the way of women; but I'm as big a Bulldog as anybody. I'd want to be at this game just as bad if they was playing it in the Methodist Church parking lot."

"OK, OK," Bonnie Faith tried to make peace. "I swear, I know you two are both crazy about them Dogs. I'd ask you if you had Bulldogs painted on your drawers if I wasn't afraid you'd drop your trousers and show me. But I think y'all are wrong about them Yankee people bein' so hateful. When I was up north, everybody was sweet as pie to me."

Andrew and Whit looked at one another.

"Bonnie Faith, when did you ever go up north?" they asked in unison.

"Why, when Wayne was still in the Marines, back before we was married. He was stationed at Camp Lejune, and I spent a whole week up there in North Carolina. I couldn't have been treated better."

"Bonnie Faith, are you on break or on vacation? If you don't get your butt back to work soon, I'll have to retrain you." The voice of Leon Huff was gruff, but everyone knew he held no real malice toward his best waitress and number one good will ambassador.

"OK, Leon. Don't get your shorts in a wad. I'm coming."

Bonnie Faith slid across the vinyl cushion of the booth and stood up, tugging on her short white skirt in an unsuccessful attempt to get it down to at least a somewhat respectable length. She smiled at her two friends and winked. "Good luck, fellas."

Before the boys even realized what she had done, Bonnie Faith picked up their lunch check, reached inside her shirt front, and tossed a ten dollar bill onto the pile of money, which was still spread across the cluttered table. Before they could protest, Bonnie Faith was gone— smiling at her customers, smacking a fresh piece of Juicy Fruit, and leaning much further across tables than necessary, to pour sweet iced tea into half full mason jars—the better to show off her most pleasing assets.

Whit stood up, too, scooping up the pile of money, which had grown to fifty-seven dollars, thanks to Bonnie Faith's generosity. He took one last swig of now watery tea, as he looked at his watch. "I got to get back to work, Andrew."

"But we didn't accomplish a thing," protested his best buddy.

"Hell, yes, we did," retorted Whit. "We got a free lunch, a free peek down Bonnie Faith's shirt, and ten dollars more than we started out with. I told Mama I'd come eat supper with her after work, and help take down her Christmas tree. Borrow your mama's station wagon and meet me at the trailer park at about eight o'clock."

"No chance," Andrew answered. "If I know your mama, she'll be feeding you fried chicken, creamed corn, mashed potatoes, and homemade biscuits, with milk gravy. Tell her to set me a plate and I'll meet you at her house at six o'clock. And I'll be driving Terri Lynn's Camaro, not any old station wagon. I'm getting all the mileage I can out of these," he said, patting his sister's purloined package of birth control pills that he'd returned to  his jacket pocket.

"Don't press your luck, man. See you at six. Hey, don't you think you ought to give those back?  I mean, isn't she supposed to have one every day, or something?"

"Why do you care?"

"No reason, man. Just asking. See you at six."

Whit, his ears beet red again, hurried out the door. Andrew stayed seated in the booth, a sly grin on his face, sipping what was left of his tea, trying to figure out a way to get his hands on some quick cash, and stealing whatever glances he could at Bonnie Faith's  rear end.

"Damn, Andrew. You gonna sit in that booth all day? You stay any longer, I'm going to charge you rent." It was Leon.

Andrew gave him a grin and a friendly salute with his middle finger. "I'm gone, Leon." The Christmas bells attached to the door frame jingled behind him as the door swung shut.

# Chapter Three

Whit Johnson was in a melancholy mood. He hummed to himself as he carefully removed the string of faded glass beads from the scrawny little scotch pine that had served dutifully as Mary Johnson's Christmas tree. He remembered helping to place that very string of colored beads on a place of honor on the family tree every Christmas of his life, and how his father, now four years dead, would sit in his recliner in the corner of the room and admonish him, "Be careful with those beads, boy. They're real glass you know. Why don't you let your mama put them on?"

Whit turned intuitively, his eyes falling on that same chair, and he could almost see Big Whit Johnson sitting there, dressed in his blue twill work pants and cotton pullover shirt, a glass of who-shot-john in his hand, taking a drag off one of the unfiltered cigarettes that finally killed him.

Whit would never forget that night as long as he lived—the last night of his father's life. It was the first Friday in September, Whit's senior year in high school. It was supposed to be Whit's big year. His teammates had elected him captain of the football team in a team meeting in the field house, just before the opening game pep rally. He had finally earned a starting position at tight end, after three years of warming the bench and holding for extra points.

He showed the team that he deserved their confidence that night by catching a twelve yard dump pass for a touchdown, with ten seconds left in the game against Mayfield County, and then throwing the key block on the two point conversion, to allow Nate Jones to score, and give Leesdale an 8-7 win.

Later that night, his high school sweetheart, Tammy Sue Willis, rewarded Whit by agreeing to leave the sock hop early to go parking out on Airport Road. She even agreed to climb into the roomy back seat of the '68 Buick Electra 225 that Big Whit Johnson had let his son drive, and lie down while making out. While not a first for Tammy Sue, it was certainly a rare concession.

Whit could tell that being a starter was going to be much better than being a bench warmer when Tammy Sue actually allowed his hands unprecedented freedom to wander at will inside her sweater and under her skirt. He knew better than to try anything more, but when he dropped her off at her house, just before her midnight curfew, Whit was the picture of contentment. He had a hickey on his neck, a warm stain on the inside front of his jeans, and a smile on his face. As he drove toward his house, in the part of town known as "the mill village," Whit couldn't imagine life ever being any better. He was at peace with the world.

Whit parked his father's Buick in its normal place, in the back yard. As was his custom, he walked to the edge of the yard, unzipped his pants, and urinated on the kudzu vines that threatened to take over the yard each summer. Something just felt right about using the bathroom outside on a cool, clear, starlit night.

Whit had been in bed for about an hour, with no hope of falling asleep. His mind was too full of all the exciting events of the day—the pep rally, the game, the unexpected liberties he'd been allowed to take with Tammy Sue. Who would even want to sleep, with so many wonderful things to think about?

He heard the toilet flush in the one bathroom of his family's small, clapboard, mill house, and then heard heavy footsteps heading toward the kitchen. Whit knew that his dad would be sitting at the kitchen table in his underwear, lighting up a smoke. He decided to join him in the kitchen and talk about the game. He knew his daddy would have words of praise for his performance—more so for the big block on the conversion than the touchdown.

Just as Whit's feet were hitting the floor, he heard a loud and sickening thud out in the kitchen. Whit's whole world had just changed without his knowing it. He ran into the kitchen and found Big Whit Johnson, all 285 pounds of him, lying face up on the kitchen floor, wearing only his boxer shorts. One hand clutched a package of cigarettes; one hand was on his chest. There was an agonized expression of surprise and pain on his face—his eyes were wide open—and he had been as dead as a hammer handle when he hit the cold linoleum of the kitchen floor.

The next few days, and in fact, the rest of Whit's senior year, had seemed like a horrible dream. He went through the motions of high school life in a fog, as things around him got worse and worse. Whit's only sibling, an older sister, was living at Ft. Sill, Oklahoma with her husband, who was an army artillery instructor. Whit and his mother were all alone, and he had to take on more and more responsibility.

Big Whit Johnson had not been able to get life insurance, even through the group plan at the cotton mill where he worked, because of the 285 pounds he carried on his five foot-six inch frame, and because of the fifty unfiltered cigarettes he smoked each day. The family's entire life savings had gone to pay for the funeral, even the U.S. Savings Bonds that Big Whit and Mary Johnson had been purchasing each month, by payroll deduction, since the Thursday after Little Whit was born, in hopes of allowing him to be the first child in either of their families to attend the University of Georgia, or any other college for that matter.

Football, which had been the most important thing in Whit's life for the past four years, and the biggest bond between him and his father, became meaningless.

After the fifth game of the season, he had felt he had to quit the team and go to work in the mill to help make ends meet at home. After the sixth game, Tammy Sue had felt she had to quit him to go out with Nate Jones. Nine months to the hour after their first date, Tammy Sue gave birth to an eleven pound, three ounce baby boy, whom she named Nathaniel Davis Jones, III, but who had the extreme misfortune of having to make his way through life, known to one and all as Little Nate.

"What the hell you daydreaming about, kicking Notre Dame's ass, or all the honeys we're going to make it with while we're way down yonder in New Orleans? I been giving it some thought, and just for the sake of experience, I might try to score with one of them Yankee women, at least if I run across one that shaves her legs."

Whit wiped a tear from the corner of his eye and forced a grin onto his face before turning around to face his friend.

"Hell, Andrew. If we even make it to New Orleans, your only hope of getting any will be your old steady, Rosie Palm."

Whit was glad to see Andrew Hawkins standing in the doorway of his mother's living room. He had a hard time being blue when Andrew was around.

"I went over our figures with a sharper pencil, and we're not quite as bad off as we thought we were. I've got all the expenses down on paper. Help me finish with this tree and I'll show them to you. Here, you take these icicles off."

The two made small talk about Georgia's chances of actually winning the big game, as they finished taking the tinsel, lights, and ornaments off the little tree. The wonderful smell of chicken frying and biscuits baking drifted into the room from Mary Johnson's kitchen, making them both eager to get through with the task at hand and sit down to supper.

"Look at this." Finished with the task of undecorating the tree, Whit sat down on the brown and beige plaid sofa that was six years older than he was. Andrew joined him, and they both studied the yellow sheet of paper that Whit held in his hand. It was covered with all sorts of figures and mathematical scribbling. Toward the bottom of the page was a neat list of words and figures.

"Here's what we'll need to get by." Whit pointed at each item on the list with the pencil he had picked up from the coffee table in front of them. "Gas—$150. Lodging—$100. That's two nights in the cheapest hotel we can find."

Andrew interrupted right away. "Wait a minute, Whit. We can't stay just two nights. The game is Thursday afternoon. We won't be able to drive home afterward. And we need to get there at the very latest by Tuesday at supper. Monday would be better. We got to soak up the atmosphere—pick up some women—get it on with some of them damnyankee Notre Dame fans. We got to have time to get our minds right for the game."

"And Whit," Andrew added, not a little unlike he was explaining a math lesson to a small child, "I doubt we'll find a place in the French Quarter for under a hundred dollars a night."

"The French Quarter?" Now Whit was about to lose his patience.

"Yeah, man. That's where all the action will be."

"Look Andrew. . ."

Andrew held up one hand to stop him. "All right, we'll compromise. Put down $200 for a room and if we come up with extra cash, we'll head for New Orleans sooner."

"Well, we'll see. I'll say two hundred. We have to eat, but we'll eat cheap. We'll eat a lot of hamburgers and get by on $15 a day. That's $50 each, or a hundred dollars for food, if we're gone three days."

"We have to drink," Andrew interjected. "And we have to help young ladies drink. After all, we will be representing the South, so we'll have to be chivalrous."

"I put down fifty dollars apiece for entertainment and extras. If you want to drink up all of yours, that's up to you. But after you spend fifty, you're on your own."

"Only fifty?"

"Andrew, this is bare bones financing, remember? Right now we don't have anything."

"All right, all right. How much are we up to so far? And I agree. It's like we said. Everything's fifty-fifty. We're completely in this together." Andrew, for once was dead serious.

"So far, that's $550, and that's everything except tickets, and I have no idea how much we might have to pay for those. Face value is $17. I say we don't go over $100. That's six times face value. If we don't get them for that, we go back to the hotel and watch it on television. We can still be in the crowd before the game and celebrate with the rest of the Georgia people afterward."

"I'm going to see the game, Whit. If I don't do one other thing before I die, I'm going to see that game." Andrew was adamant.

"Well, the bad thing is, the very least we can get by on is seven hundred more dollars." Whit tried not to sound too hopeless.

"Wrong. You obviously forgot to count the ad money." Andrew pulled a folded wad of bills from his right pocket and counted out two fifties, four twenties, and two tens. "Two hundred big ones for my main man."

"Where'd that come from?" Whit was glad to see the money, but was very, skeptical of the source.

"I told you, its ad money."

"What are you talking about, Andrew?" Whit was beyond skepticism and on the verge of suspicion.

"I just sold some ads for next year's football program." Andrew's answer was as casual as if he had claimed to have picked up a little extra money mowing lawns.

Whit took a deep breath, leaned back against the cushions of the sofa, and put both hands behind his head, interlocking his fingers. "Tell me exactly what you're talking about, Andrew," he said, but he was fairly certain that he didn't really want to know.

"It was easy, man. The cheerleaders are always in charge of selling advertising for the high school football program. They usually do it in the spring. Terri Lynn was captain of the cheerleaders last year and was in charge of keeping track of the ad sales. You know how organized Little Miss Perfect is. I remembered that she kept all her records in this one big folder, and she never throws anything away. I just dug around in her closet this afternoon until I found it."

"You sure do snoop around in her room a lot." Whit interrupted without meaning to, and hoped there wasn't any trace of anxiety in his voice.

"So what, she's just my kid sister—what's it to you?" Andrew looked at Whit sideways and cocked one eyebrow.

"Nothing, nothing at all. Just an observation. Go ahead. Tell me the rest of your sordid story."

"OK. So I went through the records, right? I found out that almost all of the places that bought ads either cut a check for the ad when they agreed to buy it, or had the school bill them later. But, six or seven places paid cash on the spot."

"Andrew, you didn't really?" The tone of Whit's voice said that he knew he really did.

"Like shooting dove over a baited field, man. I just took last year's program into all those places that had paid cash, told them I was helping my kid sister sell ads, and that we were getting an early start this year. Hell, none of them knew she was a senior last year. They just remembered how cute and sweet and responsible she was. Damn, I hate that word—responsible. Four of those old coots couldn't give me their money fast enough. 'Just renew my quarter page,' they said. The manager was out in two others. I'll get another hundred Monday morning."

Whit just looked at his buddy in disbelief. He finally managed to ask, "What happens in the spring when the cheerleaders come back and hit them up for real?"

"Oh, get real, Whit. Those old guys can't remember from week to week who they give money to. They will have forgotten all about me and sign up for another quarter page."

Whit needed to think about this. He got up off the couch and walked over to the fireplace. He turned his back to the hearth and enjoyed the warmth of the gas logs on his hands and backside.

"I got us some more money, too." Andrew dug deep into his other pocket and added another wad of bills to the rapidly growing pile on the coffee table. "Three hundred more dollars to be exact."

Whit was absolutely afraid to ask where that money had come

from, but knew he had to, anyway.

It was obvious from Andrew's expression and demeanor that he didn't want to tell him, but he also knew he had to.

"Well, this is a hundred and fifty dollars each from Calvin Clarke and Hoss Mitchell. It's their part of the gas and lodging."

This was way too much for Whit to even consider. "Damn, Andrew!" he exploded. "I'm pretty sure I ain't going to the Sugar Bowl with money you swindled from local merchants, but I'm for damn sure I ain't going to ride a thousand miles with Calvin Clarke and Hoss Mitchell.

"Now, I like Calvin all right, and he was a good guy and all when we played football together, but he's colored. I ain't going to pal around for three days and stay in the same hotel room with a colored boy.

"And Hoss Mitchell! My God, Andrew, what were you thinking about? Hoss Mitchell must weigh four hundred pounds. He hasn't had on a shirt that would cover his belly in four or five years. He's the grossest person I've ever known. He farts right out loud, in front of girls and grown ups and everybody. You remember the time he threw up in the punch bowl at the senior class prom?

"And he stinks, too. I don't mean sometimes. I mean every time I've ever been around him. Last summer, when my sister was in town, I took her two kids over to the petting zoo. Hoss was there with his little cousin. They came over to where we were petting the goat, and he smelled so bad, the damn goat ran away. Climbed way up on top of his little building and wouldn't come down 'til Hoss had been gone about fifteen minutes and the air had cleared up. And besides all that, last year, after we had lost to Wake Forest, Hoss showed up all around town wearing a Georgia Tech baseball cap. No sir, Andrew. We ain't going to New Orleans with Hoss. Or with a colored boy, neither."

Andrew was lying on the couch, holding his sides, rolling with laughter. "Boy, you're a piece of work, Whit. You can sit in the stands at the Superdome next week and pull like crazy for a black man to help your team win a national championship, but you won't ride to the game with one. No wonder all those Yankees say we're prejudiced. Hell, we are."

"It ain't the same thing, Andrew. I ain't got nothing against colored people, but . . . " Whit let his voice trail off, too honest to try to add an ending to his sentence, when he knew there was none to add.

"Well, don't worry, Whit." Andrew sat back up on the sofa and wiped his eyes, still tickled over his friend's reaction. "Neither Calvin or Hoss is really going to the game with us."

"Andrew, are you drunk already? You don't make a lick of sense. You're talking out of your head. First you tell me Calvin and Hoss gave you three hundred dollars to go to the game with us, and then you say neither one of them is going.   You're talking in riddles,  and you don't even seem drunk."

"Look here." Andrew's arms were folded in front of him. "Have you ever heard the story of the three little pigs?"

Whit could only look at him. He was convinced that the person on the couch had completely lost his mind.

"Well," Andrew continued, "in *The Three Little Pigs*, the pigs kept telling the big bad wolf that they would go with him to buy turnips, pick apples, and visit the county fair. They would set a time to meet, then the pigs would just leave every morning about an hour before the wolf was supposed to show up. We'll just tell Calvin and Hoss to meet us one morning at about seven. We'll leave at six. When we get back we just say we thought, since they didn't show up, they had changed their minds and decided not to go."

"Oh right, Andrew. I'm sure they'll be just fine with that. And they probably won't even think to ask for their three hundred bucks back. It will probably just slip their minds altogether. Are you plumb crazy? Calvin Clarke will cut us with a knife, and then Hoss Mitchell will sit on our faces and stink us to death."

"We'll have the money when we get back," Andrew stated.

"How do you figure that, Andrew?"

"Coors Beer."

"What?"

"Coors Beer."

"Oh, I see." Whit walked to the middle of the room and started pounding his fist into his open hand to emphasize his words. "You've been drinking Coors Beer. Coors Beer makes you hallucinate. That's why you're talking completely out of your mind."

"No, dumb ass," Andrew answered. "If you'd loosen up and take a drink every now and then, you'd realize that Coors Beer is not licensed for sale east of the Mississippi River. It's not really any better than any other beer, but since its not available here, people want it, and they'll pay about three times what they pay for other beer to get it."

Whit was terribly afraid he was beginning to understand a method to Andrew's madness.

Andrew continued. "We take two hundred dollars of this money and spend it for our trip." He held a hundred and two fifties in one hand and picked up a hundred dollar bill in the other. "Then we buy a hundred dollars worth of Coors with this. We bring the Coors back, sell it to these old boys around here, and bingo—we've got the money to pay back what we owe to Calvin and Hoss, so they don't have to cut us or sit on our face."

Whit slowly shook his head. "That's called bootlegging, Andrew.

They'll put us under the jail for that."

"You don't have to go through customs to get through Mississippi and Alabama, Whit. They'll never catch us."

"Yeah, that's what you thought when you stole that stupid Coke machine from the Little League concession stand and put it on the front porch of the Pepsi place. I had to get up in the middle of the night and bail your sorry ass out of jail." Whit couldn't resist an opportunity to needle his friend about a college prank gone bad.

"For your information smart ass, I didn't think at all. I was drunk. And you didn't bail me out of jail that night. I had to sit there with muggers and rapists and thieves until ten o'clock the next morning. I was scared to death that I was going to start looking good to them. Besides, the Little League people entrapped me, leaving that gate open like that with a pair of hand trucks right beside the machine."

"Well, me and Mama had to sign a property bond to get you out, and the judge didn't get in until nine. Besides, I thought it might have done you some good to spend a night in jail, but I'm not sure it did."

Whit turned back to the fireplace, propping his elbow up on the low mantle, deep in thought, his gaze fixed on Big Whit Johnson's old pocket watch, which was displayed there in a glass dome.

He slowly turned and met the eyes of Andrew, who was sitting on the edge of the couch, staring solemnly at his friend, wondering what his thoughts were. Whit let his eyes drop to the pile of bills on the coffee table, and then raised them back to Andrew's.

"Does it mean that much to you, Andrew? Is going to a football game, even this one, so important that you'll lie to people you've known all your life, and cheat, and steal, and break the law to get to go?"

Andrew dropped his head slightly and thought about the question for a moment. Then he let his gaze meet Whit's and he never blinked an eye as he answered, "Damn straight." Then he continued, "Look, I know I've been a screw up and never seem serious about anything. But I'm serious about the Bulldogs. Being Georgia fans are about the only thing my daddy and me have ever had in common. Georgia football is about the only thing we ever talked about, back when we were still talking. I've been a Bulldog all my life. I was born a Bulldog and I was raised a Bulldog. We've never been in this position before, and we may never be in this position again. It's a once in a lifetime shot, and I aim to be there, no matter what. How about you?"

Whit waited a long time to answer. "Yeah, me too." He pointed with his eyes across the room, to a framed snapshot of his father, taken in Athens, many years earlier, wearing a red shirt and a black cowboy hat. "You know, Daddy dropped out of school back during the depression. He only finished the ninth grade. He worked hard in the cotton mill all his life and we have never had much of anything. We could never afford to have tickets to Georgia games and go to Athens and on road trips like your family and some of the others. I'd never been inside Sanford Stadium until you invited me to a game in the tenth grade.

"But Daddy loved Georgia football as much as anybody. From the time I was old enough to remember, we would listen to the games on the radio together, and he'd tell me about what he called the 'Glory Days.' He'd talk about Charlie Trippi, and Frank Sinkwich, and Catfish Smith, and Wally Butts. He told me about being in Athens when Georgia beat Yale in the first game ever played in Sanford Stadium. He said that after the game they all tied fifty-five gallon drums to the back of their cars and rolled them over the cobblestone streets.

"Whenever he could get a Saturday off from the mill, he would take me to Athens and we'd sit on the railroad tracks and look down into the stadium to watch the game. He bought an old transistor radio at a yard sale, so we could keep up with the game better. Our tailgate was a Spam sandwich in a paper bag and a fruit jar of iced tea.

"Daddy used to always tell me, 'Boy, one day Georgia's going to win the National Championship. They're going to play in a bowl game somewhere, with everything on the line, and no matter what I have to do, you and I are going to the game.' "

Whit paused and looked across the room, his eyes taking in all the furniture and books and knickknacks that had not been moved since the night Big Whit had died, four years earlier. Then he turned back to Andrew.

"I had just about given up on being at the game. It's been all me and Mama could do to get by, and to keep me in school. Me graduating from Georgia was Daddy's biggest dream of all. There was no place I could turn for any extra money. When you called me last night, though, it got me all worked up again. The more I thought about going, the more I wanted to go—the more I needed to go—for me and Daddy. And I'll do anything to get there. I guess I'd even stay with a colored boy and smell Hoss Mitchell's farts, if it came to that."

Mary Johnson backed slowly down the hall, hoping that her son and his best friend had not heard her coming in from the kitchen to call them to supper, and hoping against hope that they would never know that she had overheard them both explaining why they needed to go to what she had thought of until now as just another football game. She picked up a towel from the kitchen counter to wipe away the tears that had welled up in her eyes as she'd been reminded of her late husband and one of the few passions he had known, in a hard life that had ended far too soon. She took a deep breath, managed to put a semblance of a smile on her face, and made as much noise as she could coming back down the hall to the living room.

"Supper's ready, boys. Fried chicken and hot biscuits. Come and get it."

As Mary Johnson, Whit, and Andrew bowed their heads to return thanks, as was the custom before all meals at the Johnson home, all three people at that table prayed for a way to get money to finance the boys' trip.

# Chapter Four

The two buddies stood in the back yard of Mary Johnson's house, their stomachs full, enjoying the feel of the crisp December air.

"Man, Whit, your mama sure can cook. I don't ever remember having a meal like that at home. Why in the world do you live by yourself in that dumpy old trailer when you could stay here, and eat like a king every night?"

"I love my mama too much to live with her." Whit grinned. "I stayed here the first two years after Daddy died, and by the end of the second year, we were at one another's throats all the time. I moved out to keep peace in the family."

"I guess there's no chance she could help you out with any money for the trip?"

"Don't even think about it, Andrew. She has a little bitty pension from the mill, and social security. She does good to get by, and she already feels guilty because she can't help pay for school. No, that's not an option. How about your folks? Have you asked them for any money?"

Andrew stood with his hands deep in the pockets of his jeans, staring at his shoes, as if he expected them to do tricks. "No," he finally said, still examining his feet. "I know Mama would give me the money, but then she'd have to catch hell from my old man about it, and I won't put her through that. I'm sure my dad thinks he's teaching me a lesson. He says it's for my own good. He took away my credit cards and vowed not to give me another penny until I could show some responsibility. There's that damned word again."

"All I did was total a couple of cars, and run up a seven hundred dollar phone bill, and flunk out of school. Hell, anybody could have a bad month. Besides, fall quarter is tough, with football season and all. It's hard being a fan and a student too, especially when your team is undefeated. I bet I would have passed with flying colors if we hadn't gotten Herschel. I had an easy 2.2 last fall when we were 6-5."

Andrew couldn't be serious about anything for long. He looked at Whit and grinned. "I'm going to show my dad I can be responsible, but not 'til after the Sugar Bowl."

Whit grinned back. "Well, at least your mama keeps you riding in style. You want to drive that big old station wagon over to the trailer and watch TV?"

"No thanks, man. Actually, I'm taking it back to her now. The Hendricks twins are picking me up at the house. Their brother is home from the Air Force, and the twins are going back to Auburn tomorrow, so they're having an all night keg party at their family's lake house. Free beer and both Hendricks twins. A guy would have to be crazy to pass that up. I'll catch up with you sometime tomorrow. Maybe I'll get lucky tonight, and when I see you tomorrow I'll be able to reveal the age old secret, which Hendricks twin has a mole on her tush."

"Well, tell them to watch out for that killer deer on the old lake road. And don't do anything I wouldn't do. And if you do, name it after me."

Whit was technically watching television in the small living area of his trailer, but neither his heart, nor his mind were in it. He was racking his brain for a way to get his hands on some cash, preferably a legal way.

He kept drawing blank after blank.

So far he had ruled out robbing a bank, because he was too chicken; having a yard sale, because he didn't think he had enough to sell; selling blood, because he was too chicken; and selling sperm, because he didn't think he had enough to sell. He had also ruled out driving to Atlanta to stand on Peachtree Street and beg, because he didn't have any clothes that were dirty enough or time to grow a three day beard.

Hearing a car pull up outside his door, he walked over and peeked through the crack in the living room curtains to look out the window. He was surprised to see the Ford station wagon that belonged to Andrew's mother parked outside, right beside Bobby Jacobs's pickup. Whit wondered two things at once. "Is it family night again at the trailer next door?" and "Was Andrew stood up by the Hendricks twins?"

Whit forgot both questions when he realized that Terri Lynn Hawkins, not Andrew, was driving the LTD wagon.

In a state of near panic, Whit raced through his cluttered kitchen, down the narrow hallway, and into his bedroom, which was at one end of the trailer. He grabbed a clean shirt from his small closet and went quickly into the adjoining bathroom. He frantically tried to spray his underarms, brush his teeth, gargle, coax his hair to lay down, and put on the clean shirt; all in the twenty or thirty seconds it took Terri Lynn to get out of her car and walk up the three steps leading to Whit's front door.

He made it back through the trailer and answered the door on the second knock. Terri Lynn Hawkins stood on his front stoop, looking as beautiful as ever. She walked in without an invitation, closed the door behind her, took off her coat, dropping it on the floor, threw her arms around Whit and gave him a long passionate kiss. Then she stepped back and smiled.

"Hey, Whit," she said. "What cha doing?"

Whit Johnson and his best friend's sister had become lovers six months earlier, quite by accident, at least on Whit's part. He had called Andrew to invite him swimming at the YMCA Camp outside Leesdale, where Whit worked for the summer as a swimming instructor. It was a Saturday afternoon, and the camp was between sessions. Whit had the whole camp, including the lakefront swimming area, to himself.

Terri Lynn had answered the phone at the Hawkins residence. When she recognized Whit's voice on the other end of the line, she told him that Andrew was in the shower, and offered to deliver a message. When Whit told her what he wanted, Terri Lynn asked if she could come along, too.

Whit had never given a second thought to Terri Lynn Hawkins. Even though she was only three years younger than him, she was always just "Andrew's kid sister." If he ever had occasion to picture her in his mind's eye at all, he pictured her as she had been the first time he'd met her, a skinny eleven year old with pigtails, braces, and glasses.

Whit had been looking forward to a nice long afternoon, swimming and lazing around on the dock, swapping lies with Andrew about sexual conquests that each had dreamed of, claimed to have made, but hadn't. The last thing in the world he wanted was to have some big eared and loose mouthed child around, cramping their style.

But Whit was too nice a guy to tell a kid she couldn't come swimming. So he answered Terri Lynn's request with, "Sure, I guess so. Tell Andrew I'll be down at the waterfront."

That message was never delivered.

About an hour later, Whit was floating around on an inflated tractor inner tube, his eyes closed, half-asleep, soaking up the sun and wondering why Andrew was taking so long to get out to the camp. He sensed, rather than heard, someone standing on the dock, watching him float around. He expected to be knocked off the tube at any moment by one of Andrew's famous cannon ball belly flops. When he wasn't, he opened one eye and peeked through the bright rays of the afternoon sun at the figure standing on the dock.

What he saw was a vision. No other word could describe Terri Lynn Hawkins, as she stood above him, having suddenly bloomed into full fledged womanhood. The longest day of his life, Whit would not forget how absolutely gorgeous she looked, standing on the edge of the dock, smiling down at him.

She was wearing skin tight, very short, cut off jeans, a white T-shirt, tied in a knot on the side, the better to show off a firm, flat stomach, and the sexiest belly button in existence, an inny. Her brown eyes were sparkling clear, her long, golden brown hair, which was the color of honey, was tied with a bright yellow ribbon and pulled back into a ponytail. It reached almost to her waist. Her skin was smooth and tanned and without a blemish. Her body was firm and toned and curved in exactly the right places.

The vision spoke, and her voice sounded as sweet as the honey which matched the color of her hair.

"Hey, Whit. What cha doing? Andrew couldn't come. I got my new car yesterday, so I drove myself down here. Can I come swimming?"

Suddenly conscious of how ridiculous he must look, wearing bright orange jams and lying spread eagle across the giant tube, Whit rolled off into the water and came up sputtering, wiping his eyes, and smoothing down his hair. He felt a little less conspicuous hanging onto the side of the tube. "At least," he thought, "my pot belly isn't showing."

Finally, realizing that his guest was waiting for a reply, Whit stammered, "Uh, er, sure, Terri Lynn. Do you have a suit?"

"Sure do," she replied. "I got it for my birthday, eighteen years ago."

Whit stared up from his vantage point in the water, in total disbelief. The woman-child before him slipped her leather sandals off her darkly tanned feet, untied the knot in her shirt, and pulled it over her head. She slid her shorts over her perfectly rounded hips and down her long, tanned, legs. She stepped out of the shorts and stood there for a moment—a magnificent young goddess in all her naked splendor—then dove head first into the water.

The rest of that afternoon had been every man's fantasy, lived out. And for the six months that ensued, Whit Johnson and Terri Lynn Hawkins had gotten together whenever they could do so discreetly. Both went on occasional dates with other people, but each saved their hearts, souls, and bodies for one another. At least Terri Lynn saved her body, and Whit tried hard, for the most part.

Even after half a year, Whit couldn't believe that someone as sweet and smart and beautiful as Terri Lynn could be attracted to someone as—well, average—as he was. Whit had examined himself over and over, trying to find something special about his appearance. He was of average height, average weight, had average looking brown hair, and average looking blue eyes. His facial features were average and so was his body. No other word could adequately describe Whit Johnson's appearance. Terri Lynn Hawkins was anything but average, and Whit always felt inferior around her. If she ever noticed, she never mentioned it.

"I'm doing as little as possible," Whit finally answered. "I didn't expect the pleasure of your company tonight. I thought you had some family gathering at home, to celebrate your cousin's birthday or something."

"I do," she said, taking Whit's hand and leading him over to the couch, where they both sat down. "I made up a story about having to run out and get some pantyhose for church tomorrow, before the stores closed. I had to stop by and give you a Christmas present."

"Christmas was three days ago, Goose, and you already gave me a present." Whit reached under his shirt and pulled out the fourteen carat gold cross and chain that Terri Lynn had given him.

"Well," she replied, "now I'm giving you another one." She leaned forward, kissed his nose, and tucked a neatly folded one hundred dollar bill into his shirt pocket.

Whit felt the blood rush to his face, and he had to struggle with himself to control his emotions. He stood up from the couch and walked to the center of the room, turning his face away from his girlfriend and staring unseeingly out the window. He swallowed hard before speaking. "No way, Terri Lynn." His voice was quiet, but firm, as he fought to control his anger. "I don't want your charity."

"Besides," he added as an afterthought, "I thought you told Andrew you didn't have any money."

"I didn't," Terri Lynn replied quietly, her eyes not leaving his still flushed face. "Daddy gave me my allowance tonight. Besides, I didn't want to give Andrew any money, even if half of it was going to you. Daddy's right about one thing. Andrew spends money like a Democrat in Congress, whatever that means. I just wanted to do something special for you."

"Now, how do you think that makes me feel, Terri Lynn? I live in this trailer and you live in one of the biggest houses in town. You're one of the prettiest girls in history, and I look like I look. We both say we love each other, but we have to sneak around to be together, because your daddy would pitch a fit if he knew you were dating somebody from the mill village. Boy, that's a hell of a note. I'm good enough to hang out with your daddy's son, but not his little girl."

"Whit, you know how my daddy is. I can't make excuses for him, and I can't change him. We've talked about this over and over. I've wanted to tell him, lots of times, but we both agreed we'd wait until this summer, after your graduation. If he found out now, he'd forbid me to see you. He'd watch me like a hawk and it would be even harder for us to get together. If he cut my money off, like he did Andrew's, I could never stay in school."

Whit turned and smiled at Terri Lynn. She was an absolute angel, and he couldn't stay mad at her for long. "He'd never do that," he stated softly, "but of course, you're right."

"It won't be that much longer." Terri Lynn sounded more sure than she felt. "And when he finds out I'm dating Whit Johnson, Georgia graduate, it will be completely different than if I were dating Whit Johnson from the mill village. I know that makes absolutely no sense, but Daddy doesn't have to make sense. He's just Daddy."

"Well, I appreciate the thought, but I won't take your allowance money. If Andrew can't have any of your daddy's money, I can't have any either, not even from indirect sources. You're letting us drive your car. That's help enough." Whit walked over to her and playfully put the hundred dollar bill down the front of her shirt.

Terri Lynn's bright brown eyes clouded, and she pursed her lips, as if deep in thought. She suddenly stood up, picked her coat up from the floor, and started slowly toward the trailer door. She turned at the door and addressed Whit over her shoulder. "You know, Whit, maybe you've been right all along. Maybe it is wrong to keep our relationship a secret." She reached into her jacket pocket and pulled out the birth control pills and the phony pharmacy receipts that Andrew had returned to her that evening.

"I've probably been wrong all along to lie to Daddy and spend his money all this time under the pretense of having a medical problem. My asthma's been cleared up since I was twelve. I'm certainly not ashamed of you. I should be proud to have him know about us. I think I'll go home right now and tell him the whole story, including why I've needed these pills. If he can't trust my judgment, I guess I'll just have to be on my own, too, like Andrew."

"Terri Lynn, you wouldn't dare." Whit wore half a smile, thinking, but not certain, that his girlfriend was just putting on a show.

She fished the folded bill out of her cleavage and held it out toward him, between two fingers. There was a smile on her lips, but none in her eyes. "Just try me, sweetheart."

"Now this don't make a bit of sense." Whit tried to reason with her one more time. "Andrew blackmailed you with those pills by threatening to go to your daddy. Now, you're blackmailing me with those same pills, by threatening to go to the same daddy. That don't make no sense at all."

Terri Lynn smiled more warmly, but her eyes were still serious. "I would have let y'all have my car all along. I just needed an excuse so Andrew wouldn't get too suspicious. Lucky thing I left these pills and receipts where Andrew could find them, instead of where I usually hide them.

"Andrew would never have the nerve to go to Daddy with these. Of course, I, on the other hand, would. Andrew was bluffing. I'm not. I want you to go to the Sugar Bowl game, and I want to help you."

Whit knew when to give up gracefully. He walked over and gently took the money from her hand and stuffed it in his pants pocket. He put one hand around the small of Terri Lynn's back and kissed her gently on the lips. "I love you," he said softly.

"Me, too—you. But Whit, spend my money on a ticket to the game. Don't give it to any of those hookers or strippers or other wild women down on Bourbon Street."

"Sweetheart, you know I don't even think about any other girls."

"Oh yeah? Then why do you have a stack of *Playboy* and *Penthouse* magazines hidden under the cushions of that sofa over there? And why did you tell Andrew you dreamed about making it with Gladys Gibson three nights in a row last week? Andrew's not the only person who can do any snooping around our house."

Whit knew he was turning red, and tried to come up with a reply, but could think of none. He could only look at her and blush.

"It's all right, honey." A twinkle had returned to Terri Lynn's eyes. "I don't mind if you read the menu. Just remember, you're on a restricted diet." She turned and left quickly, without another word, or a goodbye kiss.

Whit stood at the open door, watching her drive away.

Just as he was about to close the door and return to his television set, a black Chrysler New Yorker pulled up, and parked right behind Bobby Jacobs's pickup. Peter Paul Harrison himself, wearing a dark suit with a carnation in his lapel, got out and walked up the steps leading to the trailer of his estranged wife.

Whit stood transfixed, telling himself he wouldn't be surprised by anything he saw.

He was wrong.

The door of the trailer opened wide and the scene that met Whit's eyes looked like Halloween night at a whore house. Mrs. Harrison was dressed like Wonder Woman, in red tights, a short yellow skirt, fishnet hose, a cape, and no top.

Jennifer Jacobs was peeking around Mrs. Harrison and she had on stiletto heels, a garter belt, opera hose, a bow tie, a black mask,  and nothing else.

Bobby Jacobs was also standing in the doorway, dressed like Zorro. He wore a black cowboy hat, mask and cape, black leather shirt, Spandex pants, and thigh high leather boots.

Bobby reached out and shook Peter Paul's hand, and welcomed him into the trailer. Mrs. Harrison noticed Whit standing at his door, his mouth agape.

"Hey, Whit," she called, in her most neighborly voice. "I got my gas leak taken care of."

"These are strange times we're living in," Whit said to himself, shaking his head and going back into his trailer, closing the door tightly behind him.

# Chapter Five

On a good day, sloppy would be a grossly inadequate word to describe the deplorable domestic condition of Whit Johnson's living quarters. On the last Sunday of 1980, the tidiness of this dwelling had hit an all time low.

In the kitchen, every inch of available space, including the stove top, sink, table, and counters, was covered, with pots, pans, dishes, glasses, cups, and silverware. There were empty soup and Coke cans, food wrappers, pizza boxes, foil dinner trays, junk mail, magazines, unopened bills, Christmas cards, and crumpled wrapping paper, three levels high and overflowing onto the floor. The garbage can looked like a volcano that had erupted, spewing trash over its side and across the kitchen floor instead of molten lava.

Cleanliness was not a top priority with Whit, and had in fact, failed to even make his top ten list. He enjoyed telling people that he cleaned his house every month, whether it needed it or not. In reality, this was just a boast, and his cleaning binges were much less frequent. He rationalized his lack of good housekeeping habits by pointing out that every single time he had ever washed dishes, they were dirty again after only one use.

His normal modus operandi was to sacrifice one whole day, when it became absolutely necessary, to put his kitchen in some semblance of order. He would then use his dishes, pots, and pans until they were all dirty. Then he would switch to paper plates, plastic cups, and food that could be prepared and eaten in its original container. He would never clear the table. He just pushed things back until he had cleared a space large enough to accommodate his pie pan, frozen dinner tray, or sack of fast food de jour. In short, Whit's kitchen looked like it belonged to a twenty-one year old college student, who lived alone.

Getting from Whit's kitchen to his living area involved stepping from the cheap, soiled linoleum of the kitchen floor onto the cheap, soiled carpet of the living area. The living room, in its own right, was just as cluttered as the kitchen. The stereo unit, which sat against the wall, just to the left of the front door and right under the front window, was piled high with cassette tapes, record albums, and a collection of anything that Whit might have had in his pockets over the past month. This display included gum wrappers, match books, toothpicks, scraps of paper, cash register receipts, and lint. Album covers and plastic tape cases were strewn on the floor all around the unit.

The one chair in the room, which was just to the right of the front door, was piled high with a large assortment of sweat shirts, jackets, caps of every description, three towels, and a football. Determining that the object was indeed a chair was not an easy task, and actually sitting in it was out of the question.

There were sneakers, sweat socks, ripped jeans, and T-shirts tossed randomly around the room. For the literary minded, there were books and magazines of every description, as well as a week's worth of newspapers scattered over the floor. The coffee table was littered with half empty Coke cans, paper plates which held the stale remains of unidentifiable food, a deck of cards, dogeared and worn from a thousand games of solitaire, and $657 in assorted bills.

On the television, which held down a place of honor in one corner of the small room, Barney and Andy were trying to figure out a way to get rid of several dozen jars of cucumber pickles that tasted like kerosene, without hurting Aunt Bea's feelings, and on the couch, Whit Johnson, master of this domicile, was wrapped up in two blankets, holding his stomach, and moaning, hoping death would come quickly and put him out of his misery.

Whit's pain, which he assumed was just a world class stomachache, would begin in his lower abdomen and then rise, increasing in sharpness and intensity, until it reached a crescendo, seemingly at the top of his stomach. Just as the pain neared the outer limits of Whit's threshold, it would subside, leaving him to wait fearfully for the next wave.

He had experienced a similar attack about three weeks earlier. The previous bout with his lower digestive tract had occurred late at night, and had been so painful that he had actually called Andrew to take him to the emergency room at Leesdale General Hospital. That experience in itself could be a fate worse than death.

Whit and Andrew concurred that the emergency room staff they had encountered had surely undergone extensive training in torture techniques from survivors of the Hitler Gestapo. These public servants left no stone unturned in their mission to discover Whit's entire medical history, from conception to the night in question. One totally committed ward clerk got especially upset when she couldn't get Whit to admit, even under the most excruciating cross examination, that he knew what had killed his paternal grandfather, seven years before Whit had been born.

The most intense questioning was done by Head Nurse Joanna Bahlraccker. She refused to allow Whit's chart to be seen by anyone who could do him any good until she was absolutely, positively, one hundred percent certain that he was fully covered by an insurance company whose

payment record met her excruciating standards, and whose total assets
were equal to or greater than the gross national product. She made Andrew
verify his coverage also, "just to be on the safe side." She had also made the
boys sign an oath of allegiance to the United States and swear that neither
they nor any of their relatives or ancestors had ever been  involved in any
plots to overthrow the federal government. "Confederate veterans," she explained, "don't count."

By the time all the paper work was complete, and by the time Whit
had endured the obligatory ninety minutes of sitting on an examining table
with his shirt off, the pain had gone away. The emergency room doctor had
examined him anyway, of course. He told Whit that he had been suffering
from indigestion and not to eat greasy food close to bedtime. The hospital,
naturally, sent him a bill for two hundred dollars, to cover his insurance
deductible. It lay somewhere on the kitchen table, smeared with peanut
butter and ketchup, unopened.


Whit was sure he had the same problem this time, and was determined to ride it out on his own couch, under his own blankets, without
facing the intimidating Nurse Bahlraccker, and without paying two hundred dollars.  But the pains were even more severe and more frequent on
this Sunday morning than they had been three weeks before.

After downing about a fifth of thick, pink medicine and suffering
mightily for over an hour, Whit's pain had finally subsided enough to allow
him to fall asleep on the couch. When he awoke, a couple of hours later,
George Kennedy was massaging Paul Newman's shoulders on the television set in the corner, trying to help him win a bet by eating fifty boiled
eggs. "What we have here is a failure to communicate," Whit said aloud,
happy to be able to watch one of his all time favorite movies, *Cool Hand*

*Luke*, for about the umpteenth time.

A cold rain, which sounded like it had sleet mixed in, was beating a tattoo on the aluminum roof of the cluttered trailer. The noise was so loud that Whit's telephone rang several times before he realized it. "Wonder if that's Andrew," he thought as he dug the receiver out from under a pile of discarded socks and T-shirts and said, "Hello," into the mouthpiece.

"Hello, yourself. I figured I'd catch you at home. I guess you didn't go to church this morning?" It was Mary Johnson, trying very hard not to sound judgmental and self-righteous, and failing miserably.

"No, Mama, I didn't; but I talked to God, and He said I could be excused because I have a stomachache." Whit began to remember all too clearly why he had felt the need to move away from home, even if it had meant spending money that could have gone toward books and tuition.

"Did you go to church, or did you go to that other place you've been going every Sunday and Wednesday?" Whit could have bit his tongue. He honestly didn't mean to add that last sentence, but it just came out.

"There's no call to be hurtful, Whit, and I think you're being sacrilegious, too. Earl Dobbs is a good man, and the people at *The One and Only Church of the Holy Spirit* have been real good to me. I'm glad I found it, and I wish you'd come go there with me some Sunday."

"Well, what language did you speak today, or was it your week to translate? I hope nobody got snake bitten."

"Damn," he said to himself. "I can't believe I said that."

Whit truly loved his mother, and admired and respected her. He wouldn't intentionally hurt her for the world, but he simply could not understand her religious fluctuation.

When he was growing up, Whit and his family attended the small

Methodist church in the mill village, as did most of the families who earned their livelihood in the local cotton mill. The Johnsons, other than Mary, were sporadic in their attendance, but were there enough to be counted as regulars of the flock by the rest of the congregation.

During high school, Whit began to occasionally attend the more fashionable Leesdale Baptist Church, mostly because Andrew went there. Most of the time he spent at the church was of a social, rather than spiritual, nature.

After his father died, Whit got mad at God, since he had no one else to blame for his loss, and rarely attended church anywhere. His mother, on the other hand, began looking desperately for something to fill the void in her life. She felt like she needed something that didn't remind her of her years with Big Whit, which the Methodist church did.

She apparently found what she was searching for among the good people of the local "holy roller" congregation. The One and Only Church was founded by a former meat cutter who "got religion" while attending an Amway convention in Macon one summer. His church started as a Wednesday prayer circle for members of the Methodist church. The prayer circle quickly evolved into an independent church which met in an abandoned school house on the edge of town.

All the members referred to their church as "Reverend Dobbs's church" and the self-proclaimed and self-ordained minister was the sole administrator and interpreter of doctrine. Those in the congregation couldn't become full members of the church until they could prove that they had found "It," whatever "It" was, to the satisfaction of reverend Earl. Their services were big on hallelujahs, raised arms, fainting spells, speaking in tongues, and monetary contributions.

Reverend Earl was keeper of the treasury, with keeper being the operative word. The funds of the church were distributed at the sole discretion of Earl Dobbs. In the six years since Earl had quit working at the local grocery store and started working for the Lord, he had moved from a five room frame house to a four thousand square foot home in the country, complete with swimming pool and tennis court, and had traded in his four year old Pontiac for a bright yellow Porsche. "Good things happen to those who love the Lord," was Earl's motto.

Whit finally broke the long silence.

"I'm sorry, Mama. No, I haven't gone out all day. I had another one of those bad stomachaches, but its gone now."

"Well," his mother answered, "I just wanted to let you know that I'm not going to be at home today, in case you decided to stop by. I'm going to run up toward Atlanta. I need to go to the mall. I'm going to come by and see you this afternoon. I'll bring you some Jello. It will make your stomach feel better."

"OK, Mama. I love you."

"Now that is curious," Whit thought, as he hung up the phone. "I can't believe that she would drive to the mall on a terrible day like today, especially with it being Sunday. She never believed in shopping on Sunday, not even before she found 'It' at Earl Dobbs's church."

Whit looked out the window where the wintry mixture had turned to all rain. "Well," he thought, "at least she'll be warm." He allowed a little bit of pride to temper the shame he felt for deriding his mother's chosen place of worship.

Throughout the fall, Whit had, with great effort, saved as much money as he could for his mother's Christmas present. He had put a big empty pickle jar in the corner of his bedroom and made a concerted effort to stash as much money as possible into the jar. If he ate at McDonald's, he'd skip ordering fries and put fifty cents in the jar. He'd skip having a Coke in the afternoon and bring home thirty cents to add to his savings. He'd stop by the University library and look at the latest issue of *Playboy*, instead of buying his own copy at the bus station, and put two dollars in the jar. Whit was delighted when, the week after Thanksgiving, he rolled all his coins and counted all the bills. He had accumulated $185. He still hadn't a clue as to what to buy with the money. Then one evening, he stopped by his mother's house just as she was bringing groceries in from her car. It was an unusually cold day for December in Georgia, and Mary Johnson's faded old coat looked like it provided hardly any warmth at all. Whit knew immediately what he would buy with his savings.

He had Terri Lynn meet him at the mall that very evening. Her instructions were to pick out the warmest coat Rich's sold, in his price range. Together they agreed on a full length leather trench coat with a rabbit's fur lining, on sale for $178 plus tax.

Whit had never been prouder, and his mother had never been more surprised, than when she opened her gift on Christmas Eve. They both cried, and neither said anything for a long time. Mary Johnson finally spoke, and as usual, her thoughts were of her departed husband. "Oh, Whit," she said. "Now I'll be warm all winter. Don't you wish your daddy could see me in this coat?"

Whit's thoughts returned to the present as he looked around the cluttered disaster area that was his home. "Oh well," he thought. "I guess I'll spend this afternoon cleaning up this pig sty. It looks like I'll have to wait until this evening to find out which Hendricks twin has the mole."

Whit walked over and looked out his living room window to see if the rain had let up. He stood there and watched Peter Paul Harrison's big black New Yorker drive up next door. Peter Paul, who was driving, got out first, and then walked around and opened the front passenger side door to let his wife out. He then opened the back door and Jennifer Jacobs swung her long legs out and to the ground. She exited the car, followed by her husband, Bobby. All three were dressed in their Sunday finest, as if returning from services at the Baptist Church, which in fact, they all were.

"These are strange times we're living in," Whit muttered to himself, as he turned off *Cool Hand Luke*, and went to work reclaiming his trailer.

# Chapter Six

"Well, unless someone wants to perform heart surgery in here, I'd say that's good enough." Whit was very pleased with himself as he surveyed what two hours earlier had looked like a scene from the six o'clock news, depicting tornado damage.

The visible part of the trailer's living area had undergone a remarkable transformation. All adult oriented literature, including magazines, videos, and other contraband had been stored safely out of sight. Four giant trash bags of disposable toxic waste, otherwise known as Whit's garbage, were stacked behind the trailer. The dishes were washed and put away. The dirty clothes were thrown onto the waist high pile in the bedroom closet. The place looked as close to presentable as it was ever likely to look. Whit just hoped his mother didn't open either of the bedroom doors, and heaven forbid she should need to go to the bathroom.

While taking out the trash, Whit noticed that the mercury in the metal Coca-Cola thermometer on the side of his trailer had inched up to thirty-eight degrees, and the rain continued to fall steadily.

Thankful that he'd had no recurrence of his curious stomach ailment, Whit sat down on the newly accessible couch and propped his feet up on the temporarily clutter free coffee table. He picked up several sections of the Sunday issue of the *Atlanta Journal-Constitution*, which was stacked neatly beside the couch, and started looking through it for the second time that day.

He reread Lewis Grizzard's column, which on this day was about the mayor of Atlanta, Maynard Jackson, 'hizzoner' as Grizzard called him. Whit laughed harder than he had the first time he read the column. "That's telling them, Lewis," he thought to himself. "You keep giving them hell." Putting aside the Metro section, which other than Grizzard, held no interest for him, he lost himself in the special Sugar Bowl section that was a supplement to the sports page.

He closely examined every article concerning the two teams. He tried to memorize rosters and statistics and diligently studied comparisons of the strengths and weaknesses of the two teams. "Well," he finally admitted to himself, "they have the tradition, and the Pope, and they may even have a better football team, but we've got Herschel. And if Herschel don't get hurt, they ain't gonna beat us."

Herschel was Herschel Walker, Georgia's wonderful freshman running back. The target of one of the fiercest recruiting wars in Southern football annals, Walker had delayed making a decision about which college he would attend for nearly two months after national signing day. Some reports said that Herschel's mother, tired of all the attention, actually sent him to his room on Easter Sunday morning and told him not to come out until he had made up his mind between his two finalists, Georgia and Clemson, a South Carolina school a scant ninety miles from Athens. Legend had it that a lucky coin toss brought Herschel and his considerable talents to Georgia.

Walker didn't even start Georgia's opening night game against SEC rival Tennessee, in Knoxville. In fact, he was listed as third string tailback on the Georgia depth chart, and many, including Bulldog head coach, Vince Dooley, voiced an opinion that Herschel might have been overrated.

Late in the third quarter of that first game, which was being played on a sweltering night in early September, with Georgia trailing 16-2 and in possession of the ball on the Tennessee sixteen yard line, Walker was given a chance to play. On his very first play he was given an inside hand off, hit a hole in the line, and literally ran over a Tennessee defensive back, bowling him over and stepping squarely on his chest in the process. He then split two other Tennessee defenders at the goal line to score a touchdown on his very first collegiate carry.

Larry Munson, Georgia's excitable play by play announcer, known all over the South for his unique style and especially descriptive calls of big Georgia plays, was almost out of control, even for him, on the touchdown. He started screaming, "My God Almighty," and "Oh my God" into his clear channel microphone. Thousands and thousands of people across the South heard the call, and the Herschel Walker legend was born.

Later that night, Walker scored what would turn out to be the winning touchdown, and Munson never even told his audience he had scored. He simply shouted, "Herschel, Herschel Walker, Oh, you Hershel Walker!" into the mike, and all those people depending on the radio waves to bring them news of the game could only assume that Herschel Walker had become synonymous with a Georgia touchdown just that quickly.

Radio stations all across the state of Georgia broadcast replays of Munson's calls throughout the week following the Tennessee game, and by the time Georgia played their first home game against Texas A & M the following Saturday, interest in Georgia's freshman running back had reached fever pitch.

Walker didn't disappoint the crowd. Late in the game, which Georgia was winning by a big margin, he broke off tackle and outran the whole Aggie defense, for a seventy-two yard touchdown. Larry Munson didn't disappoint his listeners, either. The pattern he had started the week before of simply using Walker's name to signify a Georgia score became a tradition, as he never called the long run a touchdown. It was just, "There goes Herschel, there goes Herschel." The Georgia fans loved it.

The opportunities for the growing number of Bulldog faithful, both diehard and bandwagon variety, to hear that particular call were numerous, as Walker led his team to victory after victory. Going into the eighth game of the season, Georgia was still undefeated, as were their opponents, the University of South Carolina Gamecocks. South Carolina also featured an outstanding running back, George Rogers.

A seventy yard run by Walker gave Georgia a 13-10 lead early in the fourth quarter, but in the closing moments of the game, South Carolina appeared to be driving for the winning score. They were already in field goal range when George Rogers fumbled. Georgia recovered to preserve the victory and remain undefeated.

The next week brought the annual big game between Georgia and the Florida Gators, which had been played in Jacksonville's Gator Bowl since one day before the dawn of time. The Gator Bowl was a neutral site, as neither team played there during the regular season, and the seventy thousand seats were evenly divided between Bulldogs and Gators. Students and fans from the two schools began arriving in Jacksonville toward the middle of the week, to renew old acquaintances, party, and get their minds right for the business at hand. In fact, the game had become such a social event that it was known as the "World's Largest Outdoor Cocktail Party." Few of those who had actually experienced the game, and it was to be experienced, not witnessed, would dispute that title.

On this particular Saturday, Georgia had risen to number two in the national collegiate football polls, and only Notre Dame was ranked higher. Ironically, Notre Dame was in Atlanta that day to compete against Georgia's arch rival, the Georgia Tech Yellow Jackets. Georgia Tech had won but one game all year, so the best most Bulldog fans dared hope for was to finish the day where they started, still ranked second. Many Georgia fans wouldn't have wanted Tech to have the satisfaction of a victory over Notre Dame, anyway.

The tide of the game flowed back and forth, but late in the day it looked like Georgia's perfect season was about to come to an end. In spite of a seventy-two yard Herschel Walker touchdown run and 238 yards rushing by the freshman sensation, Georgia trailed 21-19 with less than ninety seconds to play and were backed up on their own seven yard·line.

But on third down, God smiled on the Bulldogs. There could be no other explanation. Georgia quarterback Buck Belue was almost tackled in his own end zone for a safety, but managed to scramble away from the Florida linemen and roll to his right. Throwing on the run, he completed a pass to  split end Lindsay Scott. The Florida defender who was covering Scott  fell down, allowing Scott to cut across the field and run down the far sideline. To the agony of the Gators, the delight of the Bulldogs, and the utter amazement of all, Lindsay Scott outran everybody and scored an improbable ninety-three yard touchdown, giving Georgia a 26-21 victory.

Larry Munson got so excited in the broadcast booth that he quit describing the play and started begging Lindsay Scott to run. As Scott was running down the sideline, Munson started bouncing up and down in his chair. The closer Scott got to the goal line, the harder Munson bounced. By the time Scott scored, Munson's chair—"a metal steel chair"—as he described it, lay in  pieces on the press box floor. Munson's description of that play  became his most famous call. That play became the biggest in Georgia football history.

And if any more proof were needed that God was wearing a red and black hat that day, up in Atlanta, lowly Georgia Tech tied mighty Notre Dame, 3-3. Georgia had taken over the number one spot in the polls and hadn't even had to suffer the indignation of a Tech win.

Georgia remained number one for the remainder of the regular season, and victories over Auburn and Georgia Tech gave them an 11-0 record, a Southeastern Conference title, and a chance to play Notre Dame in the Sugar Bowl to secure their first national championship.

Herschel Walker set NCAA records for a freshman by rushing for over 1600 yards and scoring fifteen touchdowns. Many thought he deserved the Heisman Trophy, which is awarded to the most outstanding football player in the nation each year, but which had never been given to a freshman or a sophomore. Senior George Rogers of South Carolina, whose fumble had allowed Georgia to hang on to their win over his team, won the award.

"What an incredible season," Whit thought. "And Herschel's just an eighteen year old freshman. Lord, I can't wait to see him when he's full grown."

"But can we beat Notre Dame?" Whit took one more look at the Notre Dame roster, filled with too many unusual names of too many players with numbers like 6-8, 322 beside their names.

"If God would let us beat Notre Dame," Whit reflected, "it would almost make up for Gettysburg."

He tossed the sports section on the coffee table, and dozed off to sleep again.

# Chapter Seven

A persistent knock on the trailer door ended Whit's catnap. A glance at the window told him it was still raining hard. He jumped up from the couch and hurried to answer the knock. Upon opening the door, Whit found Mary Johnson standing on the front stoop, in the cold rain. Her hair was protected by a clear plastic rain bonnet, the inexpensive gift of a local politician. To Whit's surprise and disappointment, she wore her old faded and threadbare overcoat on the nastiest day of the year.

"Come in the house, Mama, where its warm." Whit ushered his mother into the trailer, taking her coat and rain bonnet, and depositing them over the back of the newly accessible chair."

"Your trailer looks nice," his mother commented, looking around the tiny room. "I hope you didn't spend all afternoon cleaning up on my account."

They both knew that he had, and they both knew that the fact that he had pleased her very much.

"When are you going to take that silly old flag down?" His mother indicated the large Confederate battle flag which hung on the wall, behind the couch.

"Never, Mama. Haven't you heard?" Whit asked with a smile. "The South's gonna rise again. We start Thursday afternoon in New Orleans."

"Don't we hope?" his mother added. She was also smiling.

"Have a seat and stay awhile." Whit motioned for his mother to sit on the couch, and sat down himself on the edge of the chair.

"Why in the world did you drive to the mall on a day like today? And for goodness sakes, you ought to wear your new coat in weather like this," Whit chastised her. "That's what I bought it for. That's real leather, Mama. The rain won't hurt it."

There was a genuine tenderness in Whit's voice. He truly loved and admired his mother. He felt sorry for having hurt her feelings earlier in the day, and as he looked at her face, he could see the hard times of her life etched into every wrinkle.

Mary Rivers Johnson had not had an easy life. She was born in rural north Georgia in 1918. When the rest of the country entered the Great Depression, Mary Rivers's family and their neighbors never even noticed. They had never done more than get by. The Rivers family earned their living by coaxing food from stubborn red clay. They kept a hog when they could and chickens most of the time. What cash they had came from picking cotton for a penny a pound and selling moonshine whiskey for a dollar a gallon.

When Mary was six years old, her father, Emmett, got into a fight with a man over two gallons of moonshine and wound up killing him with an axe handle. The local sheriff visited the family's rented house that evening and called Emmett out into the yard. The sheriff told him that he understood the events leading up to the killing, but couldn't guarantee him that a jury would. He offered him twelve hours to become scarce, or face arrest for murder.

Emmett Rivers tucked his daughter into bed that evening and kissed her good night, and she never saw her father again. He left behind a wife and four children. Mary was the youngest, and her brother Leon, who was the oldest, became the man of the house. He was thirteen.

There was no work to be had in that part of the world in those days, neither for a woman with four children, nor a thirteen year old boy. The little family moved around to various communities and lived from hand to mouth. Mary's mother, Ruby, always kept a roof over their heads and for the most part there was food to eat, often thanks only to the generosity of their relatives and neighbors, most of whom were only slightly better off themselves.

Wherever the little family found themselves living, cotton was grown. Mary carried a cotton sack to the fields every summer that she could remember, from the time she was six until she was grown. She started out picking the ends of the rows and by the time she was fourteen could keep up with most grown men, sometimes earning as much as a dollar a day.

During Mary's high school days her family lived in a community called Hastings Corners. Economic conditions had not improved, and although none of the students in the school were well-to-do, Mary was easily the poorest child in her school. Her clothing always reflected her circumstances. Hand me downs were always in style for Mary as yard goods for new dresses were hard to come by and a new store bought ready to wear was an unthought of luxury.

But her mother always did whatever necessary to keep Mary in school and she became the first and only of Ruby Rivers's children to graduate from high school. She moved to Atlanta after graduation and spent six months living in a boarding house on Ponce DeLeon Avenue and working as a telephone operator. But the big city was a scary place for a girl who had never spent a night in a house with a flush toilet. She became homesick and returned to Hastings Corners to live with her mother.

The Japanese attacked Pearl Harbor at an opportune time for Mary and Ruby Rivers. With a large percentage of the male work force off to war and the country in great need of textile products, they were able to obtain jobs at the Leesdale cotton mill. They also had three rooms and a bath of their very own in one of the shotgun houses in the Leesdale mill village. Mary's two sisters also moved to Leesdale and took jobs in the mill.

Her brother Leon joined the Navy and served in the Pacific. When he came home after V-J Day, he brought with him a friend, a fellow Georgian. Whit Johnson had left his home in the North Georgia mountains to join the U.S. war effort and he left nothing behind that he ever hoped to return to. When he walked into Ruby Rivers's kitchen to meet Leon's family, Mary Rivers thought he was the best looking thing she had ever laid eyes on. He was equally taken by her. They were married less than a month after meeting.

Whit took a job on the second shift at the mill and he and Mary moved into a five room house with a screened-in porch, indoor plumbing, and a big back yard. Mary Johnson would not have been happier if she had married the King of England and moved into Buckingham Palace. The Johnsons lived a better life on cotton mill wages than either had known before. Their needs and wants were simple, and they had what everyone else in their community had, except children.

After ten years of trying, hoping, and praying, Mary and Whit were blessed with a child, a baby girl, whom they named Ruth. Four years later a son was born to the couple, and Whit became Big Whit Johnson to all who knew him. Whit Junior was Little Whit until the night his father died. God never entrusted children to more caring parents.

From the time Ruth was born, any money that might have been spent to make Mary and Big Whit's lives more pleasant went into a savings account or was used to purchase U.S. savings bonds. They gladly did without extras in their lives so that their children could have the opportunity to get a college education. They were determined that their children would live easier lives than they had.

Ruth was a good student and earned a scholarship to the Georgia Baptist School of Nursing. She chose instead to marry her high school sweetheart, Sonny Edge. They eloped two days after her graduation and three days before Sonny shipped out for a twelve month tour of duty in Vietnam. Sonny survived Vietnam and decided to make a career of the Army. Ruth followed him from assignment to assignment and never lived near her family again, except for a six month stint at Fort Benning.

Whit, while just as bright as his sister, did not apply himself as well. Although a solid student, he was never on anyone's list to receive an academic scholarship, and his athletic ability was minimal. If Whit were going to college, it would be at their own expense. As Whit's senior year in high school approached, his parents were very thankful for the modest amount of money in their college fund and for the bonds in the bottom drawer of the old oak desk in the living room.

And then Big Whit had died, suddenly and unexpectedly, leaving his widow and his son without their most constant source of companionship and stability, and after funeral expenses, without any money for college.

The two had scrimped and saved. Mary had taken in sewing and Whit had worked in the mill and at every odd job he could find. Every summer he taught swimming at the YMCA Camp and worked Saturdays and holidays at the local hardware store. Mary was used to hard work and didn't mind. Her only regrets were that her son seldom had extra money to spend on frills, as his friends did, and her husband had not lived to see their dream of a college education for their son come true.

As Whit took a long, caring look at his courageous mother, it was hard to realize that she was only sixty-two years old. Some people are very young at sixty-two. Mary Johnson was not. Whit's mother looked around the room, examining it as if she were seeing it for the first time. Then she seemed to find her hands very interesting, and stared at them for a great while. It seemed that she would rather do anything than speak. With a deep sigh, she looked up at her son through tired eyes.

"You know I love you," she started, "and I wouldn't hurt your feelings for anything in the world."

Whit couldn't imagine what this tired old lady was about to reveal.

"Whit, I know you went without to save money for my Christmas present. I loved that coat. It was the nicest one that I have ever owned and the nicest present I've ever been given. But I took it back to Rich's and got the money for it."

Now Whit was completely puzzled. He couldn't imagine what his mother could possibly have wanted or needed more than the new coat.

"Here's the money, son. I want you to use it on your trip." In her left hand, she had been clutching a small roll of bills, wrapped up in a handkerchief. Now she carefully spread it out on the coffee table.

Whit was shocked. Anger, love, embarrassment, and emotions that he couldn't identify overwhelmed him. He tried to blink back hot tears, and a lump arose in his throat, making it difficult to breathe, and impossible to speak. All he could do was shake his head, repeatedly.

His mother continued. "I know you don't want the money, but I'm going to tell you a story and then maybe you'll understand why I want you to go to the game so bad. When I graduated from high school, there were eleven of us in my senior class. Everyone else in the class was going on a trip to Jacksonville Beach, Florida. Of course, there was no way I could even think about going. But Mr. Stephens, who owned the drug store, wanted the whole class to get to go. He went to Mama and talked her into letting him pay my way.

"When it came time to go, Mama gave me all the money she had. It was a dime. We stayed in a big old house, right on the beach. Not a one of us had ever seen the ocean before. Our chaperones cooked our meals, and we just walked on the beach and played in the sand and swam in the surf, all day long. We had a big time.

"The last night, they took us to the board walk. I still had my dime. I spent a nickel on cotton candy and rode the Ferris wheel with the other nickel. I never saw a prettier sight than the reflection of the full moon on that ocean from the top of the Ferris wheel. That was the first time I'd ever tasted cotton candy, and it was the best stuff I'd ever put in my mouth.

"Whit, my Mama never did have much to give me in the way of 'things.' What little she was able to give me has long since been lost, or thrown away, or worn out. But even now, forty years later, I can close my eyes and feel the ocean breeze hitting my face and see the moonlight dancing on the water from the top of that Ferris wheel. And I can still taste that cotton candy. Mama gave me her only dime and it bought something better than gold. It bought memories, and they last a lifetime.

"I can get another coat. And if I don't, I'll get by. I've never been able to give you many 'things' either. I want to buy you some memories, Whit. Please don't be hurt about the coat, and please don't say no to the money."

Whit joined his mother on the sofa. They hugged, and for the second time in three days, cried over the same gift.

His eyes red and his face wet, Whit picked up the cash from the table and fanned through the bills. "Mama," he said, "there's two hundred dollars here. I only paid 185 for the coat."

His mother got up and walked across the room and started putting on her old, worn overcoat. Straightening out her rain bonnet, she gave her son a challenging look and said, "I held my tithe out of the offering plate today. I guess Reverend Earl Dobbs can get by without it for one week."

Whit had never loved anyone as much as he did the woman who walked out of his trailer and into the cold rain.

# Chapter Eight

"Oooooooh."

Andrew never knew a ringing telephone could hurt so bad. The last thing in the world he wanted to do was answer it and have to talk to someone. But he was alone in his upstairs bedroom, and the ringing would not stop.

"Oooooooh," he finally said into the receiver.

It was Whit. "Andrew, what are you doing, man? You sound awful."

"Oooooh. Come on Whit, can't you let someone sleep?" Andrew's voice was audible, but barely.

"Andrew, it's 4:30 in the afternoon. Don't tell me you're still in bed."

"Oooooooh."

"Come on Andrew, I've been waiting all day to find out. Karen or Sharon?"

"Oooooh. What are you talking about?" Andrew was surprised that his mouth would even move, much less form words.

"I'm talking about which twin has the mole on her tush, Karen or Sharon?"

"Oooooooh." Andrew's hair hurt. "I couldn't tell you."

"Why not? Did they swear you to secrecy?"

"No. I didn't find out. Ooooh. Whit, could we talk about this later? I want to be left alone to die right now."

"Too bad. That's the price you pay for being a lush." Whit was en-

joying his buddy's self imposed misery. "What happened, Andrew? I thought
this was a sure thing."

"OK." Andrew surrendered to the inevitable, and sat up in his bed,
which was spinning wildly. "I can see you won't leave me alone until I give
you all the dirty details. Just let me catch my balance. Damn. I feel like I'm
gonna throw up."

"Serves you right." Andrew would get no sympathy from Whit concerning hangovers. "So what happened? Did your charms fail on the
Hendricks twins?"

"It was that damned red wine," Andrew insisted.

"Red wine?"

"Hell, yes. When I got home from your mom's place, Sharon and
Karen were already waiting for me. Their brother Danny was driving his
'76 Monte Carlo. Him and his girlfriend were in the front seat and I climbed
in the back, right between the twins. It was perfect."

"So what happened?"

"Well, they had already been drinking, and they were way ahead
of me, but I tried my best to catch up on the way to the lake. Donnie's
girlfriend kept handing me cold beers from the front seat, and I kept throwing 'em down. By the time we got to the cabin, I was feeling just about
right."

"So what happened? How'd you blow it?"

"Look, Whit. You got to work your way into these things. You can't
just follow two girls into their daddy's lake house and say, 'Pardon me, but
could you ladies please drop your drawers? Rumor has it that one of you
has a mole on her ass, and I promised my best friend I'd let him know which
one of you it is.'"

"You can't do that?" Whit asked, grinning at the thought.

"No, you can't do that," Andrew shot back.

"All right," Whit coaxed. "Go on."

"Well, anyway, there were ten or twelve people there—Donnie's friends, I guess. I didn't know hardly anybody. Everything was pretty cool. They had a fire going, and some food, and the stereo was cranked up. Everybody was talking and dancing and having a good time."

"I've been to a party before," Whit interrupted. "I know what goes on. Get to the good part."

"I'm trying, ass breath," Andrew answered. "Give me time. Anyway, after we got in the house I switched from cold beer to hard liquor. I know its not good to mix beer and liquor, but my old friend Jack, Jack Daniel—you know how tight we are—was just sitting on that kitchen counter, looking so lonely. I just had to keep him company."

"Well, the twins were acting especially friendly, but old Jack was cutting up, you know, messing with my mind. I was a little fuzzy eyed and my thought process wasn't exactly clear. I was having a hard time telling one twin from the other. That's when either Karen or Sharon, I'm not sure which, hit me with the setup."

"Setup?" Whit couldn't imagine what his buddy was getting at.

"Yeah, they set me up. Can you believe it? They were really coming on to me, and I thought one while we were fixin' to be right up in the loft. And then they start in telling me how their cousin Pamela is in town, from Alabama, and how she was on her way down to the party, and would I kind of keep her company for a while?"

"They didn't come right out and say it, but they kind of hinted that if I spent some time with her they would make it up to me, and that maybe I'd leave the party knowing their 'sweet secret' as they called it."

"Well, no wonder you didn't find out," Whit said. "Sharon told me about Pamela one time. Said she weighed in at about three hundred pounds. Sharon said that she was huge."

"Hell, she was, too," Andrew agreed. "And I'd say she was closer to three-fifty."

"Andrew, you didn't!" was the unbelieving reply.

"Well, shoot. Those twins looked so fine. And they said all I'd have to do was just talk to her a little, and keep her company. Besides, I done told you, I was drunk."

"Which is just one more reason I don't drink." Whit couldn't believe what he was hearing.

"Well, they sent me out to the boathouse to wait for her. I guess they didn't want me to get my first look at her in good light."

"Andrew," Whit interrupted again, "it was cold last night."

"I wasn't feeling a thing," Andrew assured him. "I took the last little bit of Jack Daniel's and went on down there. Sure enough, 'bout fifteen minutes later, here she comes. My God, she was a big woman. Carnivals would start a bidding war if she ever declared herself a free agent."

Whit couldn't even respond, he was laughing so hard at the picture his friend was painting.

Andrew continued. "It became obvious right away that she and I had different agendas. She didn't appear to be down there to talk. I was out of liquor by this time and excused myself to go up to the house for some liquid fortification. I didn't intend to go back, but damn, when I got to the house those twins looked better than ever, and they were all over me, telling me how appreciative they were of my being so nice to their cousin."

"The only two things left in the house with alcohol in them were a bottle of red wine and a bottle of after shave lotion. I made the wrong choice. I took the wine. The last thing I remember was me and that old gal sitting in Mr. Hendricks's boat—I made sure I kept the console between us—passing that bottle of wine back and forth."

"Next thing I knew, it was daylight, and I was laying in that boat, right out in the middle of the lake. It was raining like a dog and my ass was freezing. No one else was anywhere in sight. I couldn't tell you how I got there or who did what to whom, if my life depended on it."

There was dead silence on the other end of the line.

"Whit? Whit, are you there?"

Whit couldn't answer. His receiver lay on the table. He lay on the floor, tears streaming down his face, holding his sides and laughing uncontrollably.

# Chapter Nine

When Andrew next opened his eyes, he found himself in total darkness and his mouth felt like the inside of a cotton combine at harvest time. His head was as heavy as an anvil and felt like it had been used for one. With great effort, he swung his feet to the floor and switched on the bedside lamp.

Squinting to protect his bloodshot eyes, he took a quick inventory of himself. He was surprised to discover that he had been sleeping in his jeans, and the rest of his clothes lay in a heap at the foot of his bed. He looked across the room and winced at his reflection in the mirror which sat atop his big oak dresser.

To his dismay, he heard heavy footsteps on the stairs, which could only mean one thing. Harry Hawkins was about to pay his son a visit, and Andrew was certain that it wouldn't be cordial. Of course, he could remember few private moments with his father that had been.

Harry Hawkins was one of Leesdale's most respected citizens. He owned the local dry cleaners and a ladies' fashion boutique, as well as interests in a variety of other businesses and a considerable amount of rental property. Harry was what people in Leesdale referred to as "well off."

He was very civic minded and always willing to help out with local charities and community projects. He served on the local hospital and school boards and was a past president of the Rotary Club.

Harry had moved to Leesdale shortly after World War II, with his wife Ellen, a former Mississippi beauty queen. Harry and Ellen were a perfect fit in the Leesdale community, and were welcomed with open arms. Over time, they became two of her most beloved citizens.

The people of Leesdale knew very little about Harry's past. Most knew that his father had been a high ranking military officer and that Harry himself had been a World War II pilot, whose career had ended with a post war crash.

Few people, if any, ever thought to ask for details of his life. It was enough for them that Harry had the best voice in the Baptist choir, was a generous and honest businessman, and a devoted husband and father, with a lovely wife, a treasured daughter, and a handsome, if somewhat rambunctious, son.

Those who knew Harry best would have been very surprised to learn that Harry had once been every bit as rambunctious, irresponsible, and happy-go-lucky as his eldest offspring. Harry's mother had died when he was nine and his father had been far too busy keeping the world safe for democracy to raise a son. Even if he'd been inclined to take a hand in Harry's upbringing, he wouldn't have known where to begin. Most of Harry's childhood and youth had been spent in military boarding schools. The time that Harry spent with his father was infrequent, impersonal, and very strained.

The older Harry got, the more seriously he took that part of the U.S. Constitution which guaranteed his pursuit of happiness. He set records for demerits at two separate military prep schools that would never be seriously challenged, much less broken. Only his father's good name and lofty rank kept him in a school long enough to graduate.

Upon graduation, Harry joined the Army, and his father was able to pull enough strings to get him assigned to the Air Corps and admitted to a pilot training program for noncoms. Harry took to flying like a duck takes to water. His surprising aptitude for flying fighter planes, and the fact that the country was at war with the rest of the world kept Harry in, despite his free spirited ways.

After the war, Harry was stationed in California. This suited Harry and his lifestyle. Unfortunately, his devil-may-care attitude got the best of him and his career ending crash came while trying to loop the Golden Gate Bridge in order to impress a group of young women officers he had recently met.

He was fished out of the San Francisco Bay, barely alive. Several months of lying on his broken back in a Bay Area military hospital gave Harry more time than he wanted to examine his lifestyle and his priorities. He came to the conclusion that he needed to make a 180 degree turn in the direction he was headed. His hospital stay also gave him the opportunity to meet, fall in love with, and become engaged to a beautiful young civilian nurse, Miss Ellenor Davis of the Meridian, Mississippi Davises.

Upon Harry's dismissal from the hospital, Ellen resigned her position, and the two traveled cross country to meet Ellen's family. Harry knew that his bride-to-be was an only child and from a nice Mississippi family. He was shocked to learn that her family was among the wealthiest in the entire state. The new, responsible Harry and his future father-in-law hit it off from the start. Mr. Davis was impressed by Harry's war record and his newly found no-nonsense attitude. He and his wife quickly gave their blessings, and the couple was married within weeks. Harry went to work in one of his father-in-law's dry cleaning stores. He learned the business very quickly and soon became Mr. Davis's right hand man.

Less than a year after their marriage, Ellen's parents were killed in a train derailment. Ellen, being their only heir, was suddenly very, very, wealthy. She and Harry tried to carry on the family businesses, but found that the people of the community expected them to simply continue living the Davis's lives. Neither was happy, and they decided to leave as soon as possible. When Harry found out about a dry cleaning business for sale in the small Georgia community of Leesdale, they bought it, sold all their holdings in Meridian, and moved to Georgia to make a life of their own.

A truly changed man, Harry bent over backward, nearly obsessed with his determination to be a loving husband and a good father. As for the latter, he probably went too far and tried too hard. He was determined that his children wouldn't relive his mistakes, but he had no father figure after which to model his own behavior. He was overly protective, overly demanding, and overbearing in his discipline. His daughter, Terri Lynn, inherited her mother's gentle nature. She learned by instinct, at a very young age, to pacify her father by pretending to yield to his every whim, while in reality living her life to suit herself. Her older brother, Andrew, was incapable of such deceptions. He was too headstrong and too much like his father.

Andrew started rebelling against his father's authority and confronting him at an early age, and the older he got the more frequent and the more powerfully hurtful these confrontations became. As he heard his father's footsteps getting closer, Andrew braced for another one.

If Andrew dreaded the imminent confrontation, his father dreaded it even more. He loved his son deeply, and it was a constant source of frustration that he never seemed able to communicate his true feelings. As he reached the top of the stairs he paused and took a deep breath, determined not to lose his temper, then entered Andrew's room without knocking.

Andrew, who was still sitting on the edge of his bed, looked at his father through an alcohol induced haze, and didn't speak. His father didn't either, for a long time. As soon as he took one look at his son's obviously hungover condition, anger replaced all his resolve to remain calm. He wanted desperately to allow that anger to subside before he spoke. Andrew wished his father would sit down, but he didn't.

Harry finally spoke, powerless to temper the harshness of his voice. "Damn it all, Son, look at yourself!"

Andrew also wanted to avoid a confrontation and tried hard not to turn his head and admire himself in the dresser mirror and fluff his hair and twirl his mustache. Like his father, despite his good intentions, he failed.

This, of course, infuriated his father.

"That's right. Be a smart ass. Why change now? You look like hell. I can't believe you're my son. What in the hell do you ever plan to do with yourself?"

Harry's voice got louder with each sentence. "Your mother and I have given you everything you could possibly want or need and you just fiddle faddle around and blow money like a drunken sailor on shore leave. You're an embarrassment to your mother and me, and a disgrace to this family."

Andrew had his game face on now. There would be no cute replies from him. He braced himself for the onslaught with the only effective defense he'd ever been able to muster against his father's tirades. He looked at his dad with the same insolent stare he always used in these situations and told himself that the words didn't hurt. But they did.

"Well, this time you've gone too far, Andrew. You couldn't be satisfied with wrecking *your* car. Hell no. You had to go out three nights later and destroy a thirteen thousand dollar Coupe de Ville." Harry Hawkins was roaring now.

"We pay thousands of dollars in room, board, and tuition, and you won't even work hard enough to stay in school. It's not like we sent you to Harvard or Yale. You flunked out of the University of Georgia, for God's sake.

"And this morning your mother was walking through the house in her slip, trying to get ready for church, and a total stranger walks in the front door, carrying you over his shoulder like a sack of shit. Doesn't say hello, goodbye, or kiss my ass. Just carried you upstairs, threw you on the bed, and left."

Harry's face was full of fury. His subconscious was screaming at him to stop, but he was beyond control.

"Well, by God, this crap is going to stop, and it's going to stop right now. If you can't straighten up and show some responsibility for your life, you can just . . ."

Harry caught himself before he uttered words that he knew he would regret and that his stubbornness would never allow him to take back.

Andrew finally spoke, and finished the sentence himself. "I can just what, Dad? Leave? Is that what you came up here for, to kick me out of the house?"

Harry turned his back to his son. He walked across the room and leaned with both arms on the solid oak dresser. He could see Andrew's reflection in the mirror and felt like he was looking at himself, twenty-five years earlier. Harry stood staring down at his hands for a long time, determined not to speak until he was in full control of his emotions, and praying that when he did speak, his words would reflect compassion and humility, drawn from some unknown and untapped source.

After an indeterminable silence, he turned and looked at his son with a softness in his eyes that Andrew had never seen before.

"No son," he said, his voice having found some measure of the compassion he'd been searching for. "I came up here to offer you some Sugar Bowl tickets, and some cash for the trip."

To say that Andrew was shocked would be a major understatement. A feeble, "Sir?" was the only response he could manage.

"Look, Andrew, I know that you and Whit are planning to drive Terri Lynn's car to New Orleans. Your mother said that you need two tickets. She and I canceled our trip to the game because of some business obligations. By rights, Pete Anderson should get first refusal on my seats, because we buy our tickets together and that's the understanding we have. But if you want them, I'll explain things to Pete."

Andrew couldn't believe his ears. He wasn't sure what shocked him most: his father's offer of tickets, or his gentle demeanor.

Harry wasn't through shocking his son. He continued. "I'm sure neither of you has any money, so I'll give you the five hundred dollars your mother and I would have spent on the trip."

Andrew couldn't have been more surprised if he'd learned that Hoss Mitchell was the new Avon lady.

"Are you serious, Dad?" he asked, with a catch in his throat.

"Yes, I am serious. I know that things haven't been so good between us, and I'm not sure why, but I want things to be better, and I'm willing to try and meet you half way."

"You're off to a hell of a start," Andrew thought, but said nothing.

"But . . ." Harry continued.

"But," Andrew thought. "Well, for two tickets and five hundred bucks, I can handle a few buts."

" . . . there are some conditions."

"Conditions—sure—conditions. Hell yes, conditions," Andrew

thought. "Just name 'em." Still he said nothing.

"Son, you have to straighten up and fly right. You're practically a grown man. When I was your age, hell, I was flying planes against the Japanese over the Pacific Ocean. You need to start acting a little bit like a man."

"I know Dad," Andrew agreed. For two tickets and half a grand, there was very little he wouldn't have agreed to.

"I'll give you the tickets and the money, but you have to promise to get a job when you get back, and apply for readmission for spring quarter."

"Is that all?" Andrew thought. "Is that all?" This was too good to be true.

"Sure, Dad." He couldn't get the words out quickly enough. "Look, I know I've been a screw up and probably an embarrassment to you and Mom, and I'm sorry I've wasted so much of your money, but I'll do better. I will.

"I know I need to finish school, and when I get back I'll apply myself. Whit's going to work in the mill this winter. I'll ask Mr. Reynolds if I can take over his job at the hardware store."

"We're going to New Orleans, and we're going in style," Andrew was thinking.

His father looked at him with a skeptical eye. He knew that his son was being a little too agreeable. "Don't get carried away, Andrew. I don't expect you to join a monastery when you get home. I just want you to assume a little responsibility. And you have to get a handle on your drinking. I won't stand here and tell you that I don't take a drink. When I was younger, I'm sure I overdid it myself. But I'm concerned about you. I'm concerned about your health. And I'm concerned about where your drinking might lead."

Andrew took a deep breath. "This is too easy," he thought.

He was full of humility when he spoke. "I know Dad," he conceded. "I guess I have let things get a little out of hand."

"Hot Damn," he thought. "Bourbon Street here we come."

"There's one more thing, Andrew."

"Uh oh," Andrew thought. He didn't like the tone of voice in that last comment. It contained too much of the old Harry Hawkins.

"Sure, Dad. Anything," was what he said.

Harry thought long and hard before issuing his final condition, knowing that once the gauntlet was thrown down, it could not be picked up. "I want you to cut your hair and shave off that stupid mustache." It was plainly an order, not a request or a suggestion.

Andrew bristled and felt the high tide of good will father and son had begun to experience begin to ebb away. He was again ready to do battle, if necessary. He was willing to try and avoid an engagement, but not at all costs—certainly not at the cost of his mustache.

"Dad," he reasoned, "I know I need to make some changes." He was trying to speak evenly. "But what possible difference could cutting my hair and shaving my mustache make?"

"It could make a great deal of difference," Harry countered. "Your appearance defines your whole image. It expresses your attitude toward authority and life in general. Your hair and mustache say a lot about you. Right now, I don't care for what they're saying."

"And what might that be?" Andrew knew his father could detect the insolence and sarcasm creeping back into his voice, but he didn't care.

"They say, 'I won't conform, and I'll do as I damned well please, and I don't care who doesn't like it.' That's what they say." Harry was just before losing control of himself again.

"Pretty damn good observation," Andrew thought. He said nothing.

Harry decided to make one last try at reasoning with his son. "Look," he said, "I think that if you just clean yourself up a little bit, and take some pride in your appearance, you'll be taking a giant step in the right direction. You've agreed that you need to make some changes and promised to make them. Cutting your hair and shaving off that mustache would be a show of good faith."

Years worth of repressed anger and resentment began to bubble up from some deep hidden reservoir, and threatened to rise to the surface and boil over. Andrew rose from his seat on the bed for the first time since his father had entered the room, and stood face to face with him. Andrew was actually a couple of inches taller than his father. Andrew, his face red, his bottom lip trembling, looked the older man squarely in the eye.

"Forget it, Dad. What kind of son do you think you've raised, that can be bought for five hundred bucks and two football tickets?"

Andrew abandoned all efforts to check his anger.

"I plan on working, and I plan on going back to school, once I decide what in the hell I really want to do with my life. And maybe I do drink too much. But I'll be damned if I'll change the way I look just to please you; just so you can show me to your friends and say 'look how good Andrew has turned out.' "

Tears had begun to flow from Andrew's eyes. "I don't blame you for being ashamed of how I've acted, but do I have to look a certain way before you'll claim me, before you'll love me, before you'll lower yourself to be my father again?"

Andrew's last line of defense had crumbled. He was sobbing.

"If you can't accept me just as I am, then you can go straight to hell. I wouldn't take your tickets or your money if you handed them to me on a silver platter."

Father and son, so alike and yet so different, stood face to face, having come so close to a reconciliation. Each knew that no more ground would be given on this day, by either. After a long, tense moment, Harry Hawkins turned on his heels, walked out of the room, and down the stairs. He went into his study and called Pete Anderson to offer him his tickets, before he had a chance to change his mind.

Andrew walked over to the window and stared out into the dark night for a long time. He felt a hand on his shoulder and turned to find Terri Lynn standing beside him. He couldn't remember the last time she had been in his room. Her eyes were red and wet with tears, as were Andrew's.

"I couldn't help but hear," she said. "Is there anything I can do?"

He looked down at his sister and forced himself to grin. "Yeah," he said. "If you don't mind, you can call Whit for me and tell him to meet me for breakfast at the cafe tomorrow. I don't much feel like talking to anybody right now."

"Sure thing. I understand," she answered, giving her brother's shoulder a squeeze and walking toward the door.

Andrew purposely let her get almost to the door before calling after her. "Terri Lynn," he asked softly, "don't you need his number?"

She turned back to her brother and met his smile with one of her own. "I'll look it up," she said, closing the door behind her and leaving Andrew to his solitude.

# Chapter Ten

The breakfast crowd at the Village Square Diner was large for a Monday morning, and Whit and Andrew were perturbed to find two strangers sitting in their normal spot. It was obvious that the two men in the corner booth were from out of town because they wore coats and ties and were reading menus. Whit grumbled something about them probably being Yankees to boot and sat down at an undesirable table in the middle of the room. Andrew sat across from him. The table was undesirable in that it afforded a view neither of the door, nor of Bonnie Faith Dimsdale leaning over tables.

"Hey boys, what y'all gonna have?"

The two had smelled the Juicy Fruit before hearing the voice, and their heads turned in unison, their eyes following the customary path. The legs, hips, and bosom were as magnificent as ever, but as their eyes continued upward the boys were startled to see a face completely devoid of makeup and a rat's nest of hair that was more tangled than usual.

"Bonnie Faith," Andrew teased. "Is there a shortage of cosmetics down at the drug store, or is Leon trying to wean this place of customers?"

"Oh leave her alone," Whit broke in, with a smile. "Can't you see she's trying out for a new job—haunting houses?"

"You both can just kiss my foot." Bonnie Faith put her hand over her mouth and stifled a yawn. "You wouldn't look so hot either if you had stayed up all night and then had to come in and work this morning." She yawned again.

"What kept you up, Bonnie Faith?" Andrew asked, winking at his buddy. "Did they have another dusk 'til dawn Elvis Festival on television this weekend?"

"Well, if you must know," Bonnie Faith replied, ignoring Andrew's dig, "Sally Mae Simpkins is getting married this Saturday . . ."

"She is?" Andrew interrupted. "I didn't even know she was pregnant."

Bonnie Faith stuck out her tongue at Andrew and continued, " . . . and four of us took her out last night for a bachelorette party. You know them bars in Atlanta are open on Sundays these days. Daddy says it's a sign the end of the world is at hand."

"But anyway," Whit prompted.

"But anyway, we took her to one of those places where guys dance without their clothes on. They did keep on a little G-string, but it barely covered up their you-know-whats. If you gave 'em five dollars, they'd climb up on your table and shake it right in your face."

"You didn't give any of them five dollars, did you Bonnie Faith?" Whit teased.

"Shoot, yeah, I did," Bonnie Faith replied. "By eleven o'clock I'd done spent my Saturday tip money and twenty dollars I borrowed from Barbara Jane Carter."

"Is that why you didn't get your beauty sleep?" Andrew asked. "Did you get your motor hummin' and wind up staying at that place all night?"

"Shoot, no. My motor was hummin' all right, but all you could do up there was look. Besides, I hear that most of those dancers are a little light in the loafers anyway, if you catch my drift. I made them girls bring me home to Wayne, so I could wind it out on all eight cylinders."

"Damn, Bonnie Faith," Andrew interrupted. "I don't believe I'd told that."

"Why not?" Bonnie Faith wrinkled her nose. "Daddy says that sex under the covenant of marriage is a wonderful gift from God."

"It ain't bad on top of the covers when you're single, either," Whit broke in.

Bonnie Faith tapped him on the nose with her pencil. "I said covenant, silly, not covers. Now let me finish my story so I can get back to work. Well, Wayne was asleep when I got home, but it didn't take me long to get him up, and I do mean up. We got that book out from under the bed, the one Donna Barlowe gave me for Christmas—*100 Pages to Sexual Ecstasy.* We started where we'd left off, at page twelve, and worked our way through page seventy-three. We had to skip chapters seven and eight 'cause we didn't have no honey and we were runnin' low on cooking oil."

Bonnie Faith paused to breathe.

"Wayne wanted to lay out today and finish the book, but I told him we'd have to wait 'til New Year's Eve 'cause Leon would pitch a fit if I didn't come to work. I did let him talk me into reviewing a page or two, though. That's why I didn't have time to fix my hair, or put on my face. If folks don't like the way I look, they can let Regina wait on 'em."

"I'm a little worried about Wayne, though. The last time we pulled an all nighter, he fell asleep at the saw mill and cut his right thumb off. Now he has to fish left handed. Every time he don't catch a mess I feel guilty."

Whit and Andrew just looked at one another in  amazement.

"Well, now that you know why I look like I look, what y'all gonna have?"

"I guess I'll have my usual, Bonnie Faith," Whit said.

"Two eggs over medium, bacon, toast, no jelly, grits with extra butter, coffee, and a small orange juice." Bonnie Faith rattled off Whit's usual breakfast order from memory. "You want a couple of ham biscuits?" she asked Andrew.

Andrew hadn't fully recovered from his bout with the red wine. He frowned at the thought of greasy country ham, which he dearly loved, on his delicate stomach. "I guess I'll have grits, plain toast, and a glass of milk," was his reluctant reply.

"Are you sick?" Bonnie Faith made a big show of feeling Andrew's forehead.

"No, just hungover, as usual," Whit gleefully answered for his unfortunate friend.

"I'm not hungover," Andrew insisted. Bonnie Faith didn't hear. She was already on her way to the kitchen.

"Well, here it is." Whit dug deep into the pocket of his jeans and pulled out a roll of bills, wrapped in a rubber band. $857. Not bad for two days."

Whit offered no explanation as to where the extra three hundred dollars had come from, and Andrew sensed that he shouldn't ask. He also didn't comment on how close they had come to really being able to see New Orleans in style.

"How 'bout those last two ads? Do you think they'll come through?" Whit was no longer concerned about the bogus ad campaign. If his mother could do her part for the cause, so could a few wealthy merchants.

"Already did. They both open early. I was in and out before they were wide awake this morning. They handed me cash money and were glad to do it. They won't remember a thing." He laughed as he tossed two fifty dollar bills on the table. It was just understood that Whit would keep up with the money and dole it out as needed.

"Nine hundred and fifty-seven dollars." Whit couldn't believe the total. "Guess we'll be all set to leave first thing in the morning."

"Look at all that money. Y'all rob a bank or what?" Bonnie Faith quickly placed their breakfast order in front of them.

"No," Andrew said. "We sold our bodies."

"Y'all didn't let me bid," Bonnie Faith complained, with a sparkle in her eye that assured them she was teasing. "When are you boys leaving? I might just hide in your suitcase and go, too. I'll bet Wayne would have a hissy." Bonnie Faith was still yawning, trying to fight off sleep.

"If y'all need anything else, call Regina. I'm gonna take my break before I pass out. If I don't see y'all before you leave, have fun."

The two boys began eating. Whit tore into his food like he hadn't eaten in days. Andrew sipped his milk and picked at his grits. He hadn't eaten in thirty-six hours and didn't trust his queasy stomach.

"I guess this time tomorrow we'll be on our way." Andrew spoke between nibbles. "Do you think you'll have any trouble getting off work?"

Whit grew quiet. "No," he said thoughtfully, "I don't think I'll have any trouble getting off."

"Boy, Whit, that old man Reynolds must really like you. I believe he'd give you the store if you asked him. Why do you reckon he likes you so much?" Without waiting for a reply, Andrew went off on a long dissertation on Georgia's chances of victory over Notre Dame and his chances of personal conquests of the legions of young ladies, foreign and domestic, who were at that very minute, he thought, awaiting his arrival in the French Quarter.

Whit nodded and muttered appropriate comments at appropriate times, but his thoughts were not with Andrew and they were not in the

French Quarter. They had carried him back in time, to a hot August day, ten years earlier.

Both Whit and his mother had been pleased when Frank Reynolds had called the Johnson house that Saturday morning and asked if Whit could help him make a special delivery to Atlanta. He could have asked any boy in town to make the trip with him. After all, Mr. Reynolds was a respected merchant in Leesdale, from a prominent family. He had run his family's hardware business for years, ever since his father had died suddenly of a heart attack during the community barbecue one Fourth of July. The townspeople thought it was wonderful how Frank had taken care of his poor widowed mother, and the family business, never taking time to find a wife or start a family of his own. He was the youngest of seven children, and had always showed more responsibility than his brothers and sisters. He played the pipe organ at the Episcopal church and had served as leader of the Leesdale Boy Scout troop for as long as anyone could remember.

Whit had never worked for money before, other than pulling his wagon around town and collecting Coca-Cola bottles to turn in for deposit money at the grocery store. He really felt like a big shot, riding all the way to Atlanta in the cab of the big delivery truck. He worked hard unloading the heavy boxes of nails, bolts, and other supplies at the house that was being remodeled in the Grant Park area. When the truck was empty, Mr. Reynolds had shown him the Federal Pen and then bought him two giant sandwiches at Harold's Barbecue.

On the way home, Frank Reynolds had bragged about what a good job Whit had done and how strong he was for his age. He had also told him all sorts of interesting stories about his Scout troop and Scout camp, and about how much fun Whit would have if he joined the troop.

To Whit's delight, as they neared Leesdale, Reynolds asked him if he would like to see the camp. Of course, Whit jumped at the chance. He had heard other boys talk about the camp, but had never seen it for himself. Camp was closed for the summer, but Mr. Reynolds had a key. They drove all over the camp, past the cabins where the camp staff lived, past empty campsites, all around the big dining hall, the trading post, the softball fields, and the health lodge. Finally, Reynolds parked the truck at the edge of a stand of pine trees and suggested that they walk down and look at the lake.

Whit was excited, as any eleven year old boy would have been, to walk down the narrow, pinestraw covered path, which led to the waterfront. There was an L-shaped dock that marked the swimming area, and a floating dock about thirty yards further out. The lake was calm and as smooth as glass. It looked cool and inviting as it sparkled under the hot August sun. Whit walked out to the edge of the dock, wishing he had swim trunks, or at least a pair of shorts or cut-off jeans, so he could dive in.

"Why don't we take a dip?" Frank Reynolds suggested. Whit noticed for the first time that he was carrying a rolled up towel under one arm. "Nobody but us men down here today. We don't need to worry about trunks."

Before Whit could comment, or really even comprehend what was happening, Frank Reynolds stripped off all his clothes, even his underwear, and  dove into the clear, fresh water. "Come on in," he called to Whit and then swam out toward the floating dock, executing a perfect crawl stroke.

Whit felt very confused and was more than a little self-conscious, but not knowing what else to do, he slowly began removing his clothes. He timidly turned his back to the water as he slid off his trousers and underwear. Once naked, he slid quickly into the water. At first he held onto the dock, unsure of the whole situation. But at the urging of Frank Reynolds, he soon loosened up and began to swim around and enjoy himself.

After fifteen or twenty minutes of splashing around, challenging Whit to races, and playfully dunking him a couple of times, Frank Reynolds climbed out of the water, spread out his white towel, and lay face down on the dock. "Boy, this warm sun sure does feel good," he commented. "You know, a nice firm massage sure would go good right now. Why don't you come up here and give me a good rub down. I'll show you how. Then I'll give you one."

Whit was horrified, and felt sick at his stomach. He didn't know what to do or say. He looked at the grown man, lying on the dock. His arms were folded to make a resting place for his head, which was turned sideways, facing the swimming area where Whit was treading water and contemplating what to do. The man's skin was pale and scaly looking. His legs and back were covered in thick black hair. His eyes were closed and he had a sickening little smile of anticipation on his face.

Whit made his way to the dock and cautiously climbed out on the ladder, thankful that Reynolds's eyes were closed.

"Come on," Reynolds encouraged. "Start on my legs. Rub them real hard. Just start down at my feet and work your way up."

Whit was trembling from fear and repulsion and trying not to cry or throw up. He said nothing and made as little noise as possible. He stooped down, gathered up his clothes, and ran as fast as he could up the path, toward the parked truck, ignoring the pain of the rough ground on his bare feet.

When Frank Reynolds arrived at the truck, dry and fully dressed, Whit was sitting in the cab, his clothes sticking to his wet body, staring straight ahead with a blank expression on his face. He was scared to death.

Reynolds got in without a word, started the truck, drove out of the camp, getting out of the truck to lock the gate behind him, and drove toward town. When he reached the highway he finally spoke, and spent the twenty minute drive into Leesdale trying to convince Whit that he had totally misunderstood his intentions, gotten upset over nothing, and should never say anything to anyone about their little side trip to the Scout camp.

He needn't have worried. Whit never spoke of the incident to a living soul. After a time, the horror of that day began to fade. He saw Frank Reynolds around town, and Reynolds always spoke and talked to him as if nothing had happened. Whit tried to block the whole experience from his mind, but couldn't. When he did relive that day, it was with great confusion. Thoughts of that day brought feelings of guilt and anger that he didn't understand. There came a time when he began to wonder if he had overreacted, and made much to-do about nothing.

He never joined the Leesdale Scout troop, but when he was sixteen he did accept a part time job at Reynolds Hardware. He was constantly on his guard and watched Frank Reynolds like a hawk, but Reynolds always treated him in a professional manner and was very generous with pay and time off. Whit never saw him alone with a young boy and neither of them ever acknowledged the trip to the lake.

Whit didn't know how long he had been lost in his reverie, but when he forced his mind back to the present, his partner was still babbling on about the game and the lustful pleasures of New Orleans. Andrew stopped talking in mid sentence and looked curiously at Whit. All conversation had stopped and an eerie silence befell the entire diner. Before Whit could grasp what was happening, he smelled it. A sickening, pungent odor had enveloped the whole cafeteria. Whit's eyes started burning, and he swallowed hard several times, trying not to gag. Across the table, Andrew held his hand against his chest, his dinner napkin poised near his mouth, mightily battling the reflux that was forcing itself against the opening to his esophagus.

The boys looked wildly around the cafeteria, searching desperately with their eyes for the source of the smell, cursing the strangers who had taken their table and denied them their customary view of the door. They felt betrayed by Bonnie Faith, who was sitting on a stool at the counter, her head propped up on one arm, sound asleep.

The stench got stronger and stronger and both boys fought back wave after wave of nausea. Just as he discovered the source of the awful smell, Andrew, whose stomach was already in a weakened state, heaved once, twice, and then vomited mightily into his white linen napkin. Whit twisted in his seat to make a run for the bathroom, but before he could get out of his chair a giant hand slapped him on the shoulder, pinning him to his seat.

"How 'bout them *Dawgs!*" It was Hoss Mitchell. He was blissfully unaware of the effect he was having on the patrons of the cafe.

Whit swallowed several times in quick succession, praying that his olfactory nerves would quickly acclimate themselves to the stressful conditions. He was aware of nervous coughs and choking sounds throughout the room. Andrew discreetly wiped his face and sipped from his water glass in a futile attempt to rid his mouth of the taste of regurgitated grits.

"How 'bout them Dawgs," Whit dutifully responded, once he felt he could do so without losing his breakfast.

"How's it hangin', Hoss?" Andrew called out, trying to sound enthusiastic.

Hoss Mitchell looked ridiculous, as was his custom. He wore bright yellow trousers and a a green pullover shirt, which barely covered his disgustingly large belly. He wore pointed toed cowboy boots and a large black Stetson with a red hat band. Ticket stubs from various Georgia games of the past decade were stuck in the hat band, and a large red feather adorned one side.

Although he had done nothing more strenuous than walk in the door, his face was beaded in sweat. And even though it was only 8:30 in the morning, and even though he had bathed within the hour and doused himself with great amounts of deodorant and enough Old Spice to float a ship, he smelled like the south end of a truckload of north bound hogs.

Hoss grabbed a chair from an adjoining table, whose occupants had suddenly decided that breakfast was over and left, and turned it backward to the boys' table. He sat down, straddling the chair with his fat thighs. He reached across the table for a toothpick and started gouging at his teeth and gums.

"Y'all 'bout ready to ride?" he asked, speaking loud enough for everyone in the restaurant to hear him.

"You bet, Hoss," Andrew replied.

"What time we gonna make our getaway?"

"Meet us at my trailer at eight o'clock," Whit answered.

"Eight?" Hoss sounded surprised. "We'll be getting a late start, won't we?"

"We gain an hour," Whit responded quickly. "I have some things I have to do before we can leave," he lied. "If we leave at eight, we'll be there by three."

"That's fine." Hoss seemed to be thinking about something, not an easy task for him. "Will my van be all right at your trailer?"

Andrew and Whit looked at each other, each thankful that they had been able to keep from laughing out loud. Hoss Mitchell's van would be safe left anywhere in the free world. It was an eight year old, ugly, brown monstrosity, more Bondo than metal. It had one yellow fender and was covered with bumper stickers. The van was covered, not the bumpers. The vehicle's crowning jewel was a personalized license plate which read "BIGUN." "But it runs good," Hoss was always quick to point out.

"I think it will be all right, Hoss," Whit assured him. "I guess we'd better call Calvin and tell him when to meet us."

"Oh, don't call Calvin," Hoss said.

"Why not?" Andrew questioned.

"I mean, I'll call him," Hoss said very quickly. "I'll just pick him up in the morning."

He looked around to make sure no one was listening, and lowered his voice. "You don't want Calvin's car parked at your trailer all week. It's got that 'I Have a Dream' bumper sticker on the back bumper and a 'Malcolm X' tag on front."

"Oh, Whit wouldn't want that sitting there," Andrew agreed, winking at his friend.

"Certainly not," Whit added. "OK, Hoss. You pick up Calvin and be there at eight."

"Well, I'd better be going. Got to run by the drug store and pick up about a dozen rubbers. Can't be too careful you know." Hoss grinned. He had four front teeth missing. The ones that were left were yellow and covered with plaque.

Whit and Andrew both shuddered involuntarily at the thought of any poor female being intimate with Hoss Mitchell. If she weren't crushed, she would surely die of asphyxiation.

"Tomorrow morning, dudes. Go Dawgs!" Hoss pointed his finger at the table and fired it like a pistol, then stood up, hoisting his pants in the process, and strode out of the cafe, much to the relief off the few patrons who were left.

"Maybe we'd better leave at six instead of seven, just to be on the safe side," Whit suggested.

"If we had a couple hundred more dollars we could just say to hell with it and leave today," Andrew said. "Just think about it. Do you realize that right now, even as we speak, the Georgia team is probably having breakfast, getting ready to go to the Dome and practice, and that thousands of young women, all in their very prime, are dressed in T-shirts and panties, sleeping off last night's liquor and getting ready for another round of action tonight? And we could be right there to help them find it."

"Are we going for the game, Andrew, or for you to chase women?" Whit asked.

"Primarily for the game, of course. But, hey. Nothing wrong with mixing business with pleasure."

"Let's go. I need to get to work." Whit stood up and threw a five on the table and looked around to see if Bonnie Faith was still taking a snooze. He motioned for Andrew to look toward the counter, where Bonnie Faith was looking around groggily, wiping her eyes, and trying to get her bearings.

"Bye, y'all. Be careful," she called to the boys as they blew her a kiss on their way out the door.

Just as the two stepped onto the sidewalk, Frank Reynolds parked his delivery truck at the curb, twenty feet or so up the street. A small boy, no older than twelve, got out of the passenger side of the truck and walked slowly in their direction. There was a glazed look in his eyes; a mixture of guilt and confusion that few would recognize. But Whit did.

Whit watched Frank Reynolds get out of the driver's side of the truck and walk up the street and into his hardware store as if he hadn't a care in the world. Anger welled up inside Whit. The anger slowly turned to rage, and finally Whit snapped.

Andrew hadn't noticed a thing and was shocked by the malice in his friend's voice as he said simply, "Come on," and started striding purposefully up the street. Andrew had never heard anyone speak in that tone of voice. He was completely puzzled, but followed his friend along the sidewalk and into the store.

As the boys entered the front door, they immediately saw Frank Reynolds. He was standing at the cash register, behind the cluttered counter at the front of the store, going over the previous day's invoices. Whit took the year old football program that Andrew had been carrying and slammed it down on the counter, startling his employer.

"We want to sell you an ad in the football program," Whit stated. The anger in his voice immediately put Reynolds on his guard. He started to speak, but after looking into the young man's eyes, decided to say nothing.

"In fact," Whit continued, his voice losing none of its edge, "we want you to buy the inside back cover, for $250."

Andrew's mouth flew open and he looked at his friend in total shock. He knew something was up, but had no earthly idea what it might be.

Frank attempted a weak smile. "Whit," he said, "I don't advertise in the football program."

"Then you need to start." Whit's lips were quivering. His face was red. His eyes were cold and hard.

Reynolds, like Andrew, knew something was up, but wasn't sure what. He did know that he'd never seen more anger or loathing in two human eyes. He was smart enough to be careful about what he said.

Andrew stood in silence and watched the drama unfold. He didn't know exactly what he was witnessing, but he knew that he was only a spectator.

Reynolds smiled again. It was a defensive smile. "I don't think so, Whit." He spoke quietly.

Whit took a step forward and leaned on the counter. His face was mere inches from his employer's. He looked the older man squarely in the eye. He lowered his voice so that only Reynolds could hear him, but his tone was still cold and hard. "I do think so. Or we could do one for you. Maybe we could put a nice drawing of the Scout camp on it; or maybe even a coupon for a free massage."

Andrew watched intently, straining in vain to hear his friend's words. Whatever he had said caused Frank Reynolds's face to become completely drained of color. Beads of sweat broke out on his forehead.

Reynolds measured Whit's mood for a long moment, then turned and opened the old fashioned register behind him. He took five fifty dollar bills out of the cash drawer, turned back, and placed them on the counter.

"You won't be needing a receipt, will you?" Whit asked as he picked up the money.

"No, a receipt won't be necessary." Reynolds's eyes never left Whit's. He held his breath, not sure what to expect next, and neither swallowed nor blinked.

"I won't be at work anymore," Whit said as he added the bills to the roll in his pocket.

"You won't?" Reynolds asked meekly. He wasn't sure if he should be worried or relieved.

"No, you son of a bitch. I quit."

Whit turned and left the store.

Andrew stared at Reynolds for a moment. He wasn't sure why, or what he expected to see. Reynolds sat down suddenly on the stool behind the counter. He took his handkerchief from his back pocket and began to wipe away the sweat that was flowing profusely from his pores. Finally, Andrew left the store to catch up with his buddy. "What in the hell was that all about?" he demanded, as soon as he caught up with Whit.

"Don't ever ask," was the terse reply.

Andrew took one look into his friend's eyes and knew that he never would.

"Can you get Terri Lynn's car today?" As he spoke, he didn't look at Andrew, but kept his gaze fixed on the Confederate monument across the street, in the center of the town square.

"Sure."

"Then meet me at the trailer at noon, and we'll go to New Orleans."

"Hot Damn. Now you're talking."

Whit walked away from his friend without responding. He walked around the corner, to where his car was parked. He slid behind the wheel of the big Buick Electra that had once been his father's pride and joy. He put the key in the switch and cranked the engine. Suddenly, years of repressed emotion overwhelmed him. Tears began to flow from his eyes. He lay his head against the steering wheel and cried like a baby. He might have sat there a minute, or an hour. He neither knew nor cared. He only knew that when his tears had stopped, he felt like a giant weight had been lifted from around his neck.

His only regret was that he had let Frank Reynolds off far too lightly.

He took a deep breath. "Go to hell, Notre Dame. Sugar Bowl, here we come," he said aloud as he looked over his shoulder, pulled away from the curb, and headed for the mill village to say goodbye to his mother.

# Chapter Eleven

Whit had his bags packed and was standing at his window when Terri Lynn Hawkins's candy apple red Camaro came racing through the trailer park, with Andrew at the wheel. Whit smiled as he looked at the clock on the wall. Twelve o'clock, straight up.

By the time Whit had gathered up his belongings and made his way down the steps of the trailer, Andrew had the trunk of the car open. Whit placed his battered old suitcase beside Andrew's expensive leather bag. Andrew had instructed him to pack light in order to save plenty of room for the Coors beer. The reminder hadn't been necessary. Whit's wardrobe was very simple. Limited might be a better word.

He tossed his jacket on top of the luggage and slammed the trunk lid. He glanced in the back seat and noticed a large cooler sitting on a towel. "You got any Co-Colas in that cooler?" he asked.

"Six, but they're just taking up good space that could be used for beer," Andrew answered. "But that's all right. I can use them to mix with my Jack Daniel's when we get down about Mississippi and its time for the real drinkin' to start."

"I need to get a couple more things out of the trailer." Whit hurried back inside and came out with a shoebox under his arm and the giant Confederate flag that he'd taken from the wall behind the couch.

"Can't go into battle without our banner," he said with a grin.

"What's in the shoebox?" Andrew asked suspiciously.

"Fried chicken," Whit replied proudly. "I went by to tell Mama goodbye and she had fried us up a couple of chickens to take along. I don't guess anybody in my family has ever gone on a trip of more than a hundred miles without a shoe box full of Mama's fried chicken."

"Sounds good to me, but how did she know we were leaving today?"

"Damned if I know," Whit answered. "She just knows things."

"Drape that flag behind the back seat. I wish we had some shoe polish. I'd decorate the windows. Maybe on the way back we'll be able to draw the score on the windshield. Now what in the world is she doing here?"

Andrew motioned toward the LTD wagon that was pulling into Whit's driveway. Terri Lynn Hawkins parked her mother's car right behind the Camaro and got out. Even Andrew was impressed with how gorgeous she looked. She was on her way to the mall and wore a soft red sweater, a red and black and gray plaid skirt, and black knee high stockings. Her honey brown hair was pulled back and tied with a red scarf. She looked like she should be making the trip to the Sugar Bowl.

Whit, wishing she were, greeted her with a big smile, trying hard not to be too obvious and hoping that his ears weren't turning red. He always felt self-conscious in Terri Lynn's presence when Andrew was around. He had never kept a secret from his buddy, and many times he had wanted to tell him about the relationship. He could just never seem to find the right words to make Andrew know that he really cared for Terri Lynn.

"Hey, Whit. What cha doin'?" Terri Lynn returned his smile, but was also careful not to allow her attention to linger on him for too long. "Hey, Andrew," she said to her brother. "I brought y'all something."

"You did?" Andrew and his sister had never been particularly close. He was beginning to be somewhat suspicious of her recent behavior. "What is it?"

Terri Lynn reached into the back seat of the station wagon and brought out a large piece of poster board and a roll of masking tape. The poster had *NEED TWO* printed on it in neat red letters. Terri Lynn's years of experience as a varsity cheerleader had come in handy. She climbed into the back seat of her own red car and quickly taped the sign to the inside of the back glass. Whit and Andrew watched with curiosity, big smiles breaking over their faces when they realized what was printed on the sign.

Andrew's thoughtful sister then climbed out of the car, reached back inside the LTD, and brought out two smaller signs which also read *NEED TWO*. These she taped to the inside of the two back windows. She had scrawled phrases like *GO DAWGS, GO YOU HAIRY DOGS,* and *GEORGIA DOES IT DAWG STYLE,* around the margins of these signs.

Terri Lynn reached into her mother's car yet a third time and produced two additional signs. These had been laminated, and had been made by pasting letters cut from construction paper onto squares of poster board, another old cheerleader trick. They also read *NEED TWO,* and had red twine fastened through holes in either side, near the top.

Neither boy spoke, but their expressions said that they were pleased.

Terri Lynn ceremoniously placed one of the signs around Andrew's neck, and the other around Whit's. "Here you are, guys. Y'all wear these signs everywhere you go while y'all are out yonder. Surely someone will take pity on you and sell you a ticket."

Andrew beamed at his sister as if she had hung an Olympic gold medal around his neck. Whit gave her a warm smile as well.

Terri Lynn spoke to Andrew, but her words were intended for Whit. "Have fun in New Orleans, but be careful. And don't do anything you shouldn't." Her tone was flippant but the expression in her eyes as she snuck a peek in Whit's direction was serious.

"Thanks, Terri Lynn," said Andrew. For once he was being sincere. "We'll be careful, and we'll take good care of your car. I promise."

"We'll be real good," Whit added, turning red again when Andrew shot him a curious glance.

"Bye, now." Terri Lynn got into the big LTD wagon, wishing she had five minutes alone with Whit to give him a proper send-off. She felt like he was going off to war, which, in a way, he was. She backed the wagon out of the driveway, shifted into drive, and sped away without a backward glance.

Before the boys had time to get in their car and leave, Mrs. Harrison drove up and parked right beside them. She hit a button on her console, causing the car's trunk lid to pop open. The boys watched as she got out of her car and walked around to where they were standing. She was dressed in gray slacks and a man's white dress shirt. She had a scarf tied around her head and wore sunglasses, even though the skies were cloudy and, in fact, threatened rain.

"Hello, boys," she greeted them. "I'm glad I caught y'all. Do you think you could help me tote some heavy things in the house?"

"Sure," they replied, not knowing anything else they could have said.

They followed her over and inspected the contents of her trunk. They were puzzled by what they found. Mrs. Harrison had bought two twenty-four count cases of red clover honey and four five gallon cans of Wesson oil.

"I'm having some friends over for New Year's Eve," was her only explanation.

Mrs. Harrison opened the door to her trailer and stood aside to let the boys carry her party supplies inside. She instructed them to place them on the kitchen floor. They exchanged grins when they both noticed a copy of *100 Pages to Sexual Ecstasy* on the kitchen table. An index card was on the table beside the book with the words, "12/31—Chapters 8 & 9" scrawled on it in red ink.

Whit and Andrew accepted Mrs. Harrison's thanks and exited the trailer without comment.

Andrew, since he was sober for the time being, volunteered to drive first and climbed behind the wheel of the waiting car. Whit checked the lock on his trailer door, picked up the morning paper from his front steps, and got in on the passenger side.

"These are strange times we're living in," he said as much to himself as to his friend. He glanced over his shoulder at his neighbor's front door, wondering what it would be like to be a fly on the wall in that trailer around midnight on New Year's Eve.

"Screw 'em," Andrew said, just to be saying something.

"You got your clothes?" he asked.

"Such that they are," Whit replied.

"Got the money?"

"Yep."

"Got the tickets?"

"Nope. Need two."

"We'll get 'em. You turn your iron off?"

Whit laughed. "Ain't got one."

"Then let's go to New Orleans."

Andrew cranked the red Camaro, revved the engine, swung the car backward out of the driveway and laid thirty feet of rubber as he sped up the small road leading out of the River's Edge Mobile Home Community.

They were on their way.

# Chapter Twelve

Andrew Hawkins was behind the wheel of the red Camaro and Whit Johnson was riding shotgun, which was an important job, because he was in charge of navigating, reading the paper, distributing the fried chicken and manning the cooler. The duo had traveled exactly one quarter of a mile, to the trailer park entrance, when Whit made his first navigational decision. "Turn right and let's go around the square one time," he instructed.

"For what?" Andrew questioned.

"For the hell of it. To say goodbye to Leesdale. To shoot a bird at Frank Reynolds. Maybe we'll see a Tech fan. Just to do it, man. Why the hell not?"

"Because we might see Hoss or Calvin, and they'll wonder why we're cruising around at this time of the afternoon with this flag on our back deck and these signs on our windows."

"Good point," Whit agreed. "Turn left."

Turn left, Andrew did, at something just under the speed of sound, leaving a good portion of Terri Lynn Hawkins's tire rubber on the asphalt behind him. Exactly twelve seconds later, he noticed the blue lights of a Leesdale sheriff's patrol car in his rear view mirror.

"Oh shit," he said aloud. "We're getting pulled over already."

"Damn, Andrew," was Whit's only comment.

Tommy Lee Martin, who was ten years older than Andrew and Whit, got out of the brown cruiser and sauntered up to the driver's side window of the Camaro. Tommy Lee looked like a cartoon character. He was bowlegged and so skinny that he looked like he might be blown completely away by a high wind. He walked with a limp and had lost almost all of his teeth. These maladies occurred when a car he was chasing stopped suddenly in front of him. This unexpected maneuver had caught Tommy Lee by surprise. He hadn't even been able to hit his brakes before slamming into the culprit. Tommy Lee had never believed in wearing seat belts because he was afraid he might be in a crash involving fire, or worse, drive off the road into deep water and drown before he could release his belt. When he hit the car he had been chasing, he flew through the windshield of his cruiser, over the car he had hit, and landed face first on the pavement in front of him.

Miraculously, he suffered only minor injuries, except for the loss of his teeth when his face hit the pavement.

The driver of the car he had hit thought he was dead. Thanks to a jacked up rear end and a steel bumper, his car was still drivable, and he left the scene of the accident, running over Tommy Lee and crushing his hip in the process, thus the limp. Tommy Lee vowed not to replace his teeth until the driver of the truck had been apprehended and brought to justice. So far, nine years had passed, and the driver was still at large.

"Damn, Andrew, I'm glad I caught y'all," he offered as he reached the window.

Andrew breathed a sigh of relief and returned his wallet to his hip pocket.

Whit leaned forward and smiled at the young deputy. "How's it goin', Tommy Lee?" he greeted the officer, who despite being a bit of a character, was well liked.

"Can't complain. Wouldn't nobody listen if I did. I heard you boys were headin' to the Sugar Bowl. Y'all on your way right now?"

Andrew and Whit looked at one another. Andrew answered cautiously, "We'll be headin' that way soon. Why?"

"I want y'all to bring me back one of them Sugar Bowl T-shirts and a program from the game." Tommy Lee had taken a twenty dollar bill out of his pocket and was handing it through the window to Andrew. He looked around to make sure no one had walked up beside him, leaned into the car, and lowered his voice, "and I heard they sold that Coors Beer out in Louisiana. You reckon' y'all could bring me back a case?"

"Why, deputy," Andrew tried his best to sound sanctimonious. "Wouldn't that be bootlegging?"

Tommy Lee stood straight up. "No sir," he insisted. "It would be doing a favor for a friend. The same friend, I might add, who investigated both your accidents last November, and failed to find cause to administer a test for DUI in either case."

"You got it, officer." Andrew pocketed the twenty and saluted.

Tommy Lee offered his own salute and a toothless grin. "Y'all have fun, and make damn sure the Dogs do it."

"Later, Tommy Lee." Andrew squealed tires again and headed west on the small access road that ran alongside the expressway, leaving the comical looking Tommy Lee Martin standing on the side of the road, beside his police cruiser.

"Go Dogs," he shouted to the disappearing Camaro.

"You want to get on the expressway or go the back roads for a while?" The boys had traveled less than two of the five hundred miles to New Orleans.

"Let's go expressway," Andrew suggested. "We'll make better time."

He turned right and headed across the bridge toward the interstate entrance ramp.

"Wait a minute," Whit said. "That looks like Mrs. Barnes up there." He pointed down the road a few hundred yards to where an older lady was standing beside a worn out looking Pontiac, which was seemingly crippled by a flat tire.

Andrew hit the brakes and stopped the car, but turned to reason with his companion. "Give me a break, Whit. Somebody else will come along and change her tire. We'll get up there and she won't even have a jack or a spare or anything and we'll wind up spending half the afternoon monkeying around with her."

"Come on, Andrew, it looks like rain. That could be my mama, or yours, standing out here needing help. We can change her tire in five minutes."

"Oh, all right, Mr. Dogood." Andrew gunned the car across the intersection and pulled over, right behind a very grateful Rosa Barnes. To Andrew's relief, she had a jack in her trunk and a spare, and just as Whit had predicted, the two had done their good deed and were pulling onto the westbound expressway in less than ten minutes.

"It's a sign," Whit said. "It's a sign. On the road less than two miles and a cop has pulled us over to give us money and we've done our good deed for the day. Have a piece of fried chicken." He offered Andrew a chicken leg from the foil lined shoe box, and took a thigh for himself.

"Thanks, buddy. Hand me one of these cold beers to wash it down."

"You gonna drink and drive, Andrew?" Whit knew without asking that if Andrew were going to drive on this trip that he was going to drink and drive.

"Not more than one or two," he said. "Six packs, that is."

Whit handed Andrew a brew and popped the top on a can of Coke for himself.

"I wish they still sold Co-Colas in them little bottles." Whit commented. "Nothing tastes better than a little Co-Cola, real cold, with just a slight crust of ice on top."

"Yeah," Andrew agreed. "And they make a great sound when you toss them at road signs."

"Only if you hit them," Whit answered. "Damn Andrew—how fast you going?"

"Not much more than a hundred."

"You'd better be careful. We're just about out of Tommy Lee's jurisdiction."

"Shoot, all the cops are on their two hour lunch breaks right now. Besides, no self-respecting Georgia State Patrolman would ticket somebody going out to help do their part against Notre Dame."

"I wouldn't bet my ass on that," Whit said.

Andrew lowered his window and tossed out a well cleaned chicken leg, then turned up his beer, making sure he didn't waste a drop, before tossing the empty can into the back floorboard. "How about another piece of chicken—is there a breast in there? I'm a breast man, you know."

Whit wrapped a perfectly fried chicken breast in a paper napkin and handed it across to the driver, then took another piece out for himself.

"Cold beer—cold beer—cold beer," Andrew demanded.

Whit leaned over the back seat and took another frosty can from the cooler.

"What's in the paper?" Andrew asked.

"Just more stuff about the hostage situation. President Carter ought to get some old boys from the mill village with Buck knives and tire tools and get those guys out of there."

"Jimmy Earl's a wimp," Andrew responded. "I don't care if he is from Georgia. They'll let those hostages go when Ronald Reagan gets in office or he'll kick their ass."

Whit didn't comment. He'd learned long ago not to discuss politics with his buddy. Every registered voter in the mill village had been a yellow dog Democrat. They'd vote for a yellow dog if it were running on the Democratic ticket. Most had very little now, but before the days of FDR they had nothing. They were suspicious of Republicans, even though the Republican party was beginning to be more representative of their social views. But old habits died hard, and mill workers had voted Democratic by habit for a long, long time. Andrew, on the other hand, was quick to expound his father's beliefs that the Democrats would be the ruination of the country. Rather than get into a political argument, Whit turned to the sports page.

"It says here that Pat Dye is going to be the new coach at Auburn. He's a Georgia boy. Now he'll be a turncoat. I guess it's no different than Vince Dooley being from Auburn and coaching at Georgia all these years. I'm just glad Dooley didn't take the Auburn job." Whit was a big fan of success and Dooley had been very successful.

"Hell, I wish he had gone," Andrew said. "Then maybe Erk would be the head coach. What would be wrong with that?"

Neither Whit, nor any other Georgia fan could find much wrong with the notion of Erk Russell being head coach at the University of Georgia. Russell was a powerful man, full of charisma, and a legend. He was a master of motivation. He was nicknamed Mr. Clean, because of his shaved head, which gave him a dramatic appearance. On game days Russell had been known to butt heads with his helmeted defensive players until blood flowed from his bald dome.

His players loved the big cigar-chomping coach, with the gruff exterior, and often played over their heads, far surpassing their ability, to please their mentor.

Russell had come to Georgia from Auburn with Vince Dooley when he had been named head coach in 1964 and had been with him ever since. Dooley was a pipe-smoking history professor type, often seen as being withdrawn and aloof. Many Georgia fans preferred the earthy demeanor of Russell and gave him much of the credit for Georgia's success during the Dooley era. Dooley himself would never dispute his contributions.

"What's Grizzard writing about?" Andrew asked, referring to the *Atlanta Constitution's* ultrapopular daily columnist, Lewis Grizzard, who was a Georgia man and proud of it.

"He did an interview with Herschel's mama," Whit said, rifling through the paper to the Metro section. He quickly scanned the article, chuckling at most of it, then shared the highlights with his friend.

"Christine Walker said that Herschel got the way he is by eating peas," Whit laughed. "Damn, I hope he gets plenty of them in New Orleans. She says that she'd spank Herschel sometimes, if he'd let her, and that in the eighth grade she tried to get him not to play football. Grizzard says, 'Why? Were you afraid he'd get hurt?' and she says, 'No, I was afraid he'd hurt someone else's children.' "

Andrew laughed with Whit over the comment, then asked for another beer. "Are you sure, Andrew? We've only been on the road twenty minutes."

"If I'd wanted somebody to count my drinks, I'd have brought my mama. Hand me a cold beer."

Whit reluctantly dug in the cooler for another beer, deciding that he would take the wheel sooner rather than later.

"I know one sucker that wishes Herschel had taken his mother's advice and given up football," Andrew said, turning up the beer can. "Bill Bates, the poor guy from Tennessee that Herschel ran over the first time he touched the ball. We were right there. I'll never forget it. Hot? God almighty, it was hot. Tennessee had added twelve thousand seats to Neyland Stadium with a paint brush. I went up there with my parents, and we were packed in the seats like sardines.

"We were getting killed, and all of a sudden, here comes Herschel. Just bowled that sucker over and stomped on him. Turned the whole game around."

"Yeah," Whit agreed. "I couldn't believe it. I was listening to Munson. I believe hearing him is better than being at the game. He was talking about Herschel running over people with those big thighs."

"Where were you listening to the game?" Andrew asked, trying to sound nonchalant. He took a big sip of beer and studied his friend through the corner of one eye, trying to keep the smile off his face.

Whit felt his face begin to burn, and knew it was turning a deep red. "I don't remember," he lied. "I guess I was at the trailer, by myself. I might have been at Mama's house."

"Bullshit," Andrew laughed.

"What do you mean?" Whit became defensive.

Andrew drained his beer, adding a third can to the meager but growing collection in the back floorboard.

The alcohol in his system was beginning to relax any inhibitions he might have had, and he decided to have some fun at his best friend's expense.

"I mean that while I was snooping around in Terri Lynn's room the other day, I found her 'personal journal' as she calls it. Honestly compels me to admit that I did glance at an entry or two."

Now Whit was a deep red, his ears burned, and he felt a knot forming in the pit of his stomach.

Andrew pretended not to notice and continued. "I remember that Terri Lynn didn't want to go to Knoxville because she said that she needed to stay and help Mrs. Alexander with the cheerleaders, since the high school team was playing their first game that weekend. My folks said she could stay at home. They were under the impression that Maggie Phillips was going to stay with her."

Whit's eyes were closed. His arms were folded and his head rested in one hand.

Andrew was having a great time. "According to her diary, though, she spent that Saturday night at the River's Edge Mobile Home Community. Imagine that. Maybe she just uses her journal to fantasize, I don't know, but she claimed in her journal that she listened to the Georgia-Tennessee game with you."

Whit looked skyward, still saying nothing, and covered his face with both hands. He was beyond the point of embarrassment and prepared himself for the worst. And the worst came.

Andrew turned his head and grinned at his buddy before driving home the final stake. "You know, Whit, Terri Lynn claimed in her journal that you, of all people, gave up on the Dogs. She said that y'all retreated to the bedroom in the middle of the third quarter, and she was complaining because you left the radio beside the bed on the football game instead of finding some music. She wrote that, let's see, how'd she word it? Oh yeah, she said that you were 'lost in foreplay' for a long time, but she couldn't ignore the game. She said that when the Dogs started driving, so did you."

Whit was mortified. He was trying to cover up his face and his ears at the same time.

"She said that Herschel scored at the same time you did and that Larry Munson was screaming 'Oh my God' and you were screaming 'Oh my God' and she wasn't sure if she was making it with Munson or you or Herschel Walker or all three!"

Whit could only moan. He kept his hands over his face and didn't even try to comment or defend himself.

Andrew nearly ran off the road as he drove with one hand while reaching into the back seat to fish another beer out of the cooler. The sudden swerving of the car startled Whit and he removed his hands from his face and cautiously looked at Andrew to make sure the car was under control.

He tried to make some explanation, but "Look, Andrew ..." was all he could get out.

Andrew popped the top on his beer and waved a hand at Whit. "Hell, man. You think I care what you and Terri Lynn do? I'd rather know she was with you than somebody else. Besides, did you think I didn't already know about y'all?"

"You did?" Whit was stunned. "Since when?"

"Since one day about six months ago when you called to invite me swimming. We have an old tradition at the Hawkins house. It's called eavesdropping. I picked up the phone when you called, but Terri Lynn was already talking to you, so I just listened. When she left the house, I followed her. I saw your whole encounter from the bushes at the top of the hill. It was better than the dirty movie we saw on Tenth Street in Atlanta that time."

Whit looked at his buddy in disbelieve and said nothing. The two drove on in silence—at a hundred miles an hour.

Whit was wondering what other closely guarded secrets his friend knew. Andrew was wondering where the nearest restroom was, the five beers he had drained having begun to work on his bladder.

Suddenly, he jerked the car across two lanes of traffic, having almost missed the ramp leading to I-85 South, and slowed down to eighty in deference to the sharp turn. He quickly merged with the south bound traffic, thankful for the sign which promised relief in one mile. He left the expressway for the first of many pit stops and pulled into the convenience store at the top of the exit ramp.

Andrew parked the car and jumped out, hurrying toward the restroom in back of the building. Whit stayed in the car for a moment, then got out, locking the doors behind him, and slowly made his way toward the rear of the store as well.

# Chapter Thirteen

Whit offered to drive after the rest break, but Andrew insisted that he be allowed to put in a few more miles behind the wheel while his vision was still good. They drove in silence for a long time, each lost in his own thoughts. They crossed the Chattahoochee River, and Whit broke the silence. "Alabama state line—set your watch back one hour." A couple of miles past the Alabama welcome center, the boys overtook a line of seven or eight cars, all decorated with red and black flags and banners. They were part of a caravan that was obviously heading to New Orleans. All the drivers honked their horns and the passengers gave the thumbs up sign and shouted "How Bout Them Dawgs" as the boys passed.

Whit excitedly shouted for Andrew to slow down. He had made up his mind not to worry about Andrew's embarrassing revelation. He just wondered what else Terri Lynn has written in her diary. Andrew dutifully slowed down until he was even with the last car in the convoy. Whit pushed down his window and mouthed the words, "Got any tickets?" while pointing to the sign in the back window, and holding up two fingers to indicate that the boys did indeed, need two. The red clothed passengers smiled and shook their heads no.

Andrew saw what Whit was doing and moved up beside the next car, and then the next and the next, until they had unsuccessfully tried to solicit tickets from each of the south bound cars. When it became apparent that there would be no tickets forthcoming from this particular group of travelers, Andrew blew his horn at the lead car and waved, sped up, and took over the  spot in the front of the convoy.  He decided to cruise, as they were, at only eighty-five miles per hour.

"Hand me a beer," he instructed his partner. Whit sighed and shook his head, but complied, opening another Coke for himself.

"What's the paper say about the game?" Andrew asked as he popped the top of his beer, preparing to finish off the first of many six packs.

"Most of the national media are picking Notre Dame," Whit related.

"Figures," Andrew broke in. "Bunch of damnyankees. We'll show them."

"Yeah," Whit agreed.  "All the Atlanta writers pick Georgia, and the line is three."

"Damn. I'd take that."

"Me, too."

"Here's an article about a Notre Dame player that says the line is a bunch of garbage.  He says Notre Dame will win by ten.  I'll bet he's the same SOB you saw on television the other night."

Andrew tried to hold back a smile. "Yeah, I bet that's him.  Does it have a picture of him?  Is he an ugly, Catholic-looking guy?"

"He's ugly enough, but how am I supposed to know if he's Catholic or not?"

"Oh, that's easy," Andrew insisted. "All those Catholics have a sort of pained expression, from kneeling too long on those prayer rugs."

Whit had continued to read the article, which was full of inflammatory remarks about Georgia's schedule and the weakness of Southern football in general.  His blood began to boil.

"I don't know if he's a Catholic, or a Protestant, or a Jew, or a plain out heathen, but if I get down there and some damnyankee starts running down the South in front of me, I'll kick his ass. I don't care how big he is."

"Well, you just be sure we're not out numbered if you go starting a fight," Andrew suggested.

"When have I ever started a fight?" Whit asked. He immediately wished he hadn't.

"The first time I ever met you," Andrew answered. "The first day of school, in the ninth grade."

"You started that fight," Whit shot back.

"Like hell I did," Andrew said. "I never even hit you. I was just trying to start a conversation, and you hauled off and knocked my block off."

"Well, you deserved it. You called me a linthead. My daddy had warned me that would happen when I got to the high school and had to be around town people, like you."

"I was trying to make a joke, and you broke my damn nose. And then, to make matters worse, Mrs. Tanner sent us to the principal and old man Gordon paddled us both. I never did think that was fair."

Now it was Whit's turn to smile and reveal a long kept secret. "He didn't paddle me."

"What?"

"Mr. Gordon didn't paddle me. Not many of the town kids knew it, but Mr. Gordon was raised in the mill village, too. He told me to knock the hell out of anybody that called me a linthead. I had three fights the first week."

Andrew shook his head. "Well, he was pretty smart. He made us pick up paper after school for a week, and made us carry the trash can together. We've been buddies ever since. I guess it was worth a broken nose if I got a friend like you out of the deal."

Andrew drained his beer.

"But back to you and fights. What about that time you beat up Matt Green in the locker room before baseball practice? Did he call you a linthead too?" Andrew teased.

"No, but he threatened to pull a knife on me. I didn't have a choice."

"Bullshit. You just fought him so he'd quit the team and you wouldn't have any competition for first base."

"Well, anyone can get in a fight every now and then. You can't let people push you around."

"Oh, right. What about the fight you had at the Auburn game that time?"

"The guy's girlfriend shook her pompon in my face."

"What about the Florida game when we were freshmen?"

"That guy was a typical, obnoxious Florida fan. He spilled a drink down my back."

"His date spilled the drink down your back," Andrew corrected him.

"Well, I couldn't hit her. Besides, she was from Georgia."

"What about the Tech guy that time? You broke his nose, just like you did mine."

"He didn't have any business taunting me after they beat us. Besides, all those were a long time ago. I haven't started a fight recently."

"Oh no, not since November sixth, at the Gator Bowl. The greatest play in Georgia history, and we can't enjoy it for having to keep you from killing the guy in front of us. If we hadn't pulled you off of him, you'd probably be in jail right now."

Whit shook his head. "I can explain that one. That guy had been running his mouth all day, and I warned his buddy to either shut him up or get him out of there. I was like everybody else. I had given up. When Lindsay caught that ball and started running down the sideline, I just lost it. Lindsay scored, and the next thing I knew I had the guy around the neck trying to shake his brains out of his head through his eye sockets."

"Don't I know? It took three of us to get you pried off the little asshole. If it hadn't been for Terri Lynn sweet-talking that cop, you would have spent the night in the pokey."

"Well, I won't be starting a fight on this trip, but I won't be running away from one either."

"Damn," Andrew said, hitting his brake and nearly causing a multiple car pile up.

"Did you see that billboard?"

"What billboard?" Whit asked.

"It said, 'I-85 Health Center - Truckers Welcome - Open 24 hours.'"

"So what, Andrew? You gonna stop and work out?"

"It also said, 'All Girl Staff.' It's a front. We just passed by Effie's West."

"Effies West?" Whit still didn't comprehend. "I though Effie's was a whorehouse that used to be in Athens, down near Elm Street. All the old men in the cotton mill ask me if Effie's is still there."

Andrew had been steadily watching for the next exit. "Now you're catching on. That's what it is. I heard they're popping up all along the major truck routes. They call them health clubs or massage parlors, but I heard you can get anything you want there. We've got to go back and check it out. There's the Opelika/Auburn exit. I can get off here." Andrew gunned the engine of the Camaro and whipped it off the expressway.

"Andrew," Whit complained. "We don't need to go back there. We're on our way to the sin center of the South. Get back on the expressway."

Andrew had already crossed the bridge and was heading north, back toward Opelika.

"We won't do anything. We'll just take a look. Hand me another beer."

Whit continued to argue against the detour while Andrew guzzled his beer and drove as fast as he could to the previous exit. At the top of the ramp there was a small sign with an arrow pointing to the right, directing trucks and other would-be customers to relieve stress at the I-85 Health Club.

Andrew barely slowed down for the stop sign and squealed his tires as he made the turn. Half a mile down the road he found the object of his search. On the right hand side of the road, in the middle of a large gravel parking lot, sat a newly placed, double-wide trailer, with a flashing neon sign on top proclaiming to all the world, that this was indeed the Opelika Health Center. One semi, with Texas license plates, was parked in front. There were no cars in sight, but there was a hand-lettered sign reading "Open" on the front door.

The two boys sat in the car for several minutes, contemplating their next move. Whit had given up on changing Andrew's mind, but was determined that they would only look and not participate, no matter how tempting.

"Let's go on in and get it over with," Whit suggested. "Open the trunk and give me the keys. I'm locking all our money in the trunk."

"Good idea," Andrew agreed. He handed Whit his wallet, which contained thirty dollars that his mother had handed him as he left the house that morning.

Whit hid their wallets inside Andrew's leather bag and placed the keys in his pocket. A light rain had started to fall, as they hurried up the steps leading to the door of the health center. The two boys paused when they reached the top step and looked at one another. They weren't familiar with proper massage parlor etiquette. They weren't sure if they should knock or just walk in.

Before they could do either, the door opened inward and one of the biggest men either boy had ever seen walked out. He had on jeans and cowboy boots and was tucking in his blue flannel shirt. He wore a black baseball cap, with a CAT Diesel Power logo on the front and had a toothpick sticking out of the corner of his mouth.

The stranger looked at the nervous boys and grinned. "Y'all looking to get your tally whacked?" he asked. "Pick the blonde with the red outfit and the big patooties. She's got a cute mole on her right cheek." He slapped Whit on the back, nearly knocking him off the wooden stoop, then went down the steps and climbed into the cab of his truck.

Whit and Andrew looked at one another again, shrugged, and walked in.

They found themselves in a room that looked like any living room of any double-wide trailer—it had paneled walls and cheap furniture. They were greeted by a greasy looking man in a turquoise jogging outfit, who appeared to be in his mid-thirties.

He offered a weak handshake to each boy in turn, then ushered them over and offered them a seat on the imitation leather sofa which dominated the room. The whole place smelled of air freshener, and there was a wide assortment of men's magazines on a round table in front of the couch.

"What could I do for you men?" the proprietor asked. His voice was as greasy as his appearance.

Andrew spoke up. "We've been thinking about joining a health club, and just wanted to take a look at your facilities."

The man smiled a greasy smile, showing greasy teeth protruding from greasy gums. "What we offer," he said, "is a nice, relaxing, stress-reducing massage, of a therapeutic nature. You have your choice of our lovely and well-trained therapists who will give you a full body massage using your choice of oil, lotion, or powder."

"Their fee," he continued, "is twenty dollars for a half hour or thirty for a full hour."

"Let's go, Andrew," Whit whispered to his buddy. He knew the prices sounded too reasonable and the product too promising to resist for long.

"Shhh." Andrew motioned for his buddy to wait.

"Of course, our ladies do work for tips, and of course they will show their appreciation in a most appropriate manner. The larger the tip, the more appreciative they are likely to be." He gave them another greasy smile.

"Would you like to see one of our rooms?" His Greasiness asked.

"We need to be going." Whit stood up, determined to leave the I-85 Health Center with their bankroll intact.

"We'd love to see one of your rooms." Andrew had clearly overruled Whit.

Whit rolled his eyes and followed Andrew and Mr. Greasy through one of the interior doors. They walked into a room that was lit by candles and decorated with red imitation silk wallpaper on all four walls. There was a daybed against one wall and a large gilded mirror on another. One corner of the small room held a table, laden with boxes of tissue and assorted containers of oil, lotions and powder. Soft music emitted from a cassette player on the floor.

"Thank you for your time. We need to be on our way," Whit suggested. In his mind's eye he could see twenty and fifty dollar bills, with little wings, flying away forever.

"Wouldn't you like to meet our staff?" Mr. Greasy offered.

"Of course we would," Andrew insisted, before Whit had time to say otherwise.

"Right this way."

The trio exited the room by a different door, and Whit and Andrew found themselves in another dark room. There were lamps with red bulbs in each corner, and the entire room smelled of incense. There were mirrors on three of the walls and along the fourth was a long black leather sofa. Lounging on the sofa with their feet propped on the table in front of them were four girls, each of whom appeared to be in their early twenties. They all wore lingerie and had garters around their thighs, which were filled with ten and twenty dollar bills.

The girls stood up when Mr. Greasy led the boys into the room. The first girl was exceptionally tall, skinny, and very flat chested. She had pale skin and straight red hair and was wearing a black lace teddy. She waved at the boys, showing off long, sculptured fingernails. The second girl was dark haired and very busty. She wore lavender panties and a matching bra. She smiled and winked at the boys. Her garter held a fifty dollar bill and three twenties.

The third girl, wearing a white lace camisole, was Karen Hendricks.

The fourth, wearing a red teddy, was Sharon.

Or vice versa.

The four Leesdale residents recognized one another at the same instant. The twins were mortified, as was Whit. Andrew was thrilled. Whit panicked. He turned and retraced the path he had taken into the room, through the massage room, through the reception room and out the front door. It was pouring rain by this time and Whit got soaked before he was able to fumble for the keys and get into the car. He slid behind the wheel, on the driver's side. A minute later a laughing Andrew came out of the health center and climbed in on the passenger side.

"What's wrong with you, man? You ran out of there like a bat out of hell."

Whit was embarrassed and hard-put to explain his reaction. "God, Andrew. I don't want those girls to go back home and tell people they saw us in that place."

Andrew roared. "Who do you think they'll tell and what do you think they'll say? 'You know, we were working as prostitutes in a massage parlor over near Auburn, and Andrew and Whit came in to look around.' They're a lot more worried than we are right now. If you hadn't panicked and ran out of there, we could have had anything we wanted—for free!"

As if to prove Andrew a prophet, at that same moment Karen and Sharon Hendricks came out of the double wide into the rain. They were wearing sneakers and had thrown trench coats on over their skimpy outfits. They motioned for Andrew to let them in and squeezed into the backseat with the cooler and empty beer cans. Either Sharon or Karen, neither boy could tell them apart, leaned forward and began tracing designs on Andrew's forearm with a long red fingernail. The other put her head on Whit's shoulder, lightly caressing his neck with her fingertips.

Andrew's twin spoke. "Boys, y'all won't tell anybody you saw us here, will you? It would just kill Daddy if he found out."

"And he'd just kill us," Whit's twin added.

"We don't do anything but give massages. Honest," swore the first twin.

"That's right," said the second. "We don't go topless or anything. But if y'all promise not to tell, we can give you boys a special session."

"I've heard that stuff before," Andrew broke in. "Recently. This special session won't involve your cousin Pamela or a boat will it?"

The girls giggled. "No, silly. It will just be the four of us," Andrew's twin promised.

"Sounds good to me." Andrew replied. "Let's go back inside."

Whit had been afraid something like this would happen. "Andrew," he interjected, "we need to go. We've been on the road three hours and have barely gone a hundred miles. At this rate, the game will be over before we even get to New Orleans."

Andrew was about to argue the point when the twin behind him spoke up. "Why don't y'all go on to the game and stop by here on the way back through? You'll be coming back about Friday, won't you?"

The second twin seconded that motion. "Good idea. The boss won't be here Friday, and we'll be able to have a nice long session. No charge of course."

Andrew began to waver. "Well, we can keep a secret, but before we leave, I want to know, which one has the mole?"

"That's easy," said the twin behind Andrew. "I do." With great difficulty she twisted around in the cramped quarters of the small back seat, lifted up her trench coat and pulled aside the filmy red lace of her teddy, revealing one of the most perfectly rounded rear ends either of the boys had ever seen. There was an equally perfect, reddish brown mole right in the center.

"That should hold you 'til Friday," she said, as she turned back around in the seat. "Now let us out before Eugene comes looking for us." The twins climbed out of the back seat and went running through the rain, back toward the health center.

"Wait a minute!" Andrew shouted out the window. "Which one are you?"

The twin with the mole turned back and gave the boys a sparkling smile. "I guess that's for you to find out," she shouted through the rain, before disappearing inside the double-wide.

Whit and Andrew smiled at each other and shrugged. Two log trucks pulled into the gravel parking lot, splashing mud and water onto the red car.

"Let's ride," Whit said, as he cranked the car and drove out of the parking lot, across the bridge, and down the entrance ramp—headed south.

# Chapter Fourteen

"Turn the radio on. Surely we can find a good country station in Alabama. Look, Auburn—3 miles. It's easy to find Auburn. Just go west until you smell it and south until you step in it."

"Just like Clemson without a lake," Andrew countered as he fiddled with the radio dial in search of a static-free station.

The clear sweet voice of Willie Nelson came over the speakers, singing his current hit, *On the Road Again*. "It's a sign," insisted Whit. "Another sign. We're just like that song . . . 'going places that I've never been . . . seeing things that I may never see again . .' " Whit sang along with the music in a flat voice, devoid of any semblance of pitch. "Even Willie knows we needed to get back on the road instead of hanging around that place back there."

"I don't know about that," Andrew replied. "I know we'll be stopping back by there on our way home, though."

"Damn, that redheaded sucker knows he can sing," Whit said, purposely ignoring Andrew and continuing to sing along with the radio.

"Yeah," Andrew agreed, but he's bad ugly.

"Shoot," Whit said, "I wish I looked just like him."

"Why in the world would you want to look like him?"

"'Cause he ain't average looking. People notice you, because you're good-looking and have that thick black moustache. I just blend into the scenery. If I can't be real good-looking, I'd just as soon be real ugly, like

Willie, or Johnny Cash. He's got some mileage in his face, too."

Andrew was leaning over the seat, digging yet another beer out of the rapidly emptying cooler. "You want another Coke, ugly boy?" he asked.

"Might as well."

Andrew popped the top and took a swig. He was getting real close to being very drunk. "I don't know how you stand to listen to that country crap all the time—everybody singing through their noses and whining about their mamas and their dogs and how their wives ran off with their best friend, and how  much they miss him."

"Well it's better than that disco crap you listen to, and as for that stuff you call rock and  roll—hell, there ain't been no rock and roll since Elvis sold out."

"No rock and roll?  What  about the Beatles?"

"Oh, they're all right I guess; but there wouldn't have been any Beatles if it hadn't been for Elvis."

"You sound like Bonnie Faith."

"I wish Bonnie Faith were  here."

"Yeah, you just think about trying anything with Bonnie Faith and Wayne Dimsdale would bury your remains under a fifty foot pile of sawdust."

"Might be worth it."

"Might at that."

"Say, Andrew—"

"Yeah?"

"You reckon Bonnie Faith puts that Juicy Fruit on the bedpost while they're doing it?"

"No, she probably just keeps chewing."

"Who'd you rather do it with, Bonnie Faith or Gladys Gibson?"

"Gladys Gibson? When God made her he was just showing off. I'd really love to see her in her natural state, but she always seemed like a tightass to me." Andrew paused to ponder the question. "I bet Gladys wouldn't do too much. Bonnie Faith though—I believe that dog can hunt."

"Oh shit," Whit interrupted. There were blue lights in his rear view mirror. He glanced down at his speedometer. He was only going 65. "Get rid of that beer," Whit shouted. Andrew quickly drained the can, then added it to the growing pile in the back seat. Whit placed his Coke can in the cup holder on the dash, turned on his right signal and pulled off the interstate onto the emergency lane.

An Alabama deputy sheriff pulled in behind him. He was the total package—big belly, Smoky the Bear hat, and mirror sunglasses, even though it was pouring rain.

Whit lowered his window in anticipation. The deputy slowly walked around the car, looking with disdain at the Georgia sticker and the *Need Two* signs on the car. He did allow himself to smile approvingly at the Confederate flag which was displayed inside the rear windshield. He finally walked over to the driver's window, dodging puddles, and leaned on the car with both hands. He raised his eyebrows when he saw all the empty beer cans in the back of the car.

Mr. Bear stood up, folded his arms across his chest, turned his head sideways and looked at Whit for a long time, trying to intimidate him. His efforts were hugely successful.

Whit couldn't stand the silence. He broke. "Was I speeding, officer?" Not a good opening line. The deputy took advantage of Whit's poor choice of words.

"What's wrong with you, boy? Don't you even know how fast you were going?"

Whit realized his mistake and said nothing.

After another long silence the deputy leaned closer. When he spoke, his voice was dripping with contempt. "You boys ever been out of Georgia before? In Alabama the law says you turn your lights on when it's raining. Don't you know how to turn the lights on in that fancy red car?"

To Whit's dismay, Andrew leaned across the console to answer the officer. "On most models there's a little knob beside the steering column. You just pull it out. You want me to go back and get yours for you?"

"That's a real cute remark, smartass," the deputy replied, reaching for the citation book in his hip pocket.

"Let me see your license," he said to Whit.

Whit had already been feeling in his pockets and in between the seat cushions and under the seat, but could not locate his wallet, which meant that not only could he not show Mr. Bear his license, but if he couldn't find it, he and Andrew were also out twelve hundred dollars and a trip to the Sugar Bowl.

"I can't seem to find my wallet," Whit said meekly.

"You ain't got no license?" This seemed to delight Mr. Bear. "Over here in Alabama we shoot dogs what ain't got a license."

Whit hoped he was trying to be funny.

"There sure are a lot of beer cans in the back seat. I believe you probably been doing a little drinking and driving. We got laws against that in Alabama, too. I 'spect you better step out of the car."

"No sir, sir, I haven't been drinking. I swear. My buddy here, he's been drinking. He drinks like a fish, but I haven't had a drop."

"Yeah," Andrew agreed. "I been drinking. I been drinking a lot. But Whit, he ain't been drinking a bit. Say officer, did you hear the one about the midget that was on fire—"

"Would you shut up?" Whit demanded as he got out of the car and stood in the rain.

"Stand straight up with your hands straight out beside you, then slowly touch your nose, first with your right finger and then with your left." Mr. Bear was practically salivating thinking about all the charges he could bring—driving without headlights, no license, DUI—he hadn't clocked him fast enough for a speeding ticket to stand, but all the other would take the wind out of those two Bulldogs' sails. He'd teach them to pass through Alabama on their way to the Sugar Bowl.

"Sir, if I'm going to be out here for a while, could I get my coat out of the trunk?" To Whit's horror, Andrew was leaning over the seat, getting another beer out of the cooler. He had to block the deputy's view somehow. When he opened the trunk lid he felt a flood of relief as he remembered putting his wallet in the trunk for safekeeping, back at the massage parlor. While picking up his jacket he quickly recovered his wallet, dug out his license and triumphantly handed it to the disappointed deputy. He took it from Whit and studied it closely, noting that it was current and had no telltale staple holes that would indicate past traffic violations.

"Walk that line," the officer growled, indicating a solid white line at the edge of the emergency lane. He seemed disgusted when it became obvious that Whit was not under the influence. The only thing he had him for was not turning on his head lights in inclement weather, a paltry twenty dollar fine. Deputy Bear was trying to decide if it was even worth the paperwork to write him a ticket when a red Pontiac Grand Prix came flying by, at over a hundred miles an hour. The passenger was leaning out the window, the middle finger of each hand extended skyward in a gesture that was obviously not intended for Whit or Andrew.

"Hot damn!" Deputy Bear exclaimed, his eyes glowing. He dropped

Whit's license on the ground and sprinted to his car. He barely got his door closed before fishtailing onto the highway, very nearly hitting Whit in the process.

The last the boys saw of Deputy Bear was the two tail lights of his police cruiser growing rapidly smaller and then disappearing into the rain, in hot pursuit of two other Bowl-bound Bulldog fans. Whit and Andrew knew that he would never catch them.

"It's another sign," a rain soaked Whit announced as he got behind the wheel again.

"Let me get another beer," was Andrew's response.

Whit shook his wet head, pulled on his lights, and carefully drove onto the highway, very grateful for the two strangers in the red Grand Prix.

# Chapter Fifteen

With Whit behind the wheel, and the headlights beaming, the red
Camaro and its two passengers cruised down I-85 toward Montgomery.
Occasionally other bowl bound Bulldog fans would come flying by, blowing
their horns loudly and waving. More often, the boys would pass cars that
were flying the Bulldog banner. They would always hold up two fingers and
plead for tickets. They got plenty of sympathetic expressions, shouts of "Go
Dawgs" from practically everyone, barks from a few, more than their share
of smiles from pretty girls, but no offers of tickets.

"What if we can't find tickets?" Whit worried aloud.

Andrew was feeling no pain by this time. He was well on his way to
finishing his second six-pack and was playing the car stereo like it was a
grand piano, switching stations and popping tapes in and out of the cassette player, searching for just the right song.

"What did you say, buddy?" he slurred, when he finally realized he
was being spoken to.

"I said, what if we get down there and can't get tickets?"

"Oh, you worry too much. We've been to lots of games without tickets and we've always got in. Remember the Alabama game when we were
seniors in high school?"

Whit laughed. "Yeah, I remember. We had looked everywhere for
two tickets. We finally found a place in the corner of the stadium where no
security guards were stationed. You made me climb over the fence first,

because you were chicken."

"I wish I had gone first. You made so much commotion that two cops headed that way. They grabbed my ass as soon as I hit the ground."

Whit laughed harder. "Yeah. I said 'Run, Andrew,' just as they grabbed your arms."

"By God, I ran, too."

"Well, I don't think we can climb over the fence at the Superdome. It's got a roof."

"Well, maybe we can bribe a ticket-taker like you did at the Tech game in Atlanta last year."

Whit smiled at the memory. "That was too easy. I just fell in behind the band as they marched into the stadium. I handed the guy at the gate a twenty dollar bill and said, 'does this ticket work at this gate?' He never said a word. He just put it in his pocket and motioned for me to keep moving."

"We could always do what Terri Lynn did at the Florida game," Andrew suggested. Whit just shook his head as he remembered the incident. He still couldn't believe what his girlfriend had done.

Terri Lynn had planned to stay home and study the weekend of the Georgia-Florida game. Andrew and Whit had gladly accepted the offer of the Hawkins' extra tickets. At the last minute Terri Lynn had decided to come down to Jacksonville with two of her girlfriends, hoping to find a ticket for sale outside the Gator Bowl.

She didn't find any tickets, but somehow she did find Andrew and Whit. By this time she had concocted a scheme to get in the game. She talked her brother and Whit into waiting outside with her until just before kickoff, when the crowd trying to get through the gates was at its peak. Terri Lynn got between Andrew and Whit, and just as they handed their tickets to the taker, Terri Lynn threw herself down on the ground, right in the middle of the throng of people trying to get in the gate, and started having convulsions. She rolled her eyes back in her head, held her mouth open, moved her head from side to side, and caused her body to tremble and shake.

"Oh my God, she's having another seizure," Andrew shouted.

"Get her to the first aid station," Whit screamed.

The ticket-takers just looked at one another, not sure what to do.

"Get some help!" Andrew screamed.

Two young security guards heard the commotion and came running over to the gate. One picked the convulsing girl up by her arms, and his partner slid his arms under her knees. Together they carried her into the stadium and into the bright orange first aid tent. Andrew and Whit followed closely behind.

By the time the two attendants had placed her on the canvas cot and began arguing over how many of her clothes they needed to loosen, Terri Lynn's trembling had subsided and her large brown eyes were back to normal. Several young male medics became very attentive, taking the new patient's pulse, temperature, and blood pressure, massaging her wrists, and bringing her water and orange juice.

Thanks to all of the expert attention, Terri Lynn had an amazingly quick recovery; after about five minutes she felt as good as new. She pronounced herself well, to the disappointment of the mostly male first aid staff. She put one arm through Andrew's and the other around Whit's waist and walked out of the first aid tent and directly to aisle 112 in the corner of the Gator Bowl endzone. None of the red and black clad Georgia fans minded when the three newcomers squeezed into two seats. They were in place just in time for the National Anthem, and were still in their places some three hours later when Buck Belue and Lindsay Scott combined for the biggest miracle since the first Easter.

"That wouldn't work for us," Whit said. "Those horny guys just picked Terri Lynn up and carried her in so fast because they hoped to get a free feel and maybe get to look up that short skirt she was wearing. They'd probably let us lay there while seventy thousand people walked right over us to get in the Superdome."

"Well, don't worry. We'll get in the game somehow."

Andrew twisted around in the seat and started to reach in the back for another beer, but thought better of it. "We got to find a bathroom, man. I'm about to bust."

"This is your lucky day," Whit answered, reading the large blue road sign: *Rest Area—3 Miles.*

"It had better be three fast miles. I gotta go!"

"Tie it in a knot," Whit replied, but he did pick up speed, pushing the speedometer needle past seventy-five miles per hour in an effort to get his friend some much needed relief.

"Thank God," Andrew exclaimed as Whit pulled off the expressway and parked in front of the comfort station. They were near Ft. Deposit, Alabama, between Montgomery and Mobile. They had been on the road a little over four hours and were about two hundred miles from home, less than halfway to New Orleans.

Andrew threw open the car door and hit the ground running, almost before Whit had stopped the car. Whit laughed at his buddy as he got out of the Camaro and stretched, then headed toward the rest room for a little relief of his own.

He began to notice a foul odor as he approached the big metal door marked *MEN*. It got stronger the closer he got and nearly knocked him over when he opened the door. Andrew was standing at a urinal with one hand pinching his nostrils shut. Whit approached the urinal next to him, trying hard to hold his breath in order to avoid gagging.

"Damn, it stinks in Alabama," Andrew said.

"I don't know about the whole state of Alabama, but it sure as hell stinks in here," Whit answered.

By the time they had finished their business, both boys' eyes were burning and they found themselves gasping for breath as they headed for the exit.

"Oh my God, look!" Whit shouted, pointing to the driveway that ran behind the comfort station.

Andrew turned his eyes in the direction that Whit was pointing. What he saw was a man that looked something like a giant tomato, wearing bright red pants and a bright red shirt. He also wore black cowboy boots and a black Stetson with ticket stubs and a red feather sticking in the hatband. He was displaying a large amount of butt cleavage as he climbed into an ugly brown conversion van which was covered with bumper stickers and bore a license plate reading *BIGUN*.

Whit and Andrew stepped instinctively behind the corner of the building to avoid being seen. At least Whit stepped quickly. Andrew more or less staggered.

"Hoss Mitchell," Whit thought out loud. "No wonder that bathroom stunk so bad. He looks like he's by himself. Why in the world would Hoss Mitchell be headed to New Orleans all alone?"

"That dirty double-crosser," Andrew said. "He left us before we had a chance to leave him."

Whit laughed at Andrew's logic while watching Hoss drive away from the comfort station and pull his dilapidated old van back onto the highway. "He must be up to something, but I can't imagine what. Why would he go off and leave us holding his money?"

"Well, he's out a hundred and fifty bucks, I know that. Now we just have to make enough off beer to pay Calvin back."

"Well, I don't want to overtake him until I figure out what's going on," Whit said. "Why don't we take it easy for a while and let him get ahead of us, and then we can look at the map and figure out a way to take the back roads until we're sure he's long gone."

"Whatever you say, partner." Andrew said over his shoulder. He was already headed to the car, more especially to the cooler in the back seat of the car, eager to partake of more liquid refreshment.

# Chapter Sixteen

Whit had poked along at only five miles per hour over the speed limit for several miles, being very careful not to overtake Hoss and his rusty old van. He finally turned off the expressway near Bay Minette, Alabama and headed south on a ragged two-lane blacktop, heading toward Mobile.

"How'd you like to live in this part of the world? Nothing but house trailers and cow pastures." Andrew's head was clearing up somewhat. He hadn't had a beer for nearly twenty miles.

Whit made no comment. He just drove on through the rain.

"You know why New York is full of Yankees and Alabama is full of cow shit?" Andrew asked, not aware that Whit had failed to reply to his earlier comment.

"Because Alabama got first choice," he said, not waiting to be asked.

"Look at that trailer," Andrew continued, as they passed a particularly dilapidated looking dwelling. The sides were rusted. The steps leaned, and there was no underpinning. "If that place burned, I bet three families would be homeless."

Whit's ears were turning red as he drove in silence. He knew his friend meant nothing by his comments, but his thoughtless references to poor people had hit a nerve. Since the ninth grade, Whit had been very self conscious about his family's humble little mill house. It had linoleum floors instead of carpet and bare light bulbs hanging from the ceiling in the center of each room. In fact, Andrew was one of a very few town kids that Whit had ever invited to his house during high school days.

"You know what the state motto of Alabama is?" Andrew asked, still in rare form. " 'Thank God for Mississippi.' You know what you call someone in Alabama who finds a quarter?"

Whit drove on in stoic silence.

"Wealthy," Andrew answered, howling with laughter at his own cleverness.

Whit could bear it no longer. "Everybody can't be rich like you, asshole. Some folks aren't born with lots of money. Some people have to live in trailers. Some people live in mill houses, and are damn thankful for them. Some people drive used cars and feel lucky just to get by. But that doesn't make them bad people."

Even though his brain was numb with alcohol, Andrew was still cognizant enough to be embarrassed. He loved and respected Whit Johnson and had never been one to flaunt his family's wealth. He was fully aware that it was purely by chance that he had been born to parents who were well off, and he truly judged his friends on their own worth and not on their material possessions.

"I didn't mean anything by all that, Whit. I was just popping off. I was trying to be cute."

Whit gripped the steering wheel tightly and took a deep breath. He already knew that, but still had to swallow hard a couple of times before he could speak. "Oh, I know it. I guess I'm too sensitive. You know, I never realized how little my family had until I got in high school. Everybody that went to school in the mill village was in the same boat when it came to money. None of us had any.

"I'll never forget the first time you invited me to your house. That's the first time I'd ever been in a house with carpet on the floor and light switches on the wall. I remember wondering where your heaters were, 'cause I'd never seen a home with central heat. I couldn't wait to get home and tell Mama how beautiful your house was."

"None of that means anything." Andrew was really embarrassed now. "I always envied you because you and your dad got along so well. He actually taught you how to use tools and build things and threw the football with you and took you fishing and stuff. I remember thinking how lucky you were. My old man had money, but he didn't have a clue about what to do with me."

"Well, we're about even now, aren't we? Neither of us has any money." Whit drove in silence for a couple of miles as the flat, green, lower Alabama countryside flew by.

"Andrew, what do you reckon you'll do when you finish school—work in one of your daddy's businesses?"

"No way." Andrew was adamant. "I don't know what I'll do, but I won't be working for my dad. How about you? You'll have a business degree in August. You going off to Atlanta and work for some Fortune 500 company, or you gonna stay in Leesdale and take over the cotton mill empire?"

Whit hesitated before answering. "Promise not to laugh?"

"What are you talking about?"

"I've been talking to old Mr. Gordon about getting a job at the high school, teaching business classes and coaching JV football."

"No kidding? You've never mentioned wanting to be a teacher."

"Well, I've been thinking about it for a while. Last spring I went by and talked to Mr. Gordon. I've been taking some education courses this year and he helped me get fixed up with a program that would let me get credit for student teaching and teach at the same time.

"I dreaded talking to Coach Reed about being on the coaching staff. I was afraid he wouldn't want me—you know, the way I dropped off the team my senior year. But he couldn't have been nicer. He said I could help with the offensive line and coach the JV offense."

"No kidding?" Andrew had never pictured his friend as a schoolteacher, or as anything else for that matter. Andrew was in a holding pattern, wishing that he could be a college student for the rest of his life. The somber realization that his best friend, who was his exact age, was approaching full adulthood, with plans for a career and everything, moved Andrew to reach for another brew from the back seat cooler.

"Coach Johnson," he said. "That sounds pretty good."

"What about you, Andrew? You must have given some thought to life after college."

"When I was six I wanted to be a fireman," Andrew replied. "Then I found out they had to sit around the fire station for two or three days at a time and eat their own cooking, so I gave up that notion.

"I wouldn't mind being a pilot if I thought I could spend twenty years in the Air Force without turning into my old man. Course with my luck, as soon as I got my wings, some president would get us in a war and I'd get blown to smithereens by a Russian bastard, or some towel headed dictator who had traded his country's oil for a fighter plane."

Andrew took a big swig of beer.

"You want to hear something really funny?"

"What?"

"My mama has told me all my life that she hoped I'd make a preacher one day."

"A preacher?"

"Yeah. Can't you just see that now? I'd be the only preacher in the Southern Baptist Convention that served Jack Daniel's whiskey for communion instead of grape juice." Andrew laughed at the notion.

"Well, if you were like some of those preachers on television, you'd never have to worry about getting laid. Of course, if you were like Reverend Earl Dobbs you would never have to worry about money."

"If I was going to be a preacher, I'd want to be like that guy at the Methodist church in the mill village. He seems genuine to me. He doesn't seem all pious and doesn't put on airs and he's always out in the community doing things for people. Why is he still in Leesdale, anyway? I thought Methodists moved their guys around every four years or so."

Whit also admired Gus Jackson, and sometimes felt guilty that he'd abandoned the church of his youth for the social environment of the Baptist church during his high school days. Whit hadn't been in any church since his father's funeral. This also caused him a great degree of guilt.

"Well, he came here the summer before we were freshmen in high school." Whit was counting on his fingers. "He was still here when Daddy died and he was a big help, especially for Mama. I think he was scheduled to leave that next summer, but the church was doing so good that they decided to leave him right there. Then a couple of years later, his wife died of cancer, and I think he asked to be able to retire at Leesdale. He only had a couple of years to go."

"Well, I don't think I could be a preacher," Andrew said. "I cuss too much, and I'd probably have to quit drinking and marry some ugly woman with buck teeth and thick glasses."

"I don't know about that," Whit broke in. "Most of the preachers I've known had some pretty hot-looking wives."

"Well, I still think I'll have to find some other career," Andrew said. "Maybe I can be an FBI agent, like Herschel." He was referring to a comment made by Georgia's star running back that he might pursue a career in criminal justice instead of professional football.

"I guess the pulpit's loss would be law enforcement's gain. Ooh," Whit suddenly groaned as a sharp pain cut through his abdomen.

"Uh-oh," he groaned. "Mama's fried chicken must be working on me. We got to find a bathroom—quick!"

"There you are." Andrew pointed to a building a quarter of a mile ahead. "Pull in right there."

Whit was in too much pain to do anything else. He parked the Camaro practically in the doorway of a concrete block establishment that had obviously needed a paint job for years. There were several pickups parked at various angles in the muddy yard. Neon signs advertising several brands of beer adorned the windows, which were covered from the inside with brownish blinds that had once been white.

A hand painted sign proclaimed to the world that this was Bubber's Honky Tonk and Watering Hole. A smaller sign advised that there were pool tables available inside and that the first beer was free for unescorted ladies.

Andrew and Whit warily approached the rickety front door.

"How bad do you have to go?" Andrew asked.

"Bad," Whit answered.

I believe this is one of those places where they search you at the door, and if you don't have a gun or a knife, they give you one."

"I don't care." Whit was in serious pain. "Either go in or get out of the way."

"Well, if there's blood on the floor, I'll go in. But if there's blood on the ceiling, I'm waiting in the car." Andrew pushed the door open and walked in with Whit close behind.

The boys stood in a dark room, trying to let their eyes get accustomed to the lack of light. Whit was almost doubled over with pain. He was trying to locate the men's room door. The concrete floor was covered with sawdust, the better to soak up tobacco juice from the mouths of dippers and chewers. Directly in front of them was a wooden bar with several stools in front, three of which were occupied by young men who appeared to belong to the pickups parked out front. They were all drinking beer from long neck bottles. The bartender was a heavyset older man who wore a white apron over his T-shirt and had two arms full of tattoos.

A tall blonde wearing a green leather miniskirt and a tight black sweater leaned against one corner of the bar, sipping a drink through a straw from a tall frosted glass. She carefully looked Andrew and Whit over as they stood in the doorway.

Whit searched the room frantically with his eyes for a sign indicating the bathroom. To his left was a small bandstand, with an even smaller dance floor, surrounded by a dozen or so round tables with two or three chairs at each. To his right was a pool table where two bearded men wearing jeans, T-shirts, and baseball caps advertising heavy machinery watched appreciatively as a shapely young thing in tight cutoffs, high heel shoes, and a halter top leaned over the table and lined up a shot. Even in dire pain, Whit noticed that she was dressed rather strangely for December.

One of the men who was watching the pool demonstration finally noticed Whit and the look of agony on his face. He jerked his thumb toward a door in the back corner of the bar, directly across from the jukebox. There was no sign on the door, but there was a dirty outline where on might have been at one time.

Whit thankfully nodded, and made his way toward the back corner as quickly as possible. He pushed the door open, loosened his belt, and dropped his trousers. The dirty toilet didn't look too inviting, but Whit was past the point of caring about sanitation. He closed the door behind him, unable to find any kind of latch. He had no time to search for a light switch and found himself in total darkness. He sat down on the filthy commode, his rear end finding the cold porcelain just in the nick of time. He hoped that no one barged in on him as he sat in the darkness, anticipating one of the greatest bowel movements of all time.

To his amazement, his digestive system refused to cooperate, showing no appreciation whatsoever that Whit had been so quick to find a facility. The stomachache and intestinal pain was still there, but the other end just locked up. Nothing would come out but gas. After fifteen disappointing minutes, alone in the dark, Whit felt the sharp pains subside, at least enough for him to feel safe about leaving his place of sanctuary.

When he reentered the lounge it seemed almost bright after the complete darkness of the bathroom. The first thing he saw was Andrew, standing at the bar, sipping a draft beer from a glass mug. The blonde in the green miniskirt was hanging on his arm, drawing circles on his chest with a long red fingernail. She didn't look nearly as good since Whit's eyes had grown accustomed to the dim light. Andrew didn't seem to notice. The alcohol in his system was telling him that she was a beauty queen.

"Everything come out all right?" Andrew asked his buddy as Whit approached the bar. "Meet Mary."

"Not to be confused with the virgin of the same name," the girl added.

"Her friend Ginger is playing pool right now," Andrew continued, "but as soon as her game is over they want us to visit them in their trailer. They live right out back. Isn't that a lucky thing?"

"We got to go, Andrew." Whit grabbed his friend's elbow and tried to lead him away from the bar.

Andrew's new friend put her arm around Whit's waist and leaned forward, blowing gently into his ear, causing the hair on the back of his neck to stand up.

"What's wrong?" she murmured. " Don't you want to stay and play with Mary and Ginger?"

"Sorry," Whit said. "We can't afford to play with you and Ginger."

"Sure you can," she cooed. "We'll take you around the world for fifty dollars."

"Maybe some other time. Come on Andrew. We got to go see a man about a dog."

"Fifty dollars!" Andrew exclaimed. It had just dawned on him that the lovely Mary wanted him for his money and not his charm and rugged good looks.

"Come on Reverend," Whit said, pulling on Andrew's sleeve.

This time Andrew responded. "Sure thing, coach," he replied.

When the pair opened the outside door, leaving a disappointed Mary leaning against the bar, they were surprised to see a big, black Cadillac parked beside their Camaro. A middle aged man in an expensive looking suit was propped against the fender, smoking a cigar. He had an agreeable expression on his face and very little hair on his head.

"You boys need tickets to the Sugar Bowl?" he asked, pointing to the signs in their car window with his cigar.

"We need two," Whit replied.

"We need two, bad," Andrew added.

"Well, I believe I can help you. I just happen to have two, and I'd be happy to sell them to a couple of good old Georgia boys." The man reached into his inner coat pocket and produced two colorful pieces of cardboard.

The boys just stared. These were the first actual tickets they had seen.

"Could we take a look?" Whit finally asked.

"Certainly," the man answered, handing over the tickets.

Whit gazed at the prize ducats he held in his hand. They even felt special. They were larger than regular tickets and had colorful paintings of the Superdome, a riverboat, and the New Orleans skyline. *42nd Annual Sugar Bowl Classic* was printed across the top. *Georgia vs Notre Dame. January 1, 1981* was printed underneath. The price was along the edge in bold numbers—*$17.50*.

First Whit examined them. Then Andrew looked them over and returned them to the stranger's outstretched hand.

"How much do you want for them?" Whit asked. "Face value?" he added with a smile.

"Two-fifty," the man said, blowing thick blue cigar smoke from his mouth. He didn't smile.

Whit and Andrew looked at one another.

"Excuse us a minute," Andrew said, as he pulled Whit toward the back of the car for a private conference.

"Let's take 'em," Andrew said.

"I don't know, Andrew. We said we wouldn't go over a hundred apiece. We haven't even gotten to New Orleans. They may be selling for lots less down there."

"They may be selling for lots more, too. Or they may not be selling at all. We have more money than we'd counted on. Let's go ahead and take 'em. Then we won't have to worry about finding tickets when we get there. We can concentrate on having a good time and getting fired up for the game."

"I don't know, Andrew." Whit called out to the holder of the tickets,

"Could you take a little less?"

"Sorry, buddy. That's bottom dollar. They're selling for more in New Orleans. This is the hottest ticket in years."

"See," Andrew said. "Pay the man and let's get going."

"Well, all right," Whit grumbled. With a deep sigh he took his wallet out of his hip pocket and removed two hundred dollar bills and a fifty. He and Andrew walked over to the man.

"We'll take them," Whit said, offering the bills to the stranger.

The man just looked at the three bills in Whit's hand and took another puff of his cigar. "That'd be two-fifty apiece," he stated flatly.

Whit's jaw dropped. "Five hundred dollars! For two tickets? Man, you've got to be kidding!"

"Take it or leave it, fellas." The man's expression remained pleasant.

"I'm afraid we'll have to leave it," Whit answered.

"Wait, Whit. Let's talk about this," Andrew pleaded.

"Nothing doing." Whit's mind was made up.

"Sorry, mister. That's too steep for us."

"Well, good luck." The stranger placed the tickets back in his coat pocket, climbed into his expensive car, cranked it, and drove away. There was a big Roll Tide sticker on his back windshield.

"This may be tougher than we thought," Whit commented.

"Screw it. Let's go to New Orleans," Andrew said, slapping his buddy on the back and heading for the passenger side of his sister's car.

The boys turned and waved at Mary and Ginger who stood in the doorway of Bubber's Honky Tonk, blowing kisses to their would be customers.

# Chapter Seventeen

After their little rest stop at Bubber's Honky Tonk, Whit and Andrew traveled for over an hour without incident and covered nearly seventy miles. They marveled at the bridges going over Mobile Bay and argued briefly over whether or not it was their patriotic duty to stop and tour the Battleship USS Alabama. Andrew won out and they cruised on toward the setting sun, thankful that the rain had finally stopped. Whit continued to drive, keeping close enough to the speed limit to avoid being arrested, and Andrew continued to change the radio with every new tune.

Conversation centered on the football game, mainly the availability of tickets, and Georgia's chances of winning. From time to time, it would drift to the arrogance of Yankees in general and those who were likely to be in New Orleans in particular. Of course there were the obligatory remarks about how wild the women were sure to be and the odds of actually scoring with one or more non-professionals during the trip.

The boys would continue to pass other Georgia fans, also headed to the game, and often Georgia fans would pass them. There was still lots of horn blowing, raised fists, and *How 'Bout Them Dawgs* exchanged. Many people continued to take note of the *Need Two* signs in the red Camaro, but there was still no indication that any of the fans were headed to New Orleans with extra tickets in their possession. They neither saw nor smelled any sign of Hoss Mitchell.

Andrew actually drank a Coke and went nearly an hour without a beer. He was not sober, but was closer to it than he had been in hours, which was fortunate because about fifty miles outside Mobile, which would be about fifteen miles from the Mississippi state line, Whit's stomach came under attack, suddenly and unexpectedly. The same sharp pains he had experienced several times in the past two weeks began to shoot through his digestive track. He didn't even wait for an exit ramp, but pulled onto the emergency lane of Interstate 10 as soon as the pains hit. He safely stopped the car, then held his midsection and moaned in agony.

"Whit, man. Are you gonna be all right?" Andrew asked, concern written all over his face. Andrew had seen this act before and shuddered to think of encountering an Alabama version of Nurse Bahlraccker.

Whit could hardly answer, the pain was so severe. This was not the gas pains or simple cramps he had experienced earlier in the afternoon. This was a full blown attack of something. What, he didn't know.

"I don't know," he said. "You're gonna have to drive."

With great effort, Whit got out of the car on the driver's side and walked around to exchange places with Andrew.

"Do we need to find a hospital?" Andrew asked.

"I don't know. Just drive. Oh, God, my stomach hurts."

Somehow Andrew remembered to look over his shoulder and wait for a clear lane before pulling back onto the highway. Like a Southern stock car racer of old, pulling out of a pit stop, he floored the accelerator and went from a standstill to a hundred miles an hour in no time flat, quickly overtaking and passing the same cars that had passed them while they were pulled over to change drivers.

Whit was in too much pain to notice how fast Andrew was driving. He leaned back in the passenger seat, holding his belly and gritting his teeth. After about five minutes the pains eased just as suddenly and unexpectedly as they had begun.

Whit was soaked with sweat and took several deep breaths. Afraid that the excruciating pain would return at any moment, he gingerly sat up in his seat. "I feel better now. I think I might live," he announced. He glanced to the right just in time to see a large billboard proclaiming that he had indeed lived long enough to reach *Mississippi— the Magnolia State.*

"Glad you're gonna make it," Andrew commented. "We're in Mississippi, set your watch back twenty years."

"Nothing around here but a swamp," Whit said as he peered through the darkness, hoping to use what little daylight there was to catch a glimpse of the countryside. "I'd hate to get lost out there in the dark. Don't you think you'd better slow down, Andrew?" He had just noticed that his buddy was approaching the speed of sound. "Why don't you pull over and let me drive at the next exit. You've had all that beer and I feel fine now. I'd hate for you to get pulled over."

"Oh, shit, it's too late," Andrew said, jerking his thumb over his left shoulder.

Whit turned to look behind him and didn't like what he saw—a gray Mississippi State Trooper car, blue lights flashing, fish tailing across the tree lined median, leaving a huge cloud of dust in his wake.

Andrew, instead of slowing down, actually floored the accelerator. Whit looked at the dash and was horrified to see that the needle of the speedometer had been buried past the 120 mph mark.

He looked back and the patrol car was blocked from view by a steep hill. "Slow down, Andrew!" Whit screamed as he turned back around.

"There's an exit right up there," Andrew said. "We'll jump off the expressway and maybe he'll fly right on by."

By the time he got the sentence out of his mouth, the red Camaro was at the exit ramp. Andrew eased off the accelerator and allowed the car to slow to eighty.

He barely slowed down for the stop sign at the end of the ramp, before crossing the highway and squealing his tires to a stop in the parking lot of the only gas station on that exit.

"Run in the bathroom and pretend you're sick," he said to Whit, as he put the car in park and prepared to get out.

"I won't have to pretend. Maybe I should act like I was driving. What if he charges you with DUI?"

"I'll handle it. Get in the bathroom."

Against his better judgment, Whit followed his buddy's instructions. Just as he closed the men's room door he saw the gray patrol car flying toward them up the exit ramp.

The patrolman slammed on brakes at the stop sign, then flew across the intersection and slid to a stop in the service station parking lot, throwing up dust and gravel in the process.

A young state trooper, apparently in his middle twenties, ramrod straight and hard as steel, jumped out of the car. His hand was on the pistol butt of his black service revolver. Andrew, by this time, was out of the car, arms folded across his chest, leaning on the fender of the Camaro. He wondered for a moment if he were about to be shot.

The trooper stood angrily in front of Andrew and looked him up and down before speaking. "Are you the driver of this vehicle, sir?"

"Yes sir," Andrew answered, unfolding his arms and shifting to a more respectful posture.

"Sir, are you aware of your speed as recorded on my radar device, one point fives miles due east of here?"

"No sir," Andrew answered. "I know I was probably speeding a little bit."

"A little bit!" The officer almost lost his highly prized composure.

"Sir, I clocked you at over a hundred miles an hour, and I believe you increased your speed when I crossed the median to give pursuit. Sir, were you attempting to evade an officer of the law?"

"Oh, no sir," Andrew answered. "My friend was sick and I needed to get him to a bathroom."

As if on cue, Whit chose that instant to open the bathroom door and walk across the parking lot toward the car. When he saw the trooper in Andrew's face, it wasn't hard at all to look sick.

"There he is now," Andrew said. "Don't he look sick to you?"

"Sir, is your companion ill, or is he intoxicated?" the trooper asked suspiciously.

"Oh, he's not drunk," Andrew promised. "Just sick. I was afraid he'd throw up all over my sister's car here, and we got to drive it all the way to New Orleans."

The mention of New Orleans distracted the officer and he forgot, momentarily, the strict rules of interrogation he had learned in the State Trooper school from which he had just graduated.

"Y'all headed to the Sugar Bowl?" the officer asked.

"Yes sir."

The officer looked curiously at Whit, who was now approaching the car. "Are you really sick?" the young officer asked.

"Oh, yes sir. I'm awful sick," Whit assured him. "I think it was something I ate."

The trooper remembered himself and snapped to attention once more. "Sir," he said to Andrew, "I need to see your license. I am sworn to uphold the laws of the State of Mississippi and you were driving in excess

of the speed limit." He looked at Whit, then added, "But I'm truly sorry
your friend is so sick."

Andrew handed over his license and watched as the officer placed
it on his clipboard and walked to the back of the Camaro to begin recording
information for the inevitable citation.

Andrew and Whit exchanged glances. Andrew decided to take the
initiative and walked back to join the trooper at the rear of the car.

"Sir, I'm awfully sorry I was speeding in Mississippi," he began. In
truth he was amazed that the officer hadn't questioned his sobriety. He
considered leaving well enough alone, but couldn't resist the urge to try
and talk his way out of the ticket. "Is there any way you could just give me
a warning this time?"

The officer looked at Andrew with disdain, and continued to write.
"Sir, there are no warnings in the State of Mississippi. We take the position
that the posted speed limit is warning enough for law abiding citizens."
Then, noting the big sign across the back windshield, the trooper allowed
the tiniest hint of a smile to play across his face.

"I suppose that sign means y'all need two tickets. I guess I could
just write you out two of mine and y'all would be good to go."

The trooper laughed at his own cleverness.

"Well, sir, that's just it," Andrew began, still holding out a glimmer
of hope. "We barely have enough money to get by, and we don't know how
much we'll have to pay for tickets to the game. I don't know what the pen-
alty is for speeding here in Jefferson County, Mississippi, but if we have to
pay any sort of fine at all, that might knock us out of going to the game—
and we've been waiting a long time to watch a Southern team beat those
Yankees from Notre Dame."

The word *Yankees* got the trooper's attention and he stopped writing. He looked closely at the Confederate flag behind the back seat. "You think Georgia has a chance?" he asked, doubt clearly showing in his voice.

"Damn straight," Whit answered, speaking for the first time.

"I know we can beat 'em," Andrew answered emphatically. "Hell, after all they've been saying about the South, those Georgia boys will be so fired up, there's no way we'll lose."

"What have they been saying about the South?" the trooper asked. Whit wondered, too.

"Oh, you know, wondering if teams wear shoes in the SEC and comments like that. One player said that the height of confusion was Father's Day in Mississippi, just stuff like that."

"The hell you say." The trooper was pissed now.

"Yeah. The Notre Dame coach said that they were going to fly to Texas and drive to New Orleans to avoid flying over Mississippi, just in case ignorance was contagious."

"One of them said that?"

"I heard him myself, on television last night."

"And y'all think Georgia has a chance to whip 'em."

"Damn straight."

"How good is that big colored boy y'all got at halfback?"

"Herschel?" Andrew asked. "Hell, Herschel's about the best that's ever been. Those Notre Dame boys won't know what hit 'em when Herschel gets the ball."

"And y'all are going to the game?"

"Yes sir, that is, if we can afford a ticket after we pay our fine—you know, for speeding. Of course, I never meant to be speeding. I was just trying to get my friend here to the bathroom, because he was so sick and all."

"And you say he was real sick— about to throw up in that red car?"

"Yes sir."

"And that's your sister's car?"

"Yes sir."

"Oh, to hell with the fine," the trooper said. He wrote "case dismissed" over the ticket and tore off the bottom copy, handing it to Andrew.

"My daddy's the traffic judge. I'll explain everything to him. It'll be fine. Y'all go on down there and kick those Yankees in the ass one time for me."

"Yes sir!" Andrew said.

"Well, you boys slow down while you're going through Mississippi," the officer said, then got in his patrol car, backed up, and drove away, leaving a trail of gravel and dust in his wake.

"Can you believe that?" Whit asked, utterly amazed at what he had seen and heard.

"It's a great country, isn't it?" Andrew asked.

"It's a sign," Whit insisted. "It's a sign. We can't get a ticket and Georgia can't lose."

The two friends climbed back into the car and headed west.

# Chapter Eighteen

*Catfish Heaven - Good Food* proclaimed the sign above the concrete block building as the boys pulled into what seemed like the hundredth gravel parking lot of their trip. *Catfish - All You Can Eat - 5.95* stated another sign. *Chitlins every Thursday - January thru March* read a third.

"This ain't Thursday, is it?" Andrew asked, getting out of the car.

"It must not be, we stopped," Whit answered, exiting on the driver's side.

"All of these cars have Mississippi tags and most of 'em are from Jefferson County, so I guess the locals eat here. It must be a good place," Andrew observed.

"Look at that car. It's about as out of place as a bottle of booze at a Baptist picnic," Whit said, pointing to a bright yellow Lincoln Town Car with New Jersey license plates.

"What in the world are a bunch of Yankees from New Jersey doing at a catfish place in southern Mississippi?" Andrew wondered aloud as he pushed open the door and entered Catfish Heaven. He found out as soon as he entered. They were waiting to be seated, and waiting very impatiently.

There were four of them and they all could have been cut from the same bolt of cloth. The father was tall and slender. He had greasy black hair that was combed straight back, a rather large nose, and thick black glasses. He wore a yellow Notre Dame sweatshirt, which looked rather incongruous with his black plaid slacks, black socks, and white sneakers. The teenager, who was obviously his son, was a carbon copy. He also wore a Notre Dame shirt, but instead of houndstooth plaid, his pants were black high waters that ended a good inch above his ankles, revealing white socks. He wore brown wing tip shoes and his face was covered with acne. He, too, wore glasses.

Mother and daughter were also clones. Neither was very pretty to look at. Both had red hair and thousands of freckles. Each wore a long black skirt, white blouse and a sweater tied around her neck. Each stood with a hand on one hip and her nose in the air. They both wore perpetual pouts.

"For Christ's sake, can't you people seat us? There are plenty of empty tables," the father said in a high pitched, whiny voice. The attractive middle aged lady behind the cash register answered him with as much patience as she could muster. "Chrissy will be with you in a minute," she said pleasantly. "I think she's in the back filling up some salad dressing bottles."

"Oh brother," Mr. Obnoxious said, folding his arms, tossing his head and rolling his eyes, making every effort to show his disdain.

Andrew and Whit looked around the room. The walls were utilitarian, the same concrete block as the exterior, but painted a pale green. There was a counter in one corner of the room with a cash register behind it and a large rack holding a wide assortment of candy treats to one side. On the counter was a large bowl full of pastel colored mints, a metal container of toothpicks and three or four mason jars with slits cut in the top and pictures of cute grade school girls on the front. Each jar had a note taped under the picture soliciting votes for Miss Jefferson County Elementary School. A cute little blonde with straight hair and two front teeth missing seemed to be the early leader. Her jar was nearly half full of nickels, dimes, and pennies. There were several hand lettered signs taped to the front of the counter. One read, "In God we trust—all others must pay cash." Another said, "It's nice to be important, but it's more important to be nice."

The dining area of the restaurant consisted of one large room with many formica-topped square tables scattered about in assorted configurations. Most would seat four, but some had been pushed together to accommodate six or eight people. One long table stretched across the back wall, where ten or twelve people were laughing, talking and putting away huge platters of fried catfish, french fries, and hush puppies, large bowls of coleslaw, and giant pitchers of sweet iced tea.

The tables were so close together that customers at one table could easily carry on a conversation with fellow diners at surrounding tables. Many customers seemed to be well acquainted and were visiting with several different groups at once. Three young girls, who appeared to be still in their teens, and two middle aged ladies, all wearing jeans, were busy going back and forth from the serving window to the tables. They expertly balanced huge trays that were stacked high with platters of delicious looking food. An older man was walking among the tables, a tea pitcher in one hand and coffee pot in the other, offering refills, friendly smiles and pleasant chitchat. The walls were adorned with deer heads, fishing poles, trophy fish, a large fishing net, and hand lettered signs bearing various religious slogans. The atmosphere was warm and friendly, and the food smelled delicious.

"Hey, are there six of y'all?" a friendly little pixie of a girl who couldn't have been more than eighteen years old or more than five feet tall came out of the kitchen area, carrying a stack of plastic coated menus. Her brown hair was cut short, and she had bright brown eyes and a scattering of freckles over her nose.

"No, there's not six of us. Can't you people even count to four down here?" the Yankee interloper said. His whiny, nasal voice sounded mean and hateful. There was no touch of humor in his tone and it was obvious that the girl, who was named "Chrissy" according to the name tag pinned to her red shirt, was stunned by his rudeness.

"Oh, I'm sorry. I thought y'all were together," she said, nodding toward Whit and Andrew, who were standing behind Mr. Obnoxious and his twerpy family.

"Well, we all is all by our little lonesome," the man said, mocking Chrissy's sweet Southern voice.

Whit and Andrew couldn't help but hear the exchange. Whit balled his fists in anger and took one step forward, but Andrew put a hand on his shoulder and discreetly shook his head at his buddy.

The young waitress had never encountered customers like these in her short tenure at Catfish Heaven, and she wasn't sure how to react. "I'm so sorry," she said, "why don't y'all sit right here." She led them to a table just a few feet away, on the outer perimeter of the room.

"Would y'all be needing a menu?" she asked politely as the family was taking their seats. This was a perfectly normal question to her, because most of the customers of Catfish Heaven had been coming there for years and would have been insulted by the suggestion that they didn't know what their choices were.

"Well, how else do you think we'll be able to order?" the man asked, his voice dripping with sarcasm. His redheaded daughter leaned across the table and whispered something to the mother from which she had been cloned, who in turn whispered in her husband's ear.

He rolled his eyes and turned back toward Chrissy, who was becoming more and more flustered by the minute.

"Is there a rest room in this place?" he snapped.

"Yes sir," Chrissy replied; then, "I mean, no sir. I mean, we have bathrooms, but they're outside. I mean, they're inside, but you have to go outside and around back to get to them."

The mother and daughter exchanged horrified looks, and rolled their eyes toward the ceiling.

"Are there flush toilets in Mississippi?" the man asked.

"Oh, yes sir." the poor waitress answered him.

The mother and daughter exchanged glances. The mother shook her head from side to side and continued to sit at the table. Junior hadn't opened his mouth the entire time. He sat at the table staring stupidly into space through his thick glasses.

Not knowing what else to say, Chrissy finally excused herself, promising to be back for their order in "just a jiffy."

Andrew and Whit had heard the entire encounter. Andrew was irritated. Whit was fighting mad.

"I ought to go stomp a mudhole in that Yankee son of a bitch," he said.

"Just cool it man," Andrew said. "We don't want to hunt trouble." In most situations it was Whit who had the cool head and kept Andrew out of trouble, but Andrew had learned long ago that if someone rubbed Whit the wrong way, he was ready to fight at the drop of a hat.

"Hey, how y'all doing this evening?" Chrissy tried to sound cheerful as she smiled at the boys.

"We're doing just fine," Andrew assured her.

"Don't you pay any attention to those folks," Whit told her. "They can't help the way they are. They're just Yankees."

Chrissy smiled a little smile of thanks and led Andrew and Whit to the only empty table in the room, which happened to be right beside the family from New Jersey. She smiled at them again, as if offering an apology, and shrugged her shoulders, before leaving the boys two menus and stepping over to the next table.

"All that's on here is catfish," Mr. Obnoxious snapped at Chrissy, as soon as she approached the table. "Don't you have anything else?"

"Why in the hell would someone come to a place called Catfish Heaven if they didn't want catfish?" Whit whispered to Andrew.

"Yankees," he whispered back, as if that were the only explanation needed.

Chrissy was mystified by the behavior of these foreign sounding customers.

"Well," she offered, "we have a steak plate with a salad and french fries for eight dollars, and a cheeseburger with fries for $2.50."

"Well, for Christ's sake, why aren't they on the menu?"

The young waitress was almost in tears by this time. She didn't answer. She just raised her eyebrows and shrugged her shoulders.

"What type of steak comes on your 'steak plate?' " Mr. Obnoxious asked, again mocking her accent.

"Sir?" the puzzled Chrissy replied.

"I guess you people don't understand properly spoken English. I said, 'What kind of steak does you all serve on yo steak plate?' " There was mockery in every exaggerated syllable.

Meanwhile, at the next table, Whit had had about as much as he could stomach. "It will be worth a night in jail, Andrew. I'm gonna kick his ass."

He started to rise from his seat, but Andrew reached across and put a hand on his arm.

"Just hold on," he pleaded.

Whit frowned in reply and resumed studying the various combinations of catfish platters available at Catfish Heaven.

Chrissy tried her best to appease the irate customer. She was unaware that most conversation had stopped in the immediate area. Andrew and Whit weren't the only customers who couldn't help but overhear the encounter. All were upset.

"I think we have T-bone steaks," she replied feebly.

"Well bring me a T-bone steak, and make sure it's cooked medium well. That's a gray center. Give me ranch dressing on my salad. I guess you don't serve baked potatoes?"

Chrissy shook her head in reply.

"What do you guys want?" Mr. Obnoxious whined through his nose to his family.

"I suppose I'll have the same thing," Mrs. Obnoxious whined in reply. "Bring a cheeseburger for the children."

Little Miss Obnoxious turned up her nose and junior just sat in his chair, staring stupidly into space.

"That's two steak plates, medium well with ranch, and two cheeseburgers." Chrissy made one last valiant effort to smile. "What y'all gonna drink?"

"My wife and I will have red wine."

"We don't serve spirits here." Chrissy almost winced as she said it.

The man sighed deeply. He and his wife rolled their eyes at one another.

"Well, you all can just bring us some water, honey chile." He threw down his menu in disgust.

When Chrissy turned to face Whit and Andrew there were tears in her eyes. She tried her best to blink them away. She was thankful for the bright smile that greeted her underneath Andrew's full dark mustache.

"Don't pay him any attention," Andrew said kindly. "They ain't from around here."

"What y'all gonna have?" Chrissy smiled back.

"I'll have the medium catfish—all you can eat, and sweet tea." Andrew said.

"Me, too," Whit added.

These were the kinds of orders Chrissy was used to. She smiled her thanks and headed for the kitchen.

Whit and Andrew took turns visiting the restroom outside and then sat and discussed the game and speculated about what time they would finally get to New Orleans. They tried to ignore the whiny voices of their neighbors at the next table.

Before they knew it, Chrissy was back, expertly balancing a tray laden with golden fried catfish, hand-cut fries, large bowls of slaw, and tall glasses of sweet iced tea. "Here are some lemons and a bone plate. I'll bring you back a pitcher of tea."

She turned to leave the table and Mr. Obnoxious reached out and grabbed her arm. "We ordered before them. Where's our food?" he demanded.

"It'll be right up, sir. This catfish came out first 'cause we are always cooking fish."

"Well make it snappy, would you? Jesus Christ! How long do you have to wait for a steak?"

The visitor never knew how close he had come to being knocked senseless. He let go of the waitress's arm just in the nick of time. Andrew was using all the restraint he could muster to keep Whit in his chair. He looked all around for the proprietor, but he seemed to have stepped out of the room.

"Just eat your fish, man," he finally said to Whit. "We'll be on Bourbon Street in about an hour."

"I hope I meet up with him down there," Whit said grimly.

The fish were delicious and the boys were famished. They were well on their way to making short work of the first platter when Chrissy returned with seconds for them and the food for the Yankee family. She distributed their plates and glasses of ice water as quickly as possible and departed.

She was almost to the kitchen when she was shocked to hear a loud whistle coming from the direction of the table she had just served. She turned and looked over her shoulder in amazement. The entire restaurant had turned to look as well. A million pounds of catfish had been served to the customers of Catfish Heaven without anyone needing to whistle to gain the attention of a waitress.

Mr. Obnoxious had a scowl on his face and was motioning Chrissy back toward the table with a crooked finger.

She turned and made her way back.

Every eye in the restaurant was on her.

"Didn't I order my steak medium well?" the man asked in his whiniest and most obnoxious tone.

"Yes, sir," Chrissy answered.

"Well, I don't call this medium well, do you?"

Chrissy looked down at the perfectly broiled steak with one piece removed, and was afraid to answer.

"Well, do you?

Andrew put out one hand to stop Whit from standing and stood up himself. The restaurant was completely quiet. All conversation and all eating had stopped.

Andrew walked over to the Obnoxious family's table, smiling pleasantly. He put one hand on the complaining customer's shoulder. Andrew wanted to be sure the man felt the strength of his grip. "Ladies and gentlemen," he announced to the crowd in the restaurant, who had given their undivided attention to the drama that was being played out at the small square table. "We're going to take a vote."

To the amazement of everyone, particularly the man whose shoulder he was squeezing, Andrew picked up a fork from the table, rammed it into the center of the man's steak and lifted fork and steak high above his head.

"It's time to vote," he proclaimed. "How many of y'all think this steak is medium well?"

The patrons of the restaurant, all local people who were totally unused to this type of incident, looked around at one another for a moment. Finally one seventy year old man raised his hand. Another customer followed suit; then another and another. Soon, every man, woman and child in the place, including the waitresses and cooks who had stepped out of the kitchen, had at least one hand raised toward the ceiling.

"It's unanimous," Andrew shouted triumphantly, slamming the steak down on the astounded man's plate. "This steak is hereby declared medium well—by decree." He leaned closer to Mr. Obnoxious and gave his shoulder an even firmer squeeze. "Now eat every bite," Andrew said, between clenched teeth. He spoke in the most menacing voice he could muster. Andrew returned to his seat amid thunderous applause from the other customers. He bowed deeply and waved at his admirers, before taking his seat.

"See," he said to Whit. "Violence is not the only way. The threat of violence will often  do just as well."

Whit just grinned at him.

Mr. Obnoxious entertained thoughts of leaving abruptly, but re-membering the feel of Andrew's grip on his shoulder and his instructions to clean his plate, was afraid  to go until he had done just that.

Whit and Andrew finished off two platters of fish.  Whit handed Andrew a twenty, told him to pay the bill, and headed for the door. Andrew assumed he was going to visit the head.

He ambled over to the cash register and paid their ticket, gra-ciously accepting the thanks of the woman behind the counter. He walked back to his table and left a generous tip for Chrissy and then winked at the Obnoxious family who had eaten every last crumb on their plates, but were still afraid to leave until Andrew was gone.

Andrew walked out of the restaurant into the cool night air just in time to see Whit screwing the gas cap back into place on the yellow Lincoln Town Car .

"Help me pick them up," Whit said.

Andrew looked down to find the ground littered with small white packets that had once held Dixie Crystals sugar.

"What are you doing?" Andrew asked.

"Sugar in the gas tank makes cotton candy in the carburetor," Whit explained. Andrew just laughed, and started picking up sugar packets.

They had picked up the litter and were sitting in their car when the family from the North came out of Catfish Heaven.  They watched in amused silence as the unfortunate visitors settled into their seats and drove away.

"They won't get far," Whit commented with satisfaction. "Looks like we're gonna be blessed with a little more rain," he added as he took note of the light sprinkles that were beginning to fall from the sky.

# Chapter Nineteen

"Uh oh, cooler's empty." Andrew was leaning over the seat, digging deep into the ice and water, which was all that was left in the red cooler. "Get off at the next exit and let me pick up a six pack," he instructed as he eased back into his seat.

"Come on, Andrew, the last sign said *New Orleans-- 40 miles*. We'll be there in half an hour."

"I want to make sure I feel just right when we hit the French Quarter for the first time. Pull off and let me get some more cold beer. Look at the clock. It's nearly ten, Georgia time." Andrew shook water from his hands and began turning the knobs on the car stereo, looking for just the right music. "I thought somebody said you could drive to New Orleans in less than nine hours."

"I guess you could," Whit said, "if you didn't get stopped by the cops three times and visit a massage parlor and Catfish Heaven."

"Well, it don't matter." Andrew had found an oldies station on the far end of the dial. "Bourbon Street will just be waking up when we get there. Look up yonder, on the side of the road. Is that our Yankee friend?"

Whit slowed down a little as they approached a Ford Mustang in the emergency lane with its flashers on and hood raised. A tall, leggy blonde in a miniskirt was standing in front of the car, looking helpless.

"Stop, Whit," Andrew shouted. "That precious child needs help."

Whit hit his brakes, thankful that there were no cars behind him on the dark expressway, and began to pull over into the emergency lane. He was about a hundred yards past the disabled vehicle by the time the red Camaro came to a stop.

"Andrew," Whit complained. "We don't know anything about fixing cars."

"No," Andrew agreed, "but I know lots about long legged blondes in miniskirts, and I'll bet they can be very appreciative."

"Back in Leesdale you didn't even want to change a tire for poor old Mrs. Barnes, and now you want to pull over on a dark highway for a total stranger." Whit was carefully backing up in the emergency lane.

Andrew turned and grinned at his buddy. "Old Mrs. Barnes didn't have legs like her."

He turned back to admire the damsel in distress. They were about twenty yards from her and closing rapidly when, out of the corner of his eye, Andrew noticed movement in the gully beside the car.

"Stop!" he screamed.

"Now what?" Whit asked, annoyed at his friend for startling him.

"Go, go, go!" Andrew shouted frantically.

Whit had rolled to a stop about thirty feet from the blonde's car. He turned in exasperation to see what Andrew was screaming about. Just as he did he saw a large man in dark clothes jump out of his hiding place in the roadside gully and rush toward their car.

Forgetting that the car was still in reverse, Whit hit the accelerator, causing the red Camaro to lurch backward. The miniskirted blonde, fearing that she was about to be crushed, jumped up on the hood of the Mustang. Her partner jumped out of the way of the wildly careening auto, landing in the kudzu at the bottom of the ditch.

Whit realized that he was going backward and slammed on brakes,

bringing his car to a stop just inches away from the Mustang and the terri-
fied blonde who was balanced precariously on her car's front bumper. He
jerked the gear shift lever into drive and lurched forward, burning rubber
and spraying gravel on the white Ford, the blonde on the bumper, and the
would be mugger who was picking himself up out of the ditch.

"Damn, Andrew," Whit exclaimed as he brought the car under control and pulled back onto the deserted stretch of highway.

"What did I do?"Andrew demanded. He could feel his heart pounding against the wall of his chest.

"You nearly got us robbed—and killed." Whit was scared to death.

"That was close, all right." Andrew took a deep breath, then started
giggling. Soon he was laughing out loud.

Whit wanted desperately to stay mad at his buddy, but couldn't.
He started laughing, too. Soon both boys were laughing uncontrollably,
tears streaming down their faces. From out of nowhere came the white
Mustang, passing the red Camaro like it was standing still. Whit caught a
glimpse of the blonde's face, pressed against the window as it sped by and
left them behind.

"These are strange times we're living in," Whit managed to say.

"Get off at the next exit," Andrew said. "I've got to have a cold
beer."

Whit came out of the bathroom of the Quick and Speedy, somewhere just west of the Pearl River, and paid for the gas that Andrew had
pumped, a six-pack of beer and a large Coke. The light rain that had begun
to fall was getting heavier.

"The girl at the counter said we're twenty miles away," Whit said
to Andrew who was burying five of the six beers in the melting ice of the

cooler in the backseat.

"Hot damn," Andrew responded

"Y'all need two?" The voice was sweet as sugar and came from the cab of a black pickup that had pulled up beside the Camaro.

"We need two tickets to the Sugar Bowl." Whit smiled at the young girl on the passenger side of the pickup. She appeared to be about eighteen and had a pretty face, curly black hair, and brown eyes. A slender redhead with long straight hair sat behind the steering wheel.

"That's too bad," the brunette said. "We were hoping y'all needed two of something else."

"Well, what did y'all have in mind?" Andrew walked around the Camaro and leaned in the window of the pickup, flashing a brilliant smile at the occupants, noting that the brunette wore corduroy pants and filled out her dark sweater nicely. He then shifted his gaze to her friend, whose skintight jeans covered two of the longest legs Andrew had ever seen.

"Andrew. . ."

Andrew pretended he hadn't heard his buddy.

"Y'all are going to New Orleans, aren't you?"

"Yes, we are," Andrew assured her.

"Andrew, let's go."

Andrew continued to ignore him.

"Would y'all like to have some company?" the brunette asked. The redhead said nothing, but leaned across the seat and flashed Andrew a smile that matched his own.

"Andrew, I need a word with you." Whit had walked around the car and grabbed Andrew by the arm. He had to practically pull his friend away from the truck window.

"What in the world is wrong with you?" Andrew asked Whit. "This is just another sign. We're not even in New Orleans yet, and we already have gorgeous young ladies practically begging to go with us."

"But Andrew, those girls are so young. Besides that . . ."

Whit paused in mid-sentence as a Jefferson County sheriff's car pulled up right beside the girls in the pickup. An angry looking deputy with flame red hair got out of the car and walked quickly to the window of the truck. Completely ignoring Andrew and Whit, for which they were very thankful, he lit into the driver of the truck who was obviously his daughter. The boys didn't get the entire conversation, but they heard enough to know that they needed to make themselves very scarce, and the sooner the better.

They got back in the Camaro as discreetly as possible. The deputy stood beside the pickup with his arms folded across his chest and watched as his daughter backed out of the parking space and drove off down the road, presumably toward home. The man turned and gave the boys a dirty look, but got in his cruiser and left without saying anything to them.

"Thank goodness," Whit said, breathing a sigh of relief.

"Since when is it against the law for a young man to try and pickup pretty young ladies?" Andrew asked.

"When that young man is a stranger in a strange land, and the young lady's father is the law, that's when," Whit answered. "Now, New Orleans is thirty miles away. Do you think we can go the rest of the way without having to stop?"

"You're the one holding us up. Quit running your yap and let's get going."

Whit was more than happy to comply. He started the engine then pulled the knob on the dash that should have turned on the lights. Nothing happened. He pushed the knob in and pulled it out again. Still no lights.

"Great," he said, "now the lights won't come on."

"Must be a fuse," Andrew suggested.

The boys got out of the car and lifted the hood. The on-again off-again drizzle was off for the time being. They spent thirty minutes getting in and out of the car, pulling on wires and jiggling switches. They changed every fuse on the panel. It was all to no avail. The lights would not come on.

The convenience store clerk had tried to be helpful. She even called her brother-in-law down to the store to take a look at the problem. His name was Shorty, and he claimed to be the best shade tree mechanic in the Pearl River delta. After studying the problem for about ten minutes, Shorty explained to the boys that he was "good on mechanical, but not much on electrical." He accepted ten dollars for his trouble and called his friend, Possum, to come down to the store.

Possum examined the car for another ten minutes and advised the boys that an electrical short was the cause of their problem and that the closest place to have it repaired was—New Orleans. It seemed that electrical specialists were higher paid than mechanical. Possum took twenty of the boys' dollars for his trouble.

"Looks like we're stuck here until daylight," Whit said glumly.

"Damned if that's so," Andrew replied. He strode into the convenience store and came out five minutes later carrying four very large flashlights—the kind with big square beams that people use for fishing. He opened the trunk and retrieved the roll of masking tape that Terri Lynn had tossed there when she taped the signs to the car windows.

"Andrew, you're not?"

But he was. And did. He turned on the flashlights and placed them on the hood of the car, placing two on each side. He then secured them in place by wrapping yards and yards of brown masking tape around the front of the car. The alcohol in his system had rendered Andrew totally mindless of the car's paint job, and all of Whit's protests fell on deaf ears.


It was midnight in Georgia—eleven local time—when Whit Johnson and Andrew Hawkins, riding in a mud splattered red Camaro, with four fishing lanterns lighting their way, drove across the Mississippi River Bridge and entered New Orleans, Louisiana. They exited the interstate and followed the signs to the Vieux Carre—otherwise known as the French Quarter.

Seventy hours had passed since Andrew had awakened Whit from his dreams of Gladys Gibson. Georgia's kickoff against Notre Dame was sixty-three hours away.

# Chapter Twenty

"Hey, Mister, need your shoes shined?"

"Bet I can tell your fortune."

"Go Dawgs!"

"Go you hairy Dogs!"

"Hey sweetheart, looking for a date?"

"How 'bout them Dawgs!"

"Go to hell Notre Dame, go to hell!"

"Come on in and see the show. We have the wildest girls on Bourbon Street."

"We aren't in Kansas anymore, Toto," Andrew said to Whit, as the two strolled down Bourbon Street, taking in all the sights, sounds, and smells that made the New Orleans French Quarter at midnight such an astonishing place, particularly to the first-time visitor.

"We ain't in Leesdale, either," Whit responded in amazement as a girl on a trapeze, wearing fishnet hose and little else swung right out in front of him and then back into the window of the seedy strip joint from which she had come.

It was indeed midnight in New Orleans, and Bourbon Street was wide open. The street was closed to traffic and people were everywhere. A large percentage of them were Georgia Bulldog people who were proudly displaying their school colors and greeting total strangers as if they were long lost friends.

Spontaneous pep rallies broke out on every street corner and male and female college students stood on balconies overlooking the street, offering raucous toasts to the crowd below.

New Orleans street people were out in force. There was a plethora of homeless winos, young black boys tap dancing for coins, mimes, jugglers, magicians, pimps, panhandlers, and prostitutes, all of whom did their part to give the city her soul, or if not her soul, at least her reputation. All seemed to be present and accounted for when December 29 became December 30 in 1980.

Whit and Andrew had miraculously driven the two dozen miles from the Pearl River Valley by the light of the flashlights without so much as meeting a cop. Even more miraculously, they had found their way to Canal Street, on the edge of the French Quarter, and an empty parking space.

"It's a sign," Whit had insisted.

As soon as they saw the bright lights of the city, the boys quickly forgot about being tired from the long drive and the events of the day. Neither did they give any thought to finding accommodations.

"Which way is Bourbon Street?" Andrew said to the first person they saw, a large black man in a tuxedo, who was waiting for a taxi.

"One block up and turn right," he grinned his reply.

"Anything still going on?" Whit asked naively.

The man threw back his head and laughed.

"Bourbon Street is just now waking up for the evening."

The two boys nodded their thanks and hurried off in the direction the man had indicated. They stopped at the next corner to study the street sign, which was attached to a black pole, topped with a gaslamp. "Rue de Bourbon" was engraved on the sign.

"This must be the place," Whit noted.

"Leave us go amongst them," Andrew replied.

Andrew had traveled with his family, but had never been to New Orleans. Other than a couple of trips to Jacksonville and a few camping trips to the Great Smoky Mountains, Whit had hardly been away from Leesdale. Neither was prepared for the sights they were about to see.

The first thing that caught their eyes was a wino, sound asleep, in the doorway of Woolworth's on the corner of Bourbon and Bienville. He was covered by a woolen army blanket, and Whit thought he was dead. He stopped in his tracks and stared at the unfortunate soul as if he were a sideshow at the county fair.

"Look, an oyster bar," Andrew shouted as he slapped Whit's shoulder to get his attention and pointed down the street called Iberville. "Let's check it out."

Whit tore his gaze away from the sleeping man and hurried through the crowd of people to catch up with his buddy, who was already a half a block away.

Andrew was waiting for him at the open doorway of one of New Orleans most well known landmarks. As they entered together, they were met by a chorus of voices, each vying for their attention.

"Belly up and eat some oysters," came one voice.

"Stand right here and eat oysters," said the next.

"I'll shuck you some oysters 'fore them other boys can think about it," said a third.

"Sit down here at the these stools, and I'll bring you some oysters," said a fourth voice, at the far end of the bar.

"Man, you the bartender," snapped voice number three. "Leave our customers alone."

"Yeah," said number two. "Stand up here and eat you some oysters," he said again to Whit and Andrew.

"You the worst shucker we got," snapped back the bartender. "Folks can eat oysters wherever they want to."

This spirited repartee was coming from several young black men, lined up behind a long mahogany bar. All wore identical uniforms which consisted of white slacks, white starched shirts, black bow ties, and soiled aprons which had once been white. Shuckers one, two, and three stood at the only empty spaces along the crowded bar. The bar had a foot rail along the base, but no stools. A dozen customers stood along the bar and ate oysters as fast as the men behind the counter could deliver them.

Toward the end of the bar were a dozen or so stools where customers sat and drank cocktails and beer, while eating PoBoy sandwiches. Occasionally, one of these customers would order a dozen raw, much to the delight of voice number four, who would triumphantly enter the domain of the shuckers and retrieve a dozen oysters from the large wooden crates which were stacked under the gilded mirror which ran the length of the room.

All four voices quickly turned their attention away from Whit and Andrew and began shouting at new customers who were entering the open door. The boys from Leesdale were a little intimidated by the unfamiliar environment and retreated to a spot in the corner of the room where they could survey the scene and get their bearings. They stood and watched the more experienced customers gobble up the large succulent oysters.

Whit was fascinated by the small black men behind the bar, who earned their living shucking oysters. They picked up the ugly looking brown shells, snapped them open with a sharp flat knife, set them on metal trays and placed them on the counter, a dozen at a time. Their movements were smooth and graceful, and they kept up a constant patter, talking to one another, their customers, themselves, and often, no one in particular.

Andrew studied the oyster eaters. Each person seemed to have their own unique style. A large balding man in a a camel hair sportscoat seemed to suck the oysters right out of the shell, as fast as they were placed before him.

An elderly lady in a fashionable black dress with a mink stole draped over her shoulders stood  elbow to elbow with the predominantly male crowd, daintily lifting oysters from the shells with a silver cocktail fork. A young couple stood at one end of the bar making goo-goo eyes at one another and eating oysters from the same tray.

Most dressed their oysters with cocktail sauce, hot sauce, or both. Some placed them on Saltine crackers while others ate them right off the shell and chased them with Saltines. Almost everyone was washing the oysters down with cold beer in frosted mugs.

"I'll bet the guy who ate the first raw oyster was really hungry," commented Whit.

"Or real drunk,"Andrew said. "You  ever eat a raw oyster?" he asked his friend.

"I ain't never been hungry enough," Whit replied. "You eat 'em?"

"Shoot yeah. They're better than snuff, and not half as dusty. Let's eat some."

"I'll pass. You go ahead," Whit offered.

Andrew laughed. "Let's walk. I'll eat some tomorrow."

They walked out of the oyster bar and headed back up Iberville toward Bourbon. As they headed down the street, people were everywhere. The boys tried to look in every direction at once.

A black teenager, whose skin was the color of coffee with heavy cream, came up to Andrew.

"Hey man," he said, "I bet you five dollars I can tell you where you got your shoes."

Andrew was puzzled. "Where I got my shoes?"

"Yeah, man. I bet you five dollars I can tell you where you got your shoes. In fact, I bet I can tell you the exact street, city, and state."

Andrew thought the proposition over carefully.

"It's a trick," Whit warned.

"This guy couldn't possibly know where I got my shoes," Andrew said to Whit out of the side of his mouth. "I got them at Brown's in Leesdale. He couldn't possibly know that."

Whit shrugged and shook his head.

"How 'bout it man. You wanna bet?" The youth was holding a five dollar bill.

"Sure," Andrew agreed, digging a five out of his own pocket. "Why not?"

"You wouldn't tell a lie to keep from losing five dollars would you?"

"Certainly not," Andrew insisted.

"We'll let your man hold the money." The young hustler handed Whit his five, and Andrew did likewise.

"OK," Andrew said smugly. "Tell me where I bought my shoes."

"I don't know where you bought your shoes, man. I don't even know where you stay. I said I could tell you where you got your shoes, and you got 'em on your feet, on Bourbon Street, city of New Orleans, Louisiana, US of A. Now give me my money." He held out his hand toward Whit.

"No way, man. That's a rip." Andrew insisted.

"I should have knowed you'd try to cheat me."

Whit laughed and handed over the ten dollars. "Andrew," he said, "you've been taken."

The youth flashed a big smile, showing off a gold tooth, and disappeared into the crowd.

"That was a rip-off," Andrew fumed.

"Just charge it to experience," Whit said. "Let's keep walking."

"Check that out." Andrew was pointing across the street to a night club with a garish marquee proclaiming New Orleans' sexiest dancers. A guy in a tuxedo and top hat stood outside trying to get passersby to come in and take a look.

"Come on in, gentlemen. See the show. Guaranteed to please," he said to Andrew and Whit as they approached the door. "Only a five dollar cover charge," he added.

"Pay the man, Whit," Andrew said.

With a sigh and a shake of his head, Whit handed the man ten dollars, and the two buddies walked into the dimly lit night club. The place smelled of stale beer and the boys' shoes almost stuck to the floor with each step. The club consisted of a long, narrow room with tables along one wall and a bar along the other. A long runway with chairs around it protruded into the middle of the room. It was surrounded mostly by empty chairs, but a few were occupied by a scattering of men of varying ages and descriptions. Most were smoking cigarettes and looked extremely bored.

On the runway, a middle-aged woman in a platinum wig with sagging breasts, wearing only tassels and a G-string, was bumping and grinding in time to the loud disco music that was blaring from a cheap sound system. She looked at least as bored as the men she was supposed to be entertaining. As the boys' eyes grew accustomed to the dim light they noticed that there were two men sitting in one of the booths which lined the wall, smoking cigarettes and talking to two tired looking show-girls who sat beside them.

A skinny black-haired girl with wild eyes approached Whit and Andrew who were standing just inside the front door, wishing they had their five dollars back. The girl was wearing a black skirt and a shirt with long sleeves, the better to hide the needle marks on her arms, and sheer black hose which looked baggy on her skinny legs. She had a garter on her right thigh, stuffed with five and one dollar bills, and carried a tray.

"Have a seat, gentlemen, and let me get you a drink." She sounded as sad as she looked.

Not knowing what else to do, the two buddies allowed her to seat them in two of the chairs surrounding the runway. Andrew ordered a beer and Whit a Coke. They sat and waited for their drinks, trying to avoid looking at the pathetic dancer who stood above them, rolling her hips and rubbing her worn out body in the hope of enticing a dollar tip from the new customers.

In just a couple of minutes, the washed out waitress was back with a tall thin glass of beer, which might have held five ounces, and a tiny glass of crushed ice with two ounces of Coca-Cola poured over it.

Whit and Andrew looked at one another in disbelief as she sat the drinks on the table in front of them. She bent her leg suggestively and rested her knees on the table, placing the garter of cash right in front of Andrew, at perfect tipping level.

"The drinks are five dollars," she said, in a voice completely devoid of emotion.

Andrew nodded his head, indicating that Whit would pay the tab. She twisted her body toward him, resting her knee on his thigh.

Whit placed a five on her tray and ignoring the garter, which was the customary place to leave a tip, threw a one on top of it.

"The drinks are five dollars apiece," she stated flatly, removing her knee from Whit's thigh. Without a word, Whit tossed another five on the tray. The waitress turned, also without a word and walked back to the bar.

"Let's get out of here," Whit said, draining his Coke in one swallow.

"Good idea," Andrew agreed. "I guess we can chalk this up to experience, too."

"This experience is getting pretty expensive. Maybe we'd better find a place to stay and call it a night," Whit suggested.

"Let's walk a couple more blocks."

"I don't know if we can afford to walk a couple more blocks," Whit argued, but the two walked out of the club and turned left, heading further down Bourbon.

In the ensuing two hours Whit and Andrew walked the full length of Bourbon Street, all the way to Esplanade, and the fourteen blocks back to Canal. They passed streets with exotic names like Toulouse, Dumaine, and Ursulinas. They paid five dollars to watch a man on the corner of Bourbon and St. Louis drink lighter fluid and blow flames out of his nose. They lost five dollars to a hustler playing a shell game on the corner of Bourbon and St. Anne. Andrew was convinced he knew where the pea was, but didn't. And in spite of all Whit's objections, Andrew lost five more dollars to a slick youngster who's hustle was, "you tell me your first name and I guarantee you I can spell your last name." He did. Y-O-U-R-L-A-S-T-N-A-M-E.

They went in two more seedy strip joints, each more depressing than the last. They were enticed into one by a gorgeous twenty year old blonde standing in the doorway in a tiny black bikini. The dancers inside were even worse than the first club they visited. They spent five dollars each to get in, five dollars each for drinks, and five dollars each to get the wrinkled stripper with black teeth to agree to keep her clothes on long enough for them to swallow their minuscule drinks and vacate the premises.

Twice burned, the boys nonetheless entered a third club, which enticed them with the offer of no cover charge. There was a two drink minimum, however, and a giant of a man serving as bouncer to make sure all customers paid $7.50 a piece for two tiny drinks.

During their first run on Bourbon, Andrew and Whit were also propositioned by at least six hookers and shot out of the saddle by as least six college girls that weren't impressed by their pick-up lines or their appearance, after twelve hours on the road and three hours on the streets.

They paid a street musician five bucks to play Dixie on his trumpet, and both agreed it was the best money they spent all night. They visited an establishment called The Rebel Arms which advertised rooms for fifty dollars a week, but after taking note of the bars on the windows and the padlocks on the doors, they decided it was probably overpriced. They asked no fewer than a hundred Georgia fans if they knew of extra tickets to the game that might be available. None did. They sat in the courtyard of Pat O'Briens on St. Peter and watched fire and water burst forth from the same fountain. They heard the piano man there play "Glory Glory to Old Georgia" with one hand and "The Notre Dame Fight Song" with the other, at the same time. They were there long enough for Andrew to consume two Flaming Hurricanes before Whit thought he smelled a whiff of Hoss Mitchell in the men's room and the two decided they'd better leave.

They were turned away rudely at seven French Quarter motels, before finding a room on Canal Street, five blocks north of Bourbon, for a hundred dollars a night, with a three night minimum. It was Four A.M.

when the two travelers laid their heads on the lumpy hotel pillows. They had been awake for twenty-one hours and driven five hundred miles. Andrew had gotten drunk and sober again three times and was somewhere in between when they finally found a bed. They had spent $461 of their $1200, and the only two tickets they had were the two for overparking that they had found under the windshield wipers of Terri Lynn's red Camaro when they picked it up on Canal Street.

They each climbed into bed, wearing only their drawers, and fell asleep within two minutes. Both were as happy as pigs in slop.

# Chapter Twenty-one

Andrew Hawkins and Whit Johnson had been the closest of friends for seven and a half years. They were total opposites; Whit was solid and down-to-earth while Andrew was happy-go-lucky. Whit was shy and reserved, but had a deep seated temper and was bad to want to fight when provoked. Andrew was loud and boisterous, particularly when he was drunk, which was often, but was a pacifist and would avoid physical confrontation whenever possible. Whit was a born worrier and Andrew wouldn't worry if the sun failed to come up. Whit was an early riser, always up at the crack of dawn; Andrew could sleep all day, and often did.

So, on December 30, 1980, Andrew was greatly surprised when he opened his eyes at 11:30 A.M. and felt wide awake. It was a if he had stumbled upon the exact combination of activity, alcohol, and sleep to make his system operate at peak performance level. Andrew was further surprised to discover that Whit, who would ordinarily have been awake, eaten breakfast, and read two newspapers, was still asleep. Being very careful not to wake his friend, Andrew showered quickly and dressed, then headed out in search of breakfast.

Sleeping until noon is not unusual in New Orleans, and the small coffee shop in the boys' hotel served bacon, eggs, waffles, and other breakfast fare twenty-four hours a day. Andrew ordered a ham and cheese omelet and hash browns, and made a valiant effort to flirt with the cute young waitress who had a French name printed on her name tag, a Cajun accent, and no interest whatsoever in Andrew. There were a few other travelers and business types eating late breakfasts, but they all were engaged in their own affairs. None seemed to be football fans, and none seemed likely prospects for the procurement of Sugar Bowl tickets, so Andrew ate quickly, bought a copy of the *New Orleans Times-Picayune* from the metal box outside the coffee shop, took an extra copy for Whit, and went back up to the room.

To Andrew's great surprise, Whit was still not awake but was tossing and turning and moaning in his sleep. Andrew noted the digital clock on the bedside table. It was 12:25. He tossed the two papers on the bed and shook Whit's shoulder until he opened his eyes. Whit looked at the clock for a moment, having trouble comprehending that he had slept past noon and that Andrew was actually up and about before him.

"You gonna sleep the whole day?" Andrew needled him.

"I feel terrible," Whit complained. "My stomach was cramping all night."

"It's just complaining 'cause you don't ever give it any alcohol. I must have had three dozen beers yesterday, and I feel great. I've been up since dawn, eaten twice, made love to three women—and found two Sugar Bowl tickets, free for the taking."

"No kidding!" Whit was wide awake now. He jumped out of bed. "You really got some tickets?"

"No," Andrew admitted. Whit had gotten so excited that Andrew felt sorry he had teased him.

"Don't kid about stuff like that, man," Whit called over his shoulder as he picked up one of the newspapers and headed for the bathroom.

"Don't you want to know about the women I made love to?" Andrew called after him.

"They were all fat and ugly, and after the third one you woke up," Whit shouted through the closed bathroom door.

Andrew switched on the small television set on the dresser. He turned the channels until he found a local newscast, then sat on the bed and rifled through the paper until he found the sports section. There was a picture of Herschel Walker, wearing a cowboy hat and apparently dancing at a local disco. The article on the game, underneath the picture, was mostly devoted to quotes by Vince Dooley, who made Notre Dame sound like the greatest football team since football was invented. Andrew began to wonder why Georgia even bothered to show up for the game. He looked at a couple more articles concerning the game, then turned to the want ads to see if there were any  tickets advertised for sale. He didn't find a single one.

"I feel like a new man," Whit announced as he came out of the bathroom with a towel wrapped around his waist. His hair was soaking wet and plastered to his head. "Amazing what a bowel movement and a hot shower can do for a guy."

He was holding his copy of the sports page. It was folded to an article on the third page. He walked over and shoved it under Andrew's nose, jabbing at a picture of a Notre Dame player with a huge nose. The name under the picture seemed Polish. "Look at that guy," Whit said, poking the picture with his finger. "Jerome Somethingorotherski. Says Notre Dame will win by ten. Is that the guy you saw on television?" he demanded.

"I don't remember," Andrew lied. "Could be."

"If Notre Dame beats us by ten points, I'll kiss your ass," Whit said with conviction. "And I'll give you two days to get up a crowd," he added.

"I'm on your side," Andrew reminded him. "It's not going to be easy, though. Says in the paper that no back has gained a hundred yards on Notre Dame all year."

"Notre Dame ain't played Herschel either," Whit said.

"I'm worried about Notre Dame's offensive line," Andrew said, turning back in the paper to the page with the team rosters. Those are some big ole white boys. I'm afraid they'll just get the ball and keep it all day. Herschel can't run if he ain't got the ball."

"You sound like Dooley," Whit said. "What's wrong with you? I'm the one who usually worries about everything. Erk Russell won't let us down. We're gonna kick their big old Yankee asses. Damn, I can't wait. I wonder what time Georgia practices. I wonder if people can watch."

"Nope," Andrew said. "Paper says Dooley is having closed practices."

"Now, why in the world would he do that?" Whit wondered.

"Maybe he's going to change the offense. Maybe Buck Belue will come out and throw every down," Andrew joked.

"Yeah, sure," Whit said dryly. "They'll be ice skating in hell and playing night baseball in Wrigley Field when Georgia throws every down. Damn, Andrew. We got to get some tickets. Let's put these signs Terri Lynn made around our necks and go hang out in some hotel lobbies where some of those big shots are staying. Maybe some of 'em will offer to sell us a couple of tickets."

"Suits me," Andrew said. "You gonna get dressed first or you gonna go like that?"

"I thought I'd get dressed, smartass, but I gotta call somebody at home before we go out."

"For what?"

"To find out what Grizzard is having to say. He's out here somewhere, writing about the game."

"Call Bonnie Faith," Andrew suggested. "She might have some news. Calvin's working for Wayne at the lumber yard. I wonder how he reacted to getting left."

"I feel bad about taking Calvin's money," Whit said. "I thought maybe he could catch a ride with Hoss, but Hoss left him and us. I still haven't figured that out."

"I don't feel bad about leaving Calvin," Andrew said. "He don't care nothing about Georgia. He was just wanting to come because he has some uncle or something playing for Notre Dame."

"You're kidding! I didn't know that."

"Yeah. You know those blacks have relatives all over the country. Some auntie or something married a guy from Chicago with a son at Notre Dame."

Whit had been punching numbers into the phone while they were talking. He motioned for Andrew to stop talking when it started ringing. It rang several time before a gruff voice said, "Hello" on the other end.

"Leon," Whit said into the mouth piece. "This is Whit. Can I speak to Bonnie Faith for  a minute?"

"Whit, what in the hell you calling Bonnie Faith for?  Wayne Dimsdale will you tear you a new asshole if he catches you foolin' around with her."

"Leon," Whit answered. "You know I ain't that stupid.  Me and Andrew are in New Orleans. We want Bonnie Faith to read us something from the Atlanta paper."

"Well, I hope it's your horoscope or the funnies, 'cause I guarantee you that's  all the paper she'll know anything about."

"Could you just get her, Leon? This is long distance."

In a moment Bonnie Faith was on the line.  She made sure she spoke especially loud, since she was talking all the way to New Orleans. Whit could almost smell the Juicy Fruit gum through the phone line.

"Hey, Whit. What y'all up to out there?"

Andrew grabbed the towel that was around Whit's waist. "Whit's nekkid, Whit's nekkid," he shouted into the phone.

Whit put his hand over the mouthpiece and made a face, grabbing the towel away from Andrew and rewrapping himself.

"Bonnie Faith," he said into the receiver, "I need you to do something. I want you to get this morning's paper and read Lewis Grizzard's column to me."

"The whole thing?" Bonnie Faith couldn't believe the normally frugal Whit wanted her to read an entire newspaper column over long distance.

"Yeah, Bonnie Faith. The whole thing. It'll be worth it. But hurry up."

"OK, I got the paper right here. Let me find him. Here he is. You know, that old boy looks kinda cute, even if he does wear glasses. If I wasn't married to Wayne, I might make him an offer he couldn't refuse."

"From what I hear, he doesn't refuse many. Could you just read the column? We're running up a bill."

Whit listened with a big grin on his face as Bonnie Faith read the column. Occasionally he would laugh out loud. Andrew kept asking what she was saying. After Bonnie Faith had finished she asked Whit to put Andrew on the line.

"Hey, Bonnie Faith, what's going on?" Andrew asked. "You miss me so much already?" he teased.

"Andrew," she said in a serious tone. "Something funny happened yesterday afternoon. I didn't want to tell Whit. You know how bad he is to get mad and want to fight."

"What happened?" he quizzed her, immediately arousing Whit's curiosity.

"Well," she started, "Terri Lynn stopped in here and she told me that y'all left for New Orleans at noon time."

"That's right," Andrew said. "We got here about midnight. We'll tell you all about it when we get home."

"Well, about one o'clock Calvin came in here, you know, the colored boy. He asked me if I had seen y'all. Said he'd been by Whit's trailer and the hardware store, and couldn't find him anywhere."

"What did you tell him?" Andrew asked apprehensively.

"Well, I didn't tell him nothing. I didn't figure it was any of his business."

"What's she talking about?" Whit asked.

Andrew shushed him. "Good girl," he said into the phone.

"Well, anyway, he gave me the strangest message for y'all. Said to tell you that he was going to the Sugar Bowl with his relatives and that he'd get his money from y'all when he got back. What in the world was that all about?"

"Never mind," Andrew said, a smile of relief forming on his face. "What else did he say?"

"Well, this is the part that I thought might make Whit mad. He said to tell y'all that he gave three tickets to Hoss Mitchell for the game, and he wanted to make sure y'all knew Hoss had them. Well, Hoss was in here about 11:30, braggin' about how he was gonna sell two tickets to the Sugar Bowl for $500 and that he was on his way to the game. I thought I heard Hoss say he was going to the game with y'all. I just figured it was y'all's tickets he was plannin' on sellin', but how does Calvin fit in all of this? Y'all weren't going to the game with a colored boy, were you?"

"That low down, no account, so and so," Andrew said.

"What's wrong?" Whit demanded.

"Who's low down?" Bonnie Faith wanted to know. "Hoss or Calvin?"

"Never mind, Bonnie Faith. You done good. We'll see you when we get back. We got to go." Andrew hung up the phone without waiting for a reply.

"What's going on?" Whit demanded. He was still wearing only a towel.

"Calvin had free tickets for us," Andrew said. "His uncle must have given them to him. And Hoss Mitchell took off with 'em and plans to sell them for five hundred bucks."

"No kidding? You're not kidding, are you Andrew? I'll kill that smelly son of a bitch. Let's go look for him right now."

Andrew sat down on the side of the bed and thought matters over. Then he started giggling. Then he started laughing. Finally he was rolling on the bed, laughing uncontrollably. The more he laughed, the madder Whit got.

"What's so damn funny?" Whit was about to be as mad at Andrew as he was at Hoss Mitchell.

"It serves us right," Andrew said. "We tried to screw Calvin and Hoss. Calvin treats us like a prince, and Hoss screws everybody. Looks like the jokes on us."

"Well, it's a bad joke." Whit failed to see the humor or the irony of the situation. "And I'll make that fat so and so regret it if it's the last thing I ever do."

"Get dressed, Linthead, and let's go see the sights."

Whit continued to complain about Hoss Mitchell's underhandedness the whole time he was getting dressed. He was still fuming when they walked out of the room ten minutes later. Whit was starved and wanted to find the biggest hamburger in New Orleans.

Andrew wanted a cold beer.

# Chapter Twenty-two

Andrew and Whit were experiencing their first major disagreement of the trip, and one of the few they'd had in their seven plus years of friendship. It was over a nightclub tour. Whit had booked and paid for them to go on one. Andrew insisted that he wasn't going.

"No way I'm going to get on a tour bus with a bunch of blue headed old women, and men without teeth. I'm going out and find some action."

"Yeah, we found lots of action last night, didn't we?" Whit argued. "I just think we need to see what New Orleans has to offer. Tomorrow night we can get out and party with the crowd."

"Forget it, man. I'm looking for foxes tonight. I know they're here somewhere. We just have to find them."

"Yeah, we've had a great afternoon," Whit replied sarcastically.

He did have a point.

The two had spent the entire afternoon rambling around the French Quarter, from Canal Street to Jackson Square, feeling stupid with their *NEED TWO* signs around their necks, but feeling it was worth feeling stupid if it helped them obtain tickets to the rapidly approaching game. They had gotten offers of tickets, too, but none for less then two-fifty apiece. Andrew had, of course, wanted to pay the five hundred bucks and be done with it. Whit had pointed out that they would probably get hungry again before Friday and that they probably couldn't sell any bogus ads in the Leesdale High football program to the merchants of New Orleans. His logic won out, and they turned all the scalpers down.

They had been in every lobby of every motel, hung around the huge parking lot of the massive Louisiana Superdome, and walked along the levee beside the Mississippi River. The street people of the night before were noticeably absent.

"They're like possums and coons and owls," Whit had said. "They disappear in the daylight and come out when the sun goes down."

They had seen Georgia fans by the legion, but practically all of them were of the alumni variety—middle aged and older. There were few on hand in Whit and Andrew's age range, and the students they did encounter were almost exclusively male.

"Where are all the single young women hiding out?" Andrew had wondered aloud, time and again.

"They're in TyTy, and Covington, and Bogart, and Nahunta, spending the holidays with their mamas and daddies," Whit had insisted each time.

The boys had eaten hamburgers and PoBoy sandwiches, and Andrew had wolfed down a couple of dozen oysters. He had also sampled many, many, cold beers. The pair was mortified to learn that Coors Beer was not sold in Louisiana. They were informed by more than one barkeep that it was a myth that Coors was sold universally west of the Mississippi. Texas was the closest place it could be purchased. In other words, they were out another hundred and fifty dollars. They both agreed that Hoss had forfeited his claim to a refund. In fact, Whit insisted that if Andrew didn't let him find and dismember him that he was going to set fire to his house when he got back home. They also agreed that Calvin must also be repaid as soon as they could catch up with him.

Andrew did discover a delightful alternative to Coors—Dixie Beer, in long neck bottles. He drank his share and Whit's, too. He even bought a case for Tommy Lee Martin at a package store beside the hotel and stored it in the trunk of the Camaro, which they left parked all day in the hotel parking lot. They were very relieved to see that the masking tape used to secure their auxiliary lighting system had miraculously pulled right off, without damaging the car's finish. That was the high point of the afternoon.

"Look, Andrew," Whit continued to reason with his buddy. "How bad could it be? We ride a bus to three nightclubs—a jazz club, a high class strip joint, which won't be like those sleazy places we went to last night, a night club with a floor show out near Lake Ponchatrain, and we finish up with beignets and coffee at the Cafe du Monde. For thirty dollars apiece we get all the shows and two drinks at each place. You can have my drinks. You'll get three shows, twelve drinks and donuts. I'll get to go home knowing that I saw the highlights of the city. You gotta remember, Andrew, you've been all over. I've never been anywhere."

Andrew was weakening. "But Whit, guys like us don't take tours. We'll be the only people on the bus under the age of fifty."

"So maybe some old guy and his wife will take a liking to us and give us a couple of tickets. Tomorrow night will be the big night on Bourbon Street."

Andrew knew he was whipped. "All right," he said angrily. "Since you snuck down to the lobby and bought the tickets behind my back, I guess I'll go, but under one condition."

"Name it."

"Nobody in Leesdale or in Athens ever knows we came out here and went on some damn nightclub tour with a bus full of old farts."

"There may be some other young people on the bus," Whit said.

"Gladys Gibson might be on this very tour."

Andrew grumbled, "If anyone under fifty-five gets on that bus I'll just ---"

"Kiss my ass?" Whit offered.

"No," Andrew finished. "I'll shave off my mustache."

"The hell you will." Whit knew better, or thought he did.

"I will," Andrew insisted. The two dozen or so longneck Dixie Beers were talking for him. "Any person on that bus, besides us, under the age of fifty-five and I'll go home with a bare upper lip."

"And if there isn't?"

"You tell me why Frank Reynolds gave you two hundred bucks."

"I can't." Whit's reply was definite, and left no room for discussion.

"OK," Andrew took another tact. "You eat a dozen raw oysters at lunch tomorrow."

Whit thought about the proposition, picturing in his mind a clean shaven Andrew Hawkins, something he'd never seen, and weighing it against the thought of twelve slimy raw oysters sliding down his throat.

"You want to go on the tour or not?" Andrew prodded.

"OK, shake on it." Whit extended his right hand to seal the deal.

"Remember," Andrew reminded him, "nobody ever finds out."

Whit laughed at him.

At eight o'clock sharp the silver and blue touring coach pulled up in front of Whit and Andrew's Canal Street hotel. Whit was suddenly very self-conscious. Andrew had fortified himself with another six pack of Dixie Beer and made up his mind to enjoy the evening, regardless of the circumstances. He actually took the lead and led Whit onto the bus. He stood in the aisle and surveyed the crowd on the bus while Whit handed their tickets to the friendly looking bus driver. The card above his mirror identified him as Ray, a twenty-seven year veteran of the touring company.

A big smile spread across Andrew's face. It was obvious that oysters were on Whit's menu for the next day. There wasn't a dark head of hair on the entire bus. In fact, if any of the couples were under the age of sixty-five Andrew would have been surprised. Whit glumly took one of the only two open seats left on the bus, a window seat right behind the driver. Andrew sat in the aisle seat beside him. He leaned forward and clapped the driver on the shoulder.

"Ray, my man. How many more stops will you be making before we start the tour?"

"You're the last two customers," the small, balding driver grinned his answer into the large rearview mirror which stretched across the entire front of the bus.

"Just put plenty of sauce on 'em," Andrew said with glee to his buddy, who was stone sober and feeling very uncomfortable, as all conversation on the bus seemed to stop. Andrew and Whit could feel forty sets of eyes drilling into their backs. The bus driver was cracking jokes into a hand held microphone and indicating points of interest as he drove past large Victorian homes, sad looking slums, and above ground cemeteries.

"Know why they have a fence around that cemetery?" he asked into the microphone.

Silence was the only reply.

"'Cause people are just dying to get in." He slapped the microphone against his knee and chortled at his own joke which was as old as the clientele on the bus. No one else even giggled.

Andrew and Whit, who both thought the joke was pretty funny but were too cool to laugh unless someone else did, turned to look back at the rest of the group and see why they weren't laughing. Ray, who had never failed to get a big laugh with his old standby looked up into his mirror as well.

What they saw was a group of senior citizens from Helena, Spokane, Des Moine, Valdosta and points in between, staring slackjawed at the last thing they had expected to see on their big night out in the Big Easy— a young, good looking, virile, male couple. Andrew was the first of the trio to comprehend what was bothering the bus load of would-be revelers. He stood up in the aisle, in front of the white line, in direct violation of bus company policy.

"I'll handle this, Ray," he said to the surprised bus driver.

"Hey, how y'all doin'?" he began, speaking into the driver's microphone. He gave the audience on the bus his best smile, his white teeth gleaming below his thick black mustache.

He got no response.

"I'm sorry," he continued. "This mike must not be turned on."

Andrew spit into the microphone a couple of times.

"I said, how y'all doin'?"

His smile got even bigger.

This time a few of the men and women muttered a semipolite response.

"I'm Andrew Hawkins and this is my buddy, Whit Johnson." He smiled in Whit's direction.

Whit smiled and waved.

"How 'bout them Dawgs!" he shouted with enthusiasm, trying what he thought would be a surefire icebreaker.

One couple in the back of the bus, the ones from Valdosta, smiled and started to clap, but stopped when they realized that there was absolutely no response from the other passengers. Andrew was clearly puzzled.

"These folks are here for a meeting of the Retired American's Council," Ray whispered. "I doubt they even know there's going to be a football game in town this week."

"Great," Andrew replied, his voice dripping with sarcasm.

He had gone too far to turn back now, so he continued. "Well, me and Whit are from Leesdale, Georgia. We're here in New Orleans to watch Georgia play Notre Dame in the Sugar Bowl, and I promise, we ain't queer or anything. We both like girls and love our mamas. We want to have a good time and see the city, just like y'all. Whit thought that this tour would be a good way to experience the night life and maybe meet some nice folks. We wouldn't make y'all feel uncomfortable for anything in the world. Y'all just enjoy the evening and don't pay us any mind at all." Andrew flashed one last million dollar smile, bowed deeply, and returned to his seat.

The members of the Retired American's Council smiled sheepishly at one another. They were all secretly relieved to learn that they would not be spending their evening in the company of homosexuals. A lady in a rabbit fur, from Cleveland, began to clap and soon the entire bus joined her in a round of applause. The atmosphere on the bus changed immediately. People resumed turning their heads and straining to see each building and attraction and the driver's jokes became funny again.

The first stop of the evening was in the French Quarter for some traditional New Orleans jazz. Whit and Andrew joined Ray in helping the well dressed and well mannered pillars of various American communities down the steps of the bus and onto the crowded sidewalks. Ray ushered his flock quickly into the side door of a tiny, dimly lit night club.

The crowd from the bus filled up most of the empty tables in the room. On the stage was a group of aging musicians. Most of them were black. They looked as if they had been born on that stage and soon all the tour group, including Andrew and Whit, were tapping their toes appreciatively in time to the pure, sweet jazz that the combo called forth from their clarinets, trombones, and saxophones.

Whit ordered a Coke from the waiter who came to their table wearing pleated pants, a white starched shirt, and red bow tie. The waiter smiled at Whit and then turned his attention to Andrew.

"Hi, Big Guy," he said as he balanced his tray above his head and sashayed around the table. "My name is Bruce, and I'll be your waiter tonight."

"Well, my name is Andrew, and I'll be your customer, but that's as far as it's going, Jack. I'll tell you that right now. I'll have a Jack Daniel's and Coke. Make it a double."

"My, my. Aren't we thirsty? And such a manly drink! I just love men who drink Jack Daniel's."

Andrew tried hard not to make eye contact.

"I think you made a friend, Andrew," Whit teased him. "Ask him if he can get us some tickets."

"Yeah, right. I'm sure old Bruce is just all into football."

Even Andrew had to admit that the jazz club was much more enjoyable than the places they'd visited in New Orleans so far. The rather weak drinks added to his pleasure. They didn't have a great amount of alcohol in them, but by the time he'd finished his fourth one—his two and Whit's two—he was beginning to experience a pleasant buzz. He especially enjoyed the part of the show where the middle aged piano player broke into a medley which included "Dixie," "Glory Glory," and "Sweet Georgia Brown."

Andrew was double-stepping and Whit was snapping his fingers in time to the music when Ray shepherded his group out of the brick walled night spot, across the sidewalk, and onto the waiting bus.

The martinis, daiquiris, glasses of white wine, and other drinks that the Retirees had consumed seemed to act as a social lubricant. The conversation was louder and livelier as the tour group climbed the steps of the bus and settled into their seats. They all smiled warmly at Whit and Andrew as they stood in the doorway, offering their hands and taking passengers by the arm to help them onto the bus.

Ray kept up a steady patter over the speaker as the group enjoyed the twenty minute drive out to the Fat City area of New Orleans. The next stop was a forties style night club called the Gold Room, which took up the entire top floor of a luxury hotel.

Andrew and Whit were impressed by the glass elevator which carried them to the club, and were even more impressed by the young lady who met them at the elevator door and showed them to their table. It was front and center, right beside the stage.

The hostess was very tall, her high heel shoes making her appear to be more than six feet in height. She wore a top hat and tails, tight black hot pants, and sheer hose. Her long blonde hair reached the middle of her back. She had a peaches and cream complexion, bright blue eyes, and a splendid smile.

"Now this is the New Orleans I've been looking for," Andrew commented, as he looked around the room, taking note of six or seven other waitresses and hostesses, each as gorgeous as the other.

Whit didn't even remind Andrew that he had been made to come on the tour. He was having too good a time to bring it up. Whit bought another Coke, and to the great amusement of the tour group, Andrew consumed four more rounds. The drinks at the Gold Room were much stronger than the ones at the jazz hall.

Andrew looked appreciatively down the tight Basque of the stunning blonde who brought the first of his drinks. "Bonnie Faith Dimsdale, with class," he commented, raising his glass high to no one in particular and everyone in general.

Whit was looking around the dimly lit room. Lush, golden colored curtains lined the walls. The high ceiling sparkled with hundreds of tiny lights, arranged so as to give the impression of a starlit sky. There were candles and fresh flowers on each table. A six piece orchestra warmed up on the bandstand near the rear of the stage.

Before this night, the classiest event Whit had ever attended had been the Junior-Senior Prom at the Leesdale Elks Lodge. He was impressed by the ambience of the Gold Room. Andrew was impressed by the amount of Tennessee sipping whiskey the generous Gold Room bartenders put in each of his drinks.

"I feel like we're in a Humphrey Bogart movie," Whit said as a slinky torch singer in a sequined gown came on stage and began singing.

"Here's lookin' at you, kid," Andrew replied, lifting a glass of amber colored liquid and downing half of his second drink in one gulp.

The forty-five minute floor show seemed to be over as soon as it had started. After the warmup singer finished her performance, a young guy came out and told bad jokes about the sinful side of New Orleans, obnoxious Yankee visitors, and Southern hicks. The senior citizens loved him. Whit was offended. Andrew was drunk. Real drunk. And he was getting drunker with each swallow.

The stars of the show were twin sisters who had been born and raised in Harlan, Kentucky, but had overcome it. They were billed as the Gold Room Gold Dust Twins and wore tight, short dresses with very low necklines. Their dresses were covered in gold sequins. The girls sang up-tempo popular songs and danced with lots of energy, showing plenty of leg with each number.

The Geritol set were convinced that they were experiencing the ultimate entertainment experience. Whit was convinced that he was in love, but couldn't decide with which twin. Andrew was just drunk. The Hendricks twins' two ton cousin would have looked good to him.

After the show, as the bus rolled back toward the city, the crowd was completely loose, maybe even boisterous. Whit was the only person on the entire bus who was completely sober, other than Ray. Andrew had taken over the microphone and had his captive audience in stitches with his jokes, impressions, and off-the-wall comments about anything and everything. He even tried to sing. His heartfelt rendition of "Georgia On My Mind" wasn't too bad, for a drunk guy with a bad voice.

As the tour group entered the Vieux Carre for the second time that evening, Ray reclaimed the mike and made a broad disclaimer concerning the next stop. He warned folks that the show they were about to see would not play very well on Main Street in Small Town, USA. He also reminded them that they were in New Orleans, the city that C.A.R.E. forgot, and as he put it, "Besides, folks. Out of town don't count."

The normal annual alcohol consumption for that whole group, excluding Andrew, was probably about two ounces per person. The members of the tour had each had, on an average, two or three very weak drinks and one or two very strong ones. At this point in the evening, none of them really gave a damn what the people back in Small Town, USA might think. This was their night to howl. They were out on the town and ready for some real action. They were not to be disappointed.

# Chapter Twenty-three

Ray parked the bus on a side street and once again led his flock quickly down the sidewalk. This time they entered a small side door of a very dimly lit and seedy looking nightclub. It was the kind of place that none of the tour group would be caught dead in back home. The club was packed, except for a group of tables that had been reserved for Ray's tour group. An invisible disc jockey welcomed the group to the club and announced to the high spirited crowd that it was almost show time.

Whit and Andrew took a seat at a table for two, right beside the stage. The rest of the group seemed thankful to be able to take seats at more discreet locations, further back in the room. A sexy young thing, wearing a G-string and pasties took the boys' drink orders, teasing Whit good naturedly when he ordered a Coke. She was back almost before they knew she was gone. The strong brown whiskey in Andrew's glass was cheap bourbon and not the golden elixir he had ordered by name. Andrew was so far gone by this time that it could have been kerosene and he wouldn't have cared.

Just as the last Retired Citizen was being served, the already dim house lights grew even dimmer, and two bright spotlights bathed the stage before coming together to make one bright circle on the faded blue curtain four feet in front of Whit and Andrew's faces. A recorded drum roll emitted from the club's speaker system and the curtains slowly parted, revealing a stunning black haired beauty in a long sequined gown, elbow length gloves, and four inch heels. She appeared to be in her mid-thirties, but was all woman. Her large breasts and round bottom threatened to burst the seams of her sequined gown with every move she made.

The featured entertainer strutted and swayed in time to sultry recorded music. Whit had never seen anything so sexy in his entire life. Andrew was threatening to climb onto the stage with her. By the end of the first number the dancer had removed her gloves and her gown. Her breasts were even more impressive as they strained against a low cut, sequined bra. Her matching bikini bottom hardly covered anything. Her firm legs were perfectly formed. As she kicked off her shoes and went into a series of wildly exotic gyrations, Whit couldn't decide which part of her glorious body to look at first. Andrew was struggling valiantly to stay in his seat and to keep his hands above the table. The older men in the tour group exchanged sheepish grins, and took handkerchiefs from their pockets to wipe perspiration from their bald heads and fog off of their steamed glasses.

Some of the older women looked at one another and narrowed their eyes in disgust. Some sat openmouthed, staring in disbelief. Others feared that their husbands would have heart attacks and die on the spot. Their greatest fear was that the people back in Peoria would learn the circumstances surrounding the death.

All were amazed.

After her second number the dancer, whose stage name was Susan Storm, went behind the back curtain and returned with a small vanity chair which she placed near the front edge of the stage. She sat on the edge of the chair and began to talk to the audience in a sultry voice. When she asked for a volunteer from the audience to help her with her act, Andrew was on the stage as fast as he could stagger. No one else in the crowd ever had a chance.

Susan stood up and offered Andrew her chair, then promptly sat in his lap. She wiggled her bottom playfully, then reached back and deftly unfastened the snaps holding her bra in place, flinging it into the audience with a flick of her wrist. She held one large breast against Andrew's mouth and used her free hand to press the other against one of his ears.

Andrew thought he had died and gone to heaven.

"Pretend you're on the telephone, big boy. What do you want to talk about?" Whit expected his pal to pull away or show some sign of embarrassment. He failed to take into consideration the amount of alcohol in his buddy's system. Any amount of inhibition that might have been present in Andrew's psyche was long since drowned. Instead of pulling away, Andrew made the most of the situation, nuzzling, licking, and sucking, until Susan Storm herself pulled away. She wasn't used to having such a willing accomplice.

Andrew took the microphone from the show's star and crooned, "Why don't we just talk about the first thing that pops up?"

The audience roared. The loudest laughs came from the Retired Citizens. Even the ladies were chuckling.

Susan Storm kept feeding Andrew lines, and he kept responding like a seasoned veteran of the vaudeville stage. During the entire repartee he was licking, stroking, fondling, and caressing every inch of the stripper's body he could get to. She made certain he could get to most of it.

Andrew was such a hit that instead of the two minute bit Susan usually did with her audience volunteer, she left him on stage for the entire rest of her show. The highlight of the evening came when Susan, wearing only her G-string, climbed into a giant champagne glass full of clear liquid, handed Andrew a sponge, and ordered him to give her a bath. He happily obliged.

The crowd in the club was enthralled. Most were convinced that Andrew was a plant and was a regular in the show. Ray stood at the back of the room, his eyes glued to the stage. He had seen Susan Storm's show five nights a week for years and usually stood outside and smoked while she performed, but Andrew was adding a whole new dimension to the performance. Ray had never seen anything like it, and didn't intend to miss a single moment.

At the conclusion of the show, Susan climbed out of the giant glass and one of the waitresses came on stage to hand Andrew a fluffy white towel. While he was drying her off, Susan Storm continued to make small talk with the audience.

"Be careful with that towel," she said over the microphone as Andrew continued to rub her body. "I got arrested once in Mobile, Alabama, and was fined five hundred dollars for showing one pubic hair."

"Hell," Andrew replied. "I'll show these folks a million dollars' worth."

He reached down and unsnapped the stripper's bikini bottom. The audience did indeed get an eyeful. Susan quickly grabbed the towel away from Andrew and covered herself, not because of modesty, but because of a New Orleans city ordinance which prohibited total nudity.

Susan smiled at Andrew and gave him a long, wet kiss. He pulled her tightly against his body and squeezed her bare bottom, enjoying the feeling as she slipped her tongue in his mouth and reciprocated in kind.

Susan finally broke the embrace. She motioned to a waitress who was waiting in the wings with an 8x10 glossy photograph of the show's star. Susan took the picture of herself from the girl and kissed it. Her lipstick left a bright red mark across the top. She handed the gift to Andrew, then still holding the towel around herself, she escorted him back to his table.

The audience gave him a standing ovation. Seventy year old women whistled and stomped their feet. One octogenarian from Odessa, Texas nearly fell trying to climb on his chair to applaud the performance.

Back on the bus, Andrew was a hero. Every man who boarded had to shake his hand, ruffle his hair, and admire the picture. They all told him how lucky he was, and Andrew smugly agreed.

Even Whit had to agree that his friend had outdone himself this time.

"I believe she wanted me," he confided to his buddy, who just shook his head, unable to comment.

"Whit," Andrew continued. "You've got to make sure you tell everybody in Leesdale about this when you get home. It won't sound like bragging if you tell it."

"I will," Whit agreed.

"Promise?"

"Sure."

"You swear?"

"I swear."

"Especially Bonnie Faith?"

"Especially her."

"You're a real pal."

The tour was making its final stop of the night. It pulled up right in front of the Cafe du Monde, in the French Market. The Cafe du Monde was open twenty-four hours a day and was known all over the world for its delicious beignets and cafe au lait. Beignets were fried donut-like pastries with a thick coating of white powdered sugar. Cafe au lait was strong chicory coffee, laden with generous amounts of rich cream.

Andrew was nowhere near sobriety, but he was less intoxicated than he had been earlier. He and Whit took their place at the small round table. Whit had had the time of his life and couldn't help but remind Andrew that he hadn't wanted to come along on the tour at all.

Andrew pretended not to hear as he admired the photograph of Susan Storm, and proudly displayed it to anyone and everyone who would pay any attention. He continued to accept congratulations from the people on the tour and tried to convince several of the ladies that he was indeed a tourist, just like them, and not a featured part of the night's show.

When a young waiter in a white uniform set beignets and coffee on the boys' table, Andrew put the treasured photograph on the table and hungrily tore into one of the pastries. Whit did likewise.

The waiter commented on the picture. "I see you guys have been over on Bourbon Street tonight."

Both boys nodded, unable to speak because of their mouths being full.

"Looks like you met Susan Storm."

Andrew smiled and nodded enthusiastically, taking a big sip of the rich coffee.

"You know," the waiter commented nonchalantly, "she used to be a man."

Andrew froze. Terror filled his eyes. Sharp pains ran up and down his left arm. His fingers tingled, then became numb. He broke out in a cold sweat. He exhaled forcefully, spraying powdered sugar and coffee from his mouth.

"Do what?" he finally said.

"Yeah," the waiter continued. "She's famous. New Orleans' sex change stripper. She started out as a female impersonator. She liked being a woman so much that she went to Sweden and had an operation. She's been dancing as Susan Storm for years."

Andrew jumped up from his chair and ran out the door of the Cafe du Monde and toward the waiting bus, with Whit in hot pursuit. Ray was sitting behind the wheel, keeping the engine warm.

Andrew shoved the picture of Susan Storm in his face and started jabbing it with his finger. "Tell me the truth," he demanded. "Was she . . . is he . . was this person born with something he . . . she . . . it doesn't have any more?"

Ray looked at Andrew in disbelief. Then a big grin spread across his face. Then he started laughing. Then Whit, who was standing on the steps of the bus, started laughing. Andrew was in a state of shock, and sat meekly in the front bus seat, the photograph of Susan Storm sliding from his fingers and onto the floor.

As the other passengers began to file onto the bus they couldn't imagine why Andrew looked so glum, or why Whit and the bus driver were laughing uncontrollably. Neither was able to speak and tears rolled down their cheeks.

Ray was still gasping for breath when he put the bus into gear and pulled away from the curb. He was finally able to pick up his microphone.

"Friends," he said. "I don't think I'd better try to explain what's so funny up here, but we will take one little detour on the way back to your hotels."

He drove the bus up a side street, turned right on another narrow street, then turned left onto Bourbon, which was supposed to be closed to vehicles. Ignoring the angry shouts of a policeman, Ray slowly drove two blocks and stopped in front of a nightclub which displayed several large posters of the one and only Susan Storm and a giant marquee advertising in letters four feet high that this was indeed the home of New Orleans' only sex change stripper.

"Folks," Ray said into his microphone, " I've been bringing folks through the side door of this club for five years. Our buddy here is the first person who's ever found out about Susan Storm."

The bus fell apart.


An hour later, Whit was lying on his bed. He was covering his face with a pillow and trying not to laugh. It was a lost cause. He laughed so much and so hard that his ribs ached.

Andrew was in the bathroom with a tube of toothpaste, a toothbrush, and the largest bottle of mouthwash the twenty-four hour drugstore down the street sold. Whit had listened to him brush, spit, and gargle for thirty minutes, laughing harder with each repetition of the cycle.

Finally, a distraught Andrew came out of the bathroom. He was a broken man.

"Whit," he said, desperation in his voice, "you've got to promise not to tell anyone about this."

"Aw, Andrew," Whit replied.

"I mean it. You can't tell anyone. Especially Bonnie Faith. Ever."

"Well," Whit hedged. "I won't tell anyone for at least fifteen years."

"Whit, make it twenty. Please."

"OK, I won't tell anyone for twenty years."

"Promise?"

"I promise."

"Swear?"

"OK. I swear."

"Swear on Robert E. Lee's grave?"

"Andrew . . ."

"I mean it. Say it."

"All right. I swear on Robert E. Lee's grave." Whit sincerely hoped the late general understood about crossed fingers.


Hours later, Whit was still covering his face with a pillow, trying to control his laughter. Every time he'd almost fall asleep, he'd hear Andrew in the bed beside him— spitting.

At some point, in the wee hours of the morning, Whit and Andrew both fell asleep. When they next awoke, kickoff would be little more than twenty-four hours away.

# Chapter Twenty-Four

The first vision to meet Whit Johnson's eyes on the last day of 1980 was bright sunlight flooding the room. He took his time waking up, letting his eyes grow accustomed to the brightness of the room by degrees. For a moment he couldn't remember exactly where he was, but as he began to obtain full consciousness he remembered that he was in New Orleans and that he was there to witness the most important event of his life.

Whit sat up in bed, rubbing the sleep from his eyes. The digital clock beside the bed read 10:45. He couldn't believe he had slept so late. He was even more surprised, perhaps even annoyed, when he glanced across at his buddy's bed and discovered that, for the second day in a row, Andrew was already out and gone.

As Whit stood up and headed into the bathroom to answer nature's morning call, he stopped dead in his tracks when he saw what was sitting on the counter beside the small sink in the corner of the room. It was the biggest bottle of Listerene he'd ever seen. At least, it used to be a bottle of Listerine. It was now well over half empty, most of its contents having been used by Andrew in an early morning attempt to eradicate any lingering remains from the past evening's debacle.

The images of Andrew sitting on Susan Storm's lap danced in Whit's mind, causing him to laugh out loud as he continued into the tiny bathroom. He was still laughing when he came out, several minutes later, to find Andrew sitting on one of the beds, the *New Orleans Times-Picayune* spread out all around him.

"What's so funny?" he demanded.

"You are," Whit shot back. "At least you were last night."

"I don't know what you're talking about," Andrew answered, nonchalantly.

"Oh, you know exactly what I'm talking about."

"No, I'm afraid not. That's the beauty of consuming excess amounts of alcohol. Sometimes you can't remember a thing."

"Well, if you can't remember anything from last night, what's that giant canister of mouthwash doing on the counter over there?"

Andrew looked up from his paper, a crooked smile on his face. "I don't know anything about that bottle of mouthwash, and I don't recall anything about last night. That's my story and I'm sticking to it."

With a smug smile on his face, he returned to the papers on his lap. Suddenly he jumped up from the bed and began waving the newspaper in Whit's face. "Look at this! Look at this! Look at this!" he shouted repeatedly.

"Well, if you'd hold the thing still I would."

"We've got the tickets! We've got the tickets! We've got the tickets!" Andrew was practically shouting with glee.

"What are you talking about?" Whit was suddenly very interested in the newspaper.

Andrew spread it out on Whit's bed and pointed to a small ad in the corner of the back page of the sports section.

*Sugar Bowl Tickets* was the bold heading. Andrew spoke rapidly, his words almost falling over one another in his excitement. "The Oyster Bar is having an oyster eating contest at twelve o'clock today. It's only fifty dollars to enter, and the person who eats the most oysters in thirty minutes gets a pair of tickets to the Sugar Bowl. A pair! That's two. Me and you.

We're in the game."

"Wait a minute, Andrew. We're not in the game yet. There's a little matter of winning the contest. What makes you think you can eat more oysters than anybody else in New Orleans?"

The corners of Andrew's mouth turned up in a sly smile as he looked at Whit out of the corner of his eye. "I thought maybe we'd enter you in the contest," he teased. "After all, you did lose the bet last night. There were no young people on the tour."

"I thought you didn't remember anything about last night," Whit quickly replied. "If we count on me winning an oyster eating contest, we'll never see the game, so you'll have to be the one who enters. Now, what makes you think you can win an oyster eating contest?"

"Motivation my boy, motivation. We want to see the game worse than anybody in New Orleans. We need two tickets worse than anybody in New Orleans. I'll suck down more of those slimy suckers than any other fool in this whole city if it kills me. Get dressed, boy. Let's go check out the oyster bar again."

Andrew and Whit strolled down Canal Street and turned left on Bourbon. It was not quite noon. The New Orleans French Quarter stays up late and usually sleeps late as well, but on this day the streets were already beginning to fill. Most of the pedestrians were middle aged couples and most were dressed in red and black. They were pharmacists and merchants and car salesmen from Bainbridge and Waycross and Dalton and they were growing more excited by the hour at the prospect of watching their team do battle. Most had followed Georgia football for their entire lives. They watched games on television and read the polls in the newspapers and saw the Alabamas and the Notre Dames and the Michigans of the world win mythical National Championships. And now, their team was a little more than twenty-four hours away from laying it all on the line. If successful, they would be able forever to say, "Remember the year we won it all." If unsuccessful—well, they didn't allow themselves to think about that.

Andrew and Whit turned right on Iberville and hurried into the Oyster Bar, hoping they were on time for Andrew to eat, or rather slurp, his way to two tickets. They were immediately alarmed when they saw that the place was packed with mostly loud, mostly rowdy, mostly young people. Andrew, determined not to be shut out of the contest, pushed his way through the crowd until he got to the main bar at the front of the room.

A large banner advertising the contest was stretched behind the bar. A smiling black man with a white cap, a big smile, and a gold tooth spoke to Andrew from behind the bar. The nametag pinned to his white apron identified him as Leon. "You here to enter the contest, Ace?"

"Is there still time?" Andrew asked.

"Sure, man."

"How many contestants so far?"

"You gonna enter?"

"Sure am."

"Then there are two."

"Two! You mean only one other person has entered? Why?"

"I reckon 'cause the other person is Big Jake."

"Who is Big Jake?"

"Who is Big Jake? Where you from boy? Big Jake is Big Jake Guillebeau, the Crazy Cajun. Big Jake has won the New Year's Eve Oyster Eating Contest seven years in a row. He's seen more Sugar Bowl games for free than Bear Bryant."

"Well, where is Big Jake now?" Andrew asked, looking around the crowded room, thinking that perhaps he would be a no-show.

"He's in the bathroom, cleansing his system. You want in or not?"

Andrew looked at Whit, who had made his way through the crowd in time to hear all about the legendary Big Jake.

Whit shrugged. "Your call, man. You're the one whose gotta eat those slimy suckers."

Andrew took a deep breath. "I'm in."

A big grin broke out on the face of the man behind the bar. "All right," he said excitedly. "We're gonna have a contest. That'll be seventy-five dollars."

"Seventy-five? I thought it was fifty."

"Fifty for the contest. Twenty-five to tip the shucker. You ain't planning on shucking your own are you?"

Andrew grimly shook his head and motioned to Whit. "Pay the man."

"All right," Leon announced to the patrons of the bar. "Contest is on. Somebody tell Big Jake."

The beer swilling crowd gathered excitedly as Leon began to explain the rules of the contest to Andrew. Big Jake apparently knew the rules already because he was yet to make an appearance.

"You got to stand at the bar to eat your oysters. Each oyster eater will have a shucker and a counter. Contest starts at noon and lasts thirty minutes. If an oyster eater upchucks he can start over at zero. Any questions?"

"Yeah," Andrew asked. "What's the most oysters Big Jake ever ate in thirty minutes?"

"About twenty-four."

"You're kidding! This guy only ate twenty-four oysters!"

"Twenty-four dozen."

"Oh shit," Andrew drew in his breath.

"Oh shit," Whit echoed.

Leon just grinned, his gold tooth gleaming.

"It's nearly twelve o'clock. Somebody get Big Jake."

"Big Jake! Contest gonna start." a loud voice called out.

A hush fell over the crowd near the back of the room and made its way toward the bar like a big wave. Andrew and Whit turned their eyes toward the back of the room in time to see the crowd part. The biggest human being either of them had ever seen was making his way through the crowd. He was close to seven feet tall and solid looking as a rock and as wide as Stone Mountain. He was as ugly as he was big with thick black hair, cold eyes, and a face which looked like it had never been softened by a smile.

Several people in the crowd gasped audibly as he strode past them, and Andrew shuddered as Jake took his place at the bar beside him. The newcomer looked down at him with disdain and then held up two fingers toward Leon, who quickly placed two mugs of draft beer on the bar.

Big Jake picked up one mug with his left hand and the other with his right. He drained the first in one gulp, then just as quickly guzzled the second. He then turned and glared at Andrew with piercing black eyes.

"How ya doin, Jake?" Andrew smiled at his adversary who answered him with a loud belch and wiped his mouth with the back of a dirty sleeve.

"Nice guy," Andrew said to Whit in a loud stage whisper, earning another glare from the Cajun.

"All right. Shuckers take your places. It's time for the contest to begin," Leon announced to the crowd. Two wiry looking oyster shuckers took their places, one in front of each contestant. Two counters took their places beside them. Each held a green slate with the word *DOZENS* painted across the top and a large piece of chalk. A large wooden barrel stood behind each shucker. The barrels were filled with ice and fresh oysters, still in their hard, spindly shells, waiting to be opened and consumed.

Whit stood behind Andrew, massaging his shoulders and giving him words of encouragement, just like George Kennedy did for Paul Newman during the egg eating scene in *Cool Hand Luke*. Big Jake stood alone, staring straight ahead.

The crowd behind the boys had grown. Most were dressed in red and black and all were having liquid lunches. Dixie Beer was the entree of choice.

Leon climbed up on a wooden crate, the better to be seen, and tried to quiet the crowd, to little avail. He finally gave up and began the introductions.

"On my right," he shouted above the uproar, "is the challenger. From Leesdale, Georgia, I give you Andrew Hawkins." He drug out the last syllable of Andrew's name. When the crowd heard that the challenger was from Georgia, a huge roar went up.

"On my left," Leon continued, "the seven time defending champion, from Lafayette, Louisiana, Big Jake Guillebeau."

The crowd began to boo, but Jake turned and stared over his shoulder. All it took was one look to bring total silence to the room.

The big clock above the bar was almost straight up. The second hand swept toward high noon. Leon began to count down the final ten seconds, and the crowd joined in. 5-4-3-2-1.... A giant roar drowned out the "0" as the two shuckers placed round metal trays on the counter. Andrew picked up the fork which was placed in front of him and quickly loosened the first oyster, swiped it through the big bowl of cocktail sauce on his right and placed it in his mouth. He chewed twice and swallowed while loosening the next oyster from its shell. He was amazed at how large the oysters were. He quickly developed a rhythm and was encouraged by how easily the oysters went down. Andrew's optimism turned to despair when Leon announced one minute was up just as he finished his sixth oyster. He glanced sideward and out of the corner of his eye he saw the small, wiry man who was shucking for the Crazy Cajun taking away a tray of shells and replacing it with a fresh tray of oysters.

"Damn," Andrew exclaimed. "He ate a dozen oysters in one minute."

"Shut up and eat," Whit ordered.

The crowd behind the two oyster eaters remained loud and rowdy as they continued to drink beer and to cheer sporadically for Andrew as he finished one tray and then another and another. Although Andrew was the sentimental favorite, the crowd was amazed by Big Jake. He was like an eating machine. He didn't bother with a fork. Every five seconds he tore an oyster loose from the shell, threw it in his mouth without benefit of sauce or any other dressing, and swallowed it, without chewing, while reaching for the next.

Andrew was making a valiant effort to keep up, but by the fifteen minute mark it was obvious that he was greatly overmatched. His shucker had piled up six trays on the table behind the bar. Unfortunately, the stack of trays behind Big Jake's shucker was twelve high and growing rapidly.

Leon smiled broadly with every oyster Jake ate. He had bet a day's tips that the Crazy Cajun would set a new record, and at the halfway point of the contest, he seemed to be well on his way.

Andrew paused to breathe and take a drink of water. He was beginning to feel a little green around the gills.

"Not much hope, is  there buddy?" Whit asked, massaging his buddy's shoulders. "You want to give up?"

"No way," Andrew insisted. "Don't forget the upchuck rule. If he barfs, I intend to be far enough ahead that he can't catch me."

Big Jake, who had paused to wash his palate with two more beers, overheard Andrew's remark and cast a disdainful sneer in his direction. Andrew answered the sneer with his best smile. As always, his white teeth gleamed from under his thick black mustache.

Jake turned away from Andrew and signaled his shucker, who promptly set another tray of oysters in front of him. Andrew did likewise, took a deep breath, and once again began forcing oysters down his throat. He had abandoned the cocktail sauce by now and his pace had slowed considerably. He was barely able to force down four oysters a minute over the next twelve minutes. Big Jake was still swallowing at a record pace and when Leon rang the bell signaling the two minute warning, Andrew had accumulated twelve empty trays. The Crazy Cajun had put  away twenty-two and was in striking distance of his own record.

The crowd had become disinterested at the halfway mark as it became apparent that Andrew had no chance of winning, but now they sensed that history was in the making. They began to buzz with anticipation and then began to chant, "Jake, Jake, Jake."

The  big man's hands fairly flew as he threw down six oysters in thirty seconds. Andrew ate two over the same time span, determined to play out  the string. As the second hand on the large clock over the bar began to sweep up toward twelve, the crowd suddenly stopped chanting; then became strangely silent. Everyone in the Oyster Bar began looking around in confusion.

Andrew and Jake simultaneously stopped eating, lifting their heads straight up. A foul odor had begun to permeate the air.

Leon jumped up on a stool behind the bar in order to survey the scene. He was convinced someone had done the unthinkable and lit a stink bomb. Jake forgot about eating oysters and turned to survey the crowd for himself. He had never smelled such a foul odor. As it got stronger and stronger, he began to swallow just a little bit. For the first time in his life he felt the slightest bit of queasiness, deep in the pit of his stomach.

Andrew put a hand over his mouth and nose, looking at Whit with hope in his eyes.

The second hand on the clock had reached twelve and started its final journey around the dial just as a great commotion broke out near the door at the back of the room. The crowd parted and into the Oyster Bar walked none other than Hoss Mitchell himself.

He was still dressed in the same red shirt and pants that he had been wearing at the Alabama rest area, two days earlier. He had stretched a purple garter, purloined from a Bourbon Street stripper, around his black cowboy hat. He had ripped the personalized license plate reading *BIGUN* off his van and tied it around his neck with bailing twine.

The crowd parted as Hoss strode toward the bar in a drunken stupor, bringing his wonderful stench closer and closer to the contestants. Leon began shouting at him in an undistinguishable dialect. Andrew tried to pretend the smell didn't exist, and Jake looked at the approaching Spectre with horror in his eyes. He was almost overcome by the noxious odor emitting from this creature, and twenty-two and a half dozen slimy, raw oysters began to rumble in his stomach, triggering something completely foreign to his considerable experience—reflux.

The contest was forty seconds away from its conclusion when Hoss stopped in his tracks—five feet away from the bar. Through his stupor he began to realize that he was looking at the last two people in New Orleans he needed to come in contact with—Whit and Andrew. He froze in his tracks, trying to interpret the message his brain was sending him.

Ten seconds passed, and the odor got stronger and stronger. Whit was grinning at his hometown nemesis, adding even more confusion to Hoss's muddled brain. Andrew was doubled over, holding his nose and mouth, trying as hard as was humanly possible to breathe through his ears.

Leon continued to scream at Hoss in an unknown tongue.

Twenty seconds before 12:30, Jake Guillebeau opened his mouth to scream at Hoss Mitchell and tell him to get the hell away. This was a mistake. The oysters which had been rumbling in his stomach had already started making their way up the giant Cajun's esophagus. As he opened his mouth, oysters began to pour from it. The startled man instantly leaned over as 270 unchewed, and undigested oysters flowed from his mouth like a milky white waterfall, forming a disgusting lake on the hardwood floor.

Andrew made the mistake of opening his eyes just as oysters began to flow from Jake's mouth. Oysters began to flow from Andrew's mouth as well. They were even more sickly looking than the one's Jake was barfing, having been tinted a reddish-orange color by the cocktail sauce Andrew had used early on in the contest.

The Oyster Bar quickly emptied as the patrons and spectators ran into the streets, gasping for fresh air and struggling to keep from upchucking themselves.

The oyster shuckers and other employees of the Oyster Bar ran quickly to the sanctuary of the bathrooms.

Leon stood stock still, speechless, staring in disbelief at the unprecedented scene before him.

Whit was the first one to realize the full implications of what had happened and took a menacing step toward Hoss.  Murder was his intention.  Unfortunately, the pile of regurgitated oysters was between him and Hoss.  His feet slid out from under him and deposited him squarely in the middle of the slimy mess.

Hoss had no idea what he had done, but as he saw Whit scrambling to get up he was cognizant enough to realize that he needed to get as far away from the scene as possible, and quickly.  He turned toward the door, putting his huge bulk into high gear and disappeared, leaving behind a stench that would last for days.

Jake and Andrew stared at one another.  Each was too traumatized to speak.

Leon was the first person to gain control of himself.  He walked out from behind the bar with several wet towels and began to help Whit try and clean himself up.  Then he walked over and stood in between Andrew and Big Jake, both of whom were still in shock.

"I declare this contest a draw," he said, reaching into his shirt pocket and pulling out the two Sugar Bowl tickets.  He handed the first to Big Jake who stared at it for a moment and then turned and walked out of the Oyster Bar  as if in a daze.  The second ticket Leon handed to Andrew.

He held it in his hand gingerly, like it was a great treasure.

Whit, who was still wiping himself off, stared at the prize over his buddy's shoulder.  "Well," he said, patting Andrew on the back.  "You've got your ticket.  I'd say you earned it, too."

Andrew turned and looked at Whit, then shook his head.  "Nope," he said firmly.  "We have one ticket."  He stuck the ticket in Whit's shirt pocket.

"Now we need one."

# Chapter Twenty-five

It was dusk on New Year's Eve. Andrew and Whit sat quietly in a corner booth of a small Creole restaurant near Jackson Square. They had purchased a large red marker at Woolworth's and altered the signs that Terri Lynn had made for them, marking through the word "TWO" and replacing it with the number "ONE." They had spent the rest of the afternoon walking up and down the streets of the French Quarter and, once more, in and out of the lobbies of all the major hotels, hoping against hope that they would find the one ticket they still needed. They had spent three hours and had talked to Bulldog fans from Rabun Gap to Tybee Island, and all points in between. Strangely, there were very few Notre Dame fans to be found. Wherever the Irish rooters were, they were keeping to themselves.

The boys' mission was two-fold. They had hoped to find a ticket and also hoped to find other Georgia students, preferably female, with whom to usher in the new year. As had been the case all week, Georgia alumni were everywhere, but actual students were as rare as Notre Dame fans. The boys were sure that there was a large pocket of students somewhere, partying to beat hell. They just couldn't find them.

And they had no luck finding a ticket, either. After three hours of wandering from place to place, they decided to try and get a good meal before the restaurants got really crowded. They were lucky to stumble across an uncrowded Creole restaurant housed in a building that was well over a hundred years old. The interior was brick and a huge open fire burned in the double fireplace in the center of the room. The boys chose from the simple menu offered to them by the efficient, middle-aged waitress and made small talk as they waited for their food and sipped sweet iced tea from tall glasses. Andrew hadn't fully recovered from his oyster eating ordeal and had gone all afternoon without a drink. Since he'd gone this long, he had decided to wait until after supper to begin his serious celebration.

Not long after taking their order, the waitress arrived with bowls of crisp fresh salad,  bread still hot from the oven, and large platters of succulent shrimp Creole, generously ladled over beds of steamed rice. The food was easily the best they had tasted since leaving Leesdale. Both boys were starved and devoured the delicious meal, gladly accepting their server's continuous  offers of extra bread and salad.

There was very little conversation during the meal, but as they were finishing up, Andrew noticed that Whit was much quieter than usual.

"What's wrong?" he asked his friend. "Worried that we won't get another ticket? Hell, we'll get in somehow. I been to games all over without a ticket, and I ain't never not got in."

Whit smiled at his buddy's destruction of the English language and shook his head. He examined his thoughts for a few moments before speaking. "No, it's not the ticket. I was just thinking about things. I guess I was feeling a little guilty."

"Guilty? What in hell do you have to feel guilty about? You haven't drank a drop since we've been here, and God knows you ain't got close to getting no . ."

Whit held up a hand and stopped him.

"I don't mean that kind of guilty. I'm just thinking, you know, why should I get to be out here in New Orleans? Here I sit on New Year's Eve in some fancy French restaurant eating this fancy food, and my mama is sitting by herself in Leesdale having who knows what to eat. And whatever she's having, she's having it all alone."

"Look, Linthead," Andrew replied. "In the first place, this restaurant ain't French, its Cajun. Well, maybe it's Creole or something, but I know it ain't French. And besides, your mama wants you to do things that she can't do. That's what it means to be a parent."

"I know, but my folks worked so hard all their lives and have given me so much. My daddy died without ever getting to go anywhere or do anything. Unless you count World War II. I don't know. It always depresses me a little when I get to do things they never got to do."

"Well my folks have been everywhere and done everything. It depresses me when I don't get to do something. In fact, I'm getting real depressed right now because I've spent three whole days without female companionship. Let's go find some."

The boys left a tip on the table, placed their *NEED ONE* signs back in place around their necks, and headed for the register. After Whit paid the bill, he ruefully examined the rapidly shrinking funds left in his wallet.

"If we even find a ticket to the game, we won't have enough money to buy it," he complained as they walked out of the warm restaurant into the chilly night air. "Look, Andrew," he said, "If we don't find a ticket, you can use the one we have. It would only be fair."

"I ain't going in the game if you don't," Andrew stated. "Besides, we're going to find a ticket."

"Well, its New Year's Eve. What do we do now?" Whit asked.

"Let's walk to our room and get a shower and then head back out on the town. Bourbon Street should be hopping in about an hour. Maybe we'll get lucky."

"And find a ticket?" Whit asked.

"And find some wild women," Andrew answered, pulling Whit along as they walked in the general direction of Canal Street.

An ugly yellow Toyota pulled up beside the boys as they hurried along one of the Quarter's side streets. It had a large Notre Dame decal on the back window. The car slowed to a crawl about ten feet in front of Andrew and Whit and a greasy looking twenty-something year old with pimples all over his face stuck his head out of the car. He was wearing a Fighting Irish baseball cap.

"Hey," he shouted agreeably, "Do youse guys need a ticket to tomorrow's game?"

"We sure do," Whit answered, hurrying to catch up with the slow moving car.

The driver waited until Whit was even with the passenger side window, then sped away. "Hope you get one!" the greasy looking Irish fan shouted back toward the pair on the sidewalk.

Andrew shot them a bird.

"We gonna kick y'all's Yankee asses!" Whit shouted at the disappearing import.

"Just like a damn Yankee," he said to Andrew.

"Just like one," Andrew agreed. The boys shook their heads and continued on their way.


Two hours later Andrew and Whit made the now familiar turn at the intersection of Canal and Bourbon and headed north.

"My God Almighty!" Andrew exclaimed.

"Hot damn," Whit cried excitedly. "The whole state of Georgia must be down here tonight."

Bourbon Street was wide open, and it was red—Dawg red. It was eight o'clock in the evening, there were four hours left in 1980, and Georgia fans had consumed Rue de Bourbon. They were everywhere. They filled every bar and restaurant. They lined wrought iron railings on hotel balconies. They spilled from the sidewalks onto the street. They were singing. They were screaming. They were cheering. They were drinking. Most especially, they were drinking.

"Let's go," the boys said to one another as they hurried toward the crowd which began about two blocks away and continued as far as the eyes could see.

"How 'bout them *Dawgs!*"

"Woof! How *bout* them Dawgs!"

"Woof ! Woof! Woof! Woof! Woof!"

"Goooooo Dogs!"

"Go you Hairy Dawgs!"

*"How 'bout them Dawgs!"*

The cries came from every direction. They were screamed and shouted by people from all walks of life. Whit and Andrew answered each and every bark with barks of their own as they jostled their way through the crowd. The atmosphere was surreal and magical. They pushed their way through an entire block, solid with people, giving high fives to every single person they met.

"By God, them Yankees might win the game tomorrow, but this town belongs to us tonight," Andrew screamed over the roar of the crowd.

"Damn straight!  Go Dawgs!" Whit screamed back.

"I need a drink." Andrew suddenly realized that he'd spent an entire day in New Orleans without benefit of imbibement.

"Well you're in a damn good place to get one!" Whit reasoned, still shouting to be heard.

"Gooooo Georgia Bulldawgs!" screamed the French Quarter as a whole.

"Go Dawgs! Woof, Woof, Woof!" screamed Whit and Andrew in reply.

"I can't stand it. This is great!" Whit screamed.

"I need a drink!" Andrew screamed in reply.

"Let's go to Pat O'Brien's," Whit suggested.

"Suits me."

The boys continued to inch their way through the red and black mob, loving every minute. Even the panhandlers and prostitutes had abandoned the streets in deference to the Red Sea which was sweeping through the French Quarter.

"Look at that!" Andrew shouted, pointing to the corner of Bourbon and St. Louis.

A  man was standing beside the gas streetlamp. He was red. All of his clothes were red. His face and hair had been been sprayed bright red. Even his eyes were red and bloodshot.  Standing on his shoulders was a young girl in a red sweater and black skirt. The skirt was very short. The man and the girl were surrounded by people screaming over and over, "Go Dogs!"

Every time the crowd said "Dogs" the girl would lift her skirt as high as she could, revealing  red panties with a picture of a Bulldog imprinted on them.

"Let's stay right here for the next couple of days," Whit suggested.

"I need a drink," Andrew replied.

The boys continued to snake their way through the crowd. Georgia people were everywhere. Sometimes they could hardly move. In fact, when they reached Toulouse and Bourbon, they could not move at all. The street was a solid mass of red clad humanity. The crowd was facing a hotel on the east side of the street. There were balconies overlooking the street, and each was filled with Georgia people. Most were either drunk or well on their way. Almost to a person, they held large cups, glasses, mugs, or cans of liquid libation and were toasting the crowd below.

An especially intoxicated man appeared on a third floor balcony. Most of the time he was a well respected young attorney from Griffin. On this particular night he was drunker than he had ever been in his life. He started waving and screaming at the crowd below through a bullhorn he had borrowed from the junior high band director back home, for just such an occasion. He quickly got the attention of most of the revelers below. He was resplendent in a red Georgia jersey with the number 34 on the front, red and black boxers, and red socks. He appeared before the crowd without benefit of pants.

His wife was on the balcony with him. She was worried to death that someone from home would see and recognize her husband and was pleading with him to come back inside. Unfortunately, two other couples were on the balcony also, and they were all as drunk as the counselor and were enthusiastically egging him on. Once he had the attention of most of the crowd, the man climbed onto the wrought iron railing of the balcony.

"Oh my God, he's going to fall to his death wearing boxer shorts," screamed his wife.

"Don't jump, brother!" shouted someone in the crowd.

"Herschel!" shouted the attorney into his megaphone.

The crowd was a little slow. They simply cheered wildly, which was not the response the lawyer had hoped for.

"HERSCHEL!" He shouted again, even louder this time.

Andrew, who was sober and not at all happy about it, was the first person to catch on. From his spot on the periphery of the crowd he screamed back, as loudly as he could, "WALKER!"

That was the response the man with the bullhorn was looking for.

Again he yelled into his mouthpiece, "HERSCHEL!"

This time most of the crowd below joined in. "WALKER!" they shouted back.

Now the attorney's friends and even his wife joined in as he shouted again, "HERSCHEL!"

Everyone within earshot shouted back, "WALKER!"

The next time he shouted, all the people on all the balconies joined him, and for the next ten minutes the crowd on the balconies shouted "HERSCHEL" and were answered by the crowd below screaming, "WALKER" at the top of their lungs.

The attorney's wife finally decided that she couldn't convince her husband to come down from the balcony so she climbed up beside him and joined in.

"I ain't going to be the only sober person in New Orleans on New Year's Eve," Andrew insisted when he saw the woman climb up on the rail. "You don't count," he said to Whit, before he could say anything. "Let's go to Pat O'Brien's."

With great effort, they made their way through the mob in front of the hotel. By the time they had made their way to the next block and turned right on St. Peter's, the crowd behind them had changed their chant and were screaming as one, "GO TO HELL NOTRE DAME, GO TO HELL!" There were as many people packed in front of Pat O'Brien's as there were in front of the hotel on Bourbon Street. "We'll never get in there," Whit observed.

"You just watch me," Andrew answered. "I'm going to have a Flaming Hurricane, and then I'm going to have another and then I'm going to have several more. Just stay with me."

Andrew lowered his shoulder and plowed through the crowd like a fullback, with Whit hanging onto his shirt tail. He completely ignored the angry shouts of the people he stepped on, ran into, and pushed aside. He refused to acknowledge the two attendants at the door as he hurled himself and Whit into the crowded courtyard.

The interior of the famous nightclub was just as packed as the street outside. Just like in the rest of the French Quarter, the color red dominated, with just a smattering of green and gold here and there. Dixieland music sounded forth from the piano, which was being played by a very talented young man who had never encountered an audience such as this. He had learned very early in the evening that they would be happy as long as he played either "Dixie" or "Glory Glory" between every number. Once he made the near fatal mistake of sounding out the first few bars of the "Notre Dame Fight Song." He was immediately assaulted by a barrage of boos, shouts, and threats, not to mention cherries, orange slices, and other unidentified garnishes.

Whit and Andrew inched their way through the crowd and found a few square inches in which to stand near the flaming fountain in the center of the courtyard. "This is great," Whit shouted above the crowd. He was trying to look in every direction at once.

Andrew was also looking in every direction, for a waitress. He wanted a drink and wanted one bad. "What do you have to do to get a drink in here?" he wondered aloud.

Whit couldn't hear him above the laughing, singing, cheering crowd. He just smiled and shrugged at his buddy, pointing to his ears to indicate he hadn't heard him.

The tables in the bar were filled with laughing, smiling, drinking people. Many of them were the college coeds which had been eluding Whit and Andrew. Most were drinking potent Hurricanes from tall glasses. Most seemed very intoxicated. All seemed to be escorted by intoxicated young men.

Andrew made several unsuccessful attempts to flag down one of the dozens of waitresses who were hurrying to and fro, trying to keep the thirsty crowd of celebrants satisfied. Finally, he managed to get the attention of a sweet young thing from Bugaloosa who was working her way through school at Tulane. She explained to him that she couldn't serve him unless he was seated at a table. She suggested he wait in line at one of the bars situated around the room and with an apologetic smile disappeared into the crowd.

Suddenly the piano player broke into another medley of Georgia fight songs. The place was up for grabs. People were screaming and shouting and banging glasses and mugs on the table in time to the music. A male pharmacy student from Hazlehurst climbed on top of his table and began doing a wild dance. At least it was as wild a dance as a male pharmacy student from Hazlehurst could do. Across the room, to the delight of the crowd, an elementary education major from Tiger climbed onto her table and started dancing, too. She matched the future pharmacist, gyration for gyration.

Whit was in heaven.

Andrew was miserable. "I need a drink," he insisted.

"Go to the bar and get one," Whit said, paying much more attention to the future kindergarten teacher than to her male counterpart.

"Are you kidding? They are lined up twenty-deep at the bar. Let's go somewhere else."

"Are you crazy?" Whit shouted above the crowd. "This place is jumping. Why do we want to go somewhere else?"

The piano player had finished his medley of Georgia songs and was doing his best Jerry Lee Lewis imitation, pounding out "Great Balls of Fire," his fingers flying over the ivory keyboard. The whole place was up and dancing. Tables became filled with uninhibited young college students who would one day be nurses, merchants, bankers, and respected pillars of their communities. Tonight they were just college students in New Orleans having a night they would never forget, if indeed they could remember it at all.

Whit began dancing to the music. A short, chunky redhead who had been trying to make her way back to her table from the restroom joined him. Andrew couldn't stand it. "A whole city full of drunks," he screamed, "and I'm stone sober!"

The place continued to rock and roll as the piano man followed "Great Balls of Fire" with "Johnny B. Goode" and then "Chantilly Lace." Whit's partner danced off toward her table after one number, but was replaced by several more honeys who were making their way through the club. Each would dance for thirty seconds or so, then go on her way, to be quickly replaced by another. Whit was having the time of his life.

Andrew was having withdrawals. He watched good-naturedly as a tall brunette from Baxley kissed Whit on the cheek and wiggled her way through the crowd as a song ended. Before another could begin, Andrew tugged on Whit's sleeve. "Let's find another place. It will be midnight soon. I need a drink, and I'll never get served in here."

With a deep sigh, Whit reluctantly agreed, and followed his buddy through the dancing, clapping crowd and out the door of Pat O'Brien's.

The street outside was even more crowded than before, if that were possible. The French Quarter was saturated. People were shoulder to shoulder. No one seemed to mind, however. Everyone was full of anticipation of the next day's battle and glad to be a Bulldog on this Wednesday night. Whit and Andrew struggled through the crowd until they had made their way back to the corner of Bourbon Street. They paused there, pressed up against people they didn't know, but who didn't seem to mind.

"I'd love to hear Munson describe this scene," Whit shouted.

"Yeah," Andrew agreed, temporarily forgetting his quest for alcohol. "I can hear him now." He broke into his best imitation of the legendary Georgia announcer. "Get the picture. Bourbon Street all in red—red jackets, red sweaters, black pants, red faces, and red eyeballs. The street? Well the street fell apart. They'll have to replace this entire area  tomorrow. Do you know how big this thing is tomorrow?  It's going to be a war. A total nuclear war."

Andrew had inspired those people within earshot and yet another huge cry of "Gooooo Dogs!" arose from the crowd, answered by a thousand voices screaming, "How 'Bout Them Dawgs! Woof ! Woof ! Woof !"

"Let's go back up the street," Andrew suggested. "It's getting close to midnight."

He became even more frustrated as they continued through the crowd at a snail's pace. All the people they struggled past had drinks, and Andrew reasoned that they had to have gotten them somewhere. But each club they inched past was packed. To even think of getting in was prohibitive.

"Ten minutes to midnight!" someone in the crowd shouted.

"Look where we are," Whit said to Andrew. They were directly underneath the balcony where the impromptu pep rally had taken place earlier. The balconies above were absolutely filled with people, all wearing red, and all holding glasses, ready to toast the new year.

"Ain't that Uga?" a drunken voice asked from somewhere in the crowd.

"Damn sure is!" came an equally drunk reply.

Andrew and Whit joined the rest of the crowd as they searched the balconies above them. Finally, on the third floor they spotted a man holding up a solid white English Bulldog, wearing a red sweater with a big block G.

"If that ain't Uga, it's a good impostor," Andrew suggested.

"If that is Uga, they need to get him inside and put him to bed," Whit reasoned. "We need all the help we can get tomorrow."

"My God Almighty, look up yonder!" Andrew was shouting and pointing and jumping up and down.

"My Lord! Is that who I think it is?" Whit was as stunned as Andrew.

"It is indeed," Andrew answered. "Its a sign. Its a by damn sign."

What it was was Gladys Gibson, Leesdale High School Homecoming Queen of 1974, and the ultimate fantasy of every male in Leesdale who was old enough to have one and young enough to remember. She was the object of every wet dream Whit and Andrew had ever had. The contents of her sweaters had been discussed wherever two or more Leesdale males had gathered since the precious child had reached puberty.

And now, she was standing on a balcony, a scant three stories above Whit and Andrew. She was obviously drunk. She wore a short plaid skirt with plenty of her shapely legs visible below the hemline. Of course she wore her trademark sweater. Tonight's version was red and very tight and very full. She was drinking beer from a plastic cup, and had been for most of the night. She was also dancing, very suggestively, to the music which was blaring through the closed doors of a night club across the street.

"Five more minutes!" someone shouted excitedly.

A large portion of the great throng below, particularly the males, had turned their attention to Gladys Gibson, the pride of Leesdale, and her wild gyrations on the balcony above. Four minutes before midnight, someone screamed the inevitable. "Take it off!" Within seconds the male portion of the populous below had begun to chant the phrase in unison, begging the object of Whit and Andrew's fantasies, to "Take it off."

To the delight of the men below, and to the horror of her date who was on the balcony with her, two minutes before the end of 1980, Gladys Gibson began to do exactly that. With a sensuous movement that would have rivaled that which the very best exotic dancer the French Quarter had to offer, the inebriated young woman grabbed the hem of her tight sweater and slid it slowly up her body, over her shoulders, over her head and off. She drew tremendous cheers as she tossed it into the street below. Andrew and Whit stood below with mouths wide open, refusing to believe what they were seeing.

The chant below turned to "Take it all off." With ninety seconds remaining in the year, Gladys was determined to oblige them. She reached behind her back and unsnapped her silky black bra and let it drop at her feet beside her. Her date, who had disappeared into the hotel room as her sweater was coming off, ran back onto the balcony with a large white towel which he flung around the drunken brunette, who was struggling with the fastener of her skirt. He hauled her back into the room, but not before all of the men below had witnessed two large rubber pads float to the street below and not before they had caught a glimpse of two of the flattest breasts any of them had ever had the privilege of seeing.

The two boys looked at one another in disbelief. Then a smile broke across Andrew's face. Then he started laughing, and Whit joined in. Someone in the crowd started counting down the last ten seconds of the year and the entire mass of people who had packed Bourbon Street beyond capacity joined in. 8 - 7 - 6 - 5 - 4 - 3 - 2 - 1, and then pandemonium erupted. "Auld Lang Syne" could be heard coming through doors of night clubs and lounges up and down the street. People were throwing confetti from wrought iron balconies. Men were exchanging high fives and couples were kissing. Whit and Andrew just looked at one another, not knowing exactly how to act or what to say. They were still both in a bit of a state of shock from the revelation of a few moments before.

Then amidst the cheers and whistles came a deep cry from somewhere far down the street. "GOOOOOO GEORGIA BULLDAWGS ! !" It was echoed by a dozen voices and then a hundred and then a thousand. "HOW 'BOUT THEM DAWGS" quickly replaced "Happy New Year" on the lips of the legions of Georgia fans who controlled the Vieux Carre.

"Want to go find that drink?" Whit said to his buddy.

Andrew's reply shocked him more than the minuscule size of Gladys Gibson's mammary glands. "Why don't we go back to the room and rest up. Tomorrow's not gonna be just a game. Tomorrow's gonna be for forever."

It was not yet one o'clock when the two boys exited the elevator back at their Canal Street Hotel. When they did, they found a twenty year old Georgia coed lying in the hallway, right beside their room. She was so intoxicated that she had passed out and was wearing little more than a Confederate flag which someone had considerately draped over her practically nude body.

"Is that a sign?" Whit asked.

"Naw," Andrew replied. "Just a drunk girl."

"Shouldn't we do something for her?" Whit asked.

"The best thing we could do for her is just let her sleep it off, right where she is," Andrew replied as he opened the door and stepped over the supine girl and into their room.

Whit shrugged. "These are strange times," he thought to himself as he also stepped over the unfortunate young lady and followed Andrew into the room, closing the door behind him.

It was 1981, and kickoff was less than thirteen hours away.

# Chapter Twenty-six

Whit was the first to awaken on New Year's Day. The clock beside the bed told him it was 8:00 A.M. He had been bothered all night by stomach cramps and awakened with a full and bloated feeling. He looked over at his buddy who was still out like a light, and shook his head. "That don't make no kind of sense," he said to himself. "Andrew drinks like a fish and is up at the crack of dawn. He goes to bed stone sober and sleeps like a baby."

Whit dressed quietly and left the room, in search of a cup of coffee and the morning paper. Canal Street was still and quiet. Only a few hours earlier there had been swarms of people. Now those people were tucked quietly away in their rented rooms, sound asleep. Whit bought a copy of the *Times-Picayune* and entered the hotel coffee shop. It was completely deserted except for a sleepy looking waitress who was sitting at the counter, smoking a cigarette. Whit took a seat in a corner booth and turned the coffee cup that was already there right side up. The waitress walked over and filled his cup without speaking then returned to her seat at the counter. She took a long drag off her cigarette and began to rub her temples, trying to wish away her headache. Like thousands of others across the city, she was wondering if the night before had been worth the morning after.

Whit studied the laminated menu that was on his table, but the queasy feeling in his stomach caused him to decide against food. He sipped his coffee and studied the sports page, taking in every syllable dealing with the upcoming game. His blood started tingling in anticipation of the impending battle. "Can we really do it?" he asked himself over and over. "Will God let us win?" He allowed his mind to drift back to other seasons and other disappointments. He couldn't help but remember the Auburn game of 1973.

Both teams had entered the next to the last game of the season undefeated and the Georgia student body had stayed awake the entire night in anticipation of the showdown for the SEC championship. Auburn's All-American passing combination of Pat Sullivan to Terry Beasley had proven too much for the Dogs on that day. Whit had been fourteen years old. He could remember almost every play. He let his mind drift back in time and for a moment he was sitting at the kitchen table of his family's home in the mill village. His dad was sitting across from him, and Larry Munson was calling the play-by-play over the old Philco radio which sat on a shelf beneath the window. A touch of melancholy overcame Whit as he thought about his father. Then his thoughts turned to his mother.

"I'll bet she's sitting at that same table, drinking coffee," he thought. He started to get up from the booth and find a phone so he could call to wish her a Happy New Year, but didn't. He returned his attention to the paper and stared at a picture of a smirking Notre Dame lineman with a name that Whit couldn't pronounce. His mind wandered to another game. This game had taken place a couple of years ago. Alabama had been carrying the South's torch that day and had things seemingly under control. Notre Dame was third and forever, backed up on their own goal line. They threw a long pass and made the first down. Then they went on to score and win the game and the National Championship. "Damn Yankees," Whit muttered to himself.

He looked in the direction of the waitress, hoping for a refill of his now empty coffee cup. She was sound asleep at the counter, her head resting on folded arms. Whit just smiled and shook his head. He tossed a dollar on the table, picked up the sports section, leaving the rest of his paper, and headed back to the room.

When he arrived there, Andrew was up and in the bathroom. "Don't ever let me do that again," Andrew shouted from behind the closed bathroom door.

"Do what?" Whit replied, having a seat on the bed and spreading the paper out before him. He wished the bloated feeling in his stomach would subside.

"Let me go a whole day and night without a drink," Andrew answered, walking out of the bathroom. He was drying his hair with a towel and already had on his game day drawers—red boxers that hadn't been washed since the Tennessee game. Andrew took a look at himself in the mirror. He brushed his thick black mustache lovingly. "I can't wait until tomorrow," he said.

"Why tomorrow?" Whit asked.

Andrew turned and smiled at his buddy. "Because I get better looking every day."

"Yeah," Whit replied. "You and Joe Willie. I wish we had Joe Namath playing for us today. I'd feel lots better about things."

"Hell," Andrew answered, "Buck Belue can give the ball to Herschel just as good as Joe Namath could. We don't have to complete a single pass to beat Notre Dame. Herschel's gonna kick their ass."

Whit looked up from the paper. "It says here that no back has gained a hundred yards against Notre Dame all year long. This guy predicts that Notre Dame will win by ten points."

"Screw him," Andrew said. "We need to find out what the Atlanta papers are saying. I'm gonna call Bonnie Faith and get her to read the paper to us."

"Are you going to call her house?   You must have a death wish. Wayne will rip your heart out."

"It's almost ten o'clock at home. She'll be at the cafe helping Leon. You know he always cooks up a big mess of collards and black eyed peas on New Year's Day. He takes 'em to the folks at the old folks home."

Whit again thought of his mother and felt guilty. He hoped she was having her New Year's dinner with some of her friends from church. He continued to look at the paper while Andrew, who had sat down on the other bed, fumbled through his wallet in search of the diner's telephone number.

"Look, Andrew. The paper says that the game will be delayed fifteen minutes to allow Jimmy Carter and his secret service entourage time to get into the stadium."

"What a crock," Andrew shot back.

"Well, he is the President of the United States," Whit replied defensively.

"For three more weeks," Andrew reminded him. "Don't forget, we still need a ticket. Those secret service guys might take up a seat that we could have bought."

"Look at the bright side," Whit responded. "Now we have fifteen extra minutes to look for a ticket."

Andrew had dialed the number,  and the phone was ringing on the other end. After several rings, Bonnie Faith finally answered.

"Village Square Diner. Happy New Year. We ain't open."

"Happy New Year, yourself. It's me, Andrew. How you doing?"

Bonnie Faith immediately began to talk louder. "Hey, Andrew. Are y'all still out yonder? I'm doin' without. That's how I'm doin'."

"Doin' without?" Andrew purposely spoke loudly enough for Whit to hear him. He grinned at his buddy and motioned for him to come over and listen in on the conversation. "What's wrong?" Andrew teased. "Did Wayne run off with some old red haired gal?"

"Might as well have," Bonnie Faith responded, "for all the good he done me last night. It was New Year's Eve out here, you know."

"Yeah, Bonnie Faith, we know. They had it here, too."

"Well, I had a big evening planned. I cooked him up his favorite meal—chipped beef on toast. He never could get enough of it in the Marine Corps. I had put on his favorite nightie, the one with the tassels, and had candles on the table and everything. He drags himself home two hours late. Says he had to go and see old Dr. Palmer. Says he threw his back out moving some logs at the lumber yard on account of all the colored boys laid out and he was trying to do some work by hisself."

Andrew and Whit were biting their arms to keep from laughing.

"Anyway, old Doc Palmer had Wayne all trussed up and full of dope. He laid down on the couch and was sound asleep before nine o'clock. He didn't even eat the special dinner I had fixed him."

"Bonnie Faith," Andrew broke in, "did you have to sit there and watch the new year in all by yourself?"

"Well, no, as a matter of fact, I had some unexpected company. About ten 'til twelve Mrs. Harrison, you know, Whit's next door neighbor, came knocking on my door. Liked to scared me to death. It was so close to midnight that I just invited her in to watch Dick Clark with me. We toasted one another with champagne and watched that big ball drop. At first I was embarrassed on account of I still had my nightie on, but you know what? She opened up her coat and she had on one just like it. Only she had the green one and I had the black one. I had wanted the green one, but they only had it in a small, and I just couldn't fit all I have into a small."

Bonnie Faith finally stopped for breath, which gave Andrew time to speak. "What in the world was Mrs. Harrison doing at your house at midnight on New Years Eve?"

"Oh," said Bonnie Faith. "She wanted to borrow some honey and some cooking oil for a party she was hosting.  She said she had bought a bunch of each the other day and that nosy old Mr. Evans had told her that I had bought a lot of honey and cooking oil, too.  I didn't buy all that much, though. Mr. Evans ought to mind his own business. But I was glad to give it to her. I sure didn't need it. Wayne just slept right through everything. In fact, he was still sleeping on the couch when I got up to come to work this morning."

Andrew and Whit looked at one another. No matter how many of her stories they heard, they were always amazed by Bonnie Faith.

"I'm sorry you had such a disappointing night," Andrew said. "Trust me. We didn't do any better."

"Terri Lynn will be glad to hear that," Bonnie Faith said. "She's been in here every day, asking if I've heard from y'all. I never knew you and her were so close," Bonnie Faith teased. She might have been a few bricks shy of a load, but was smart enough to add two and two and get four, and had done so.

Whit began to blush and drew his ear away from the phone, suddenly deciding he needed to go to the bathroom. Andrew, to his credit, hadn't mentioned his sister since the incident concerning the diary. Whit was very grateful and wished Bonnie Faith hadn't mentioned her either. He picked up the paper from the bed and retreated to the bathroom, leaving Andrew to find out the rest of the news from home.

"Bonnie Faith," he said, finally getting around to the real reason for the call, "we want to know what the Atlanta paper is saying about the game. Do you think you could read me some of the highlights?"

"Leon figured y'all would be calling. He didn't want me to stay on the phone all day, so he wrote down everything y'all needed to know. I got the list right here." Bonnie Faith was proud of herself for being prepared. "The paper said that there was a bunch of drunk, crazy, and wild Georgia fans on Bourbon Street last night."

"Tell us something we don't know," Andrew complained.

"It also said that Jesse Outlar and Ron Hudspeth said Georgia was gonna win. Furman Bisher said they might, if Buck Belue has a good day. And Lewis Grizzard said they'd better."

"That's all?" Andrew asked.

"That's all. Hey, I'd better go. Leon is hollering at me. Him and Regina are back in the kitchen, up to their hineys in collard greens. Y'all be sweet and call and tell me who won."

Just like that, Bonnie Faith was gone.

Whit had come out of hiding and was packing his suitcase, eager to get back on the streets in search of one more ticket. "What'd the paper say?" he asked.

"Who knows?" Andrew answered. "Whit, why can't we stay here tonight? After Georgia wins, this town will be up for grabs. We need to stay and celebrate."

"The town was up for grabs the last two nights. Little good it did us. I told you, we'll stay and celebrate as long as you want to, but then we'll head toward home and find a cheaper place to spend the night. We're about out of money."

"How much do we have left?" Andrew asked.

"I'm not sure. Let's count it up and see." Whit sat on the bed and opened up his wallet. "How much is in your wallet?"

A short laugh was the only reply he got. It was also the only one he expected.

Whit shook his head. "We have to give $150 back to Calvin since we couldn't buy any beer to bootleg. I'm glad we haven't run into him. Maybe we won't. Who cares about Hoss's money? When I catch up to him, I'm going to take that much more out of his sorry hide. It looks like we have a little over two hundred dollars, not counting what we owe Calvin. We should be fine."

"All right," Andrew jumped up from the bed and began throwing clothes into his overnight bag. "Let's check out of this place and go find a ticket. We got a ballgame to watch."

"It's way more than a ballgame," Whit replied, holding his stomach, which had begun to cramp again.

# Chapter Twenty-seven

The boys had checked out of their hotel and had driven around the city, which was slowly coming awake in anticipation of the big game, which was by now a scant four hours away. They had parked the red Camaro in restricted zones several times, risking a ticket in order to canvas the lobbies of several fashionable hotels. Andrew was dressed in khakis and a red Izod sweater. Whit wore his best Georgia sweatshirt. Their altered signs hung from their respective necks. As always, they got lots of salutations and sympathetic looks, but no tickets. There were none to be had, apparently, at any price.

They finally decided that outside the stadium would be the best place to continue their search. Andrew insisted they stop for breakfast at a McDonald's. Whit's stomach still hurt, so all he ordered was a Coke. Andrew also had to stop at a liquor store to buy a bottle of Jack Daniel's to carry in the game. They spent thirty minutes stalled in traffic, looking for a parking place near the massive structure on Claiborne Avenue known as the Louisiana Superdome. They kept trying to turn the wrong way up one way streets, much to the dismay of other drivers, who were just as confused as they were. They got more than their share of angry shouts from New Orleans policemen, many of whom rode large horses and wore white helmets. The boys finally parked in the parking lot of a huge hospital building, in direct violation of posted regulations, of course. They then walked to the stadium. The distance wasn't so great, but they had to make their way under an expressway viaduct and across four lanes of slowly moving traffic on Claiborne.

"Finally," Andrew exclaimed, as they made their way through the huge throng that was mingling all around the expansive promenade which surrounded the stadium. Some had been there for hours, waiting for the gates to open. The legions of Georgia fans seemed more subdued than they had been the night before. They wore grim expressions. It was easy to tell the Georgia fans from the Notre Dame fans. The Irish followers wore mostly nondescript shades of clothing and looked relaxed, as if they were attending a sporting event. The Georgia faithful were dressed almost exclusively in red and looked as if they were going to war.

"Look at that," Whit said, pointing to two Georgia fans who were parading around the promenade. Between them they carried a huge banner which proclaimed, "You've got the hunchback—We've got the tailback." Another Georgia fan followed behind, dragging a toy leprechaun tied to a rope. A gorgeous coed from Colquitt trailed behind, barely sober from the night before. An occasional "Go Dawgs!" would punctuate the air, but the mood was mostly anticipatory, and very tense.

Whit was overcome by a sudden surge of panic. He grabbed Andrew's arm. "Have you got our one ticket?" he asked.

"No," Andrew replied, "I thought you had it."

"Oh, my God," Whit said, clutching his throat. "Now we need two again. Where do you think it could be?"

"It could be right here," Andrew replied, his bright teeth gleaming beneath his thick mustache. He reached in his shirt pocket and produced their one ticket.

"Damn, Andrew," Whit admonished him. "Don't do stuff like that. I'm already about to die, I'm so nervous. I don't know where we'll get another one."

"We'll get one," Andrew insisted. "Come on, let's walk around in this direction." He led the way as they circled the stadium in a counterclockwise direction. The closer it got to game time the more excited the crowd got. At one point a giant roar went up from the crowd, and the boys craned their heads to see if the team bus was approaching, but the fans were just responding to the giant gates being swung back to start letting them in the stadium.

"I can't believe this," Whit said. "I haven't seen a single ticket for sale."

"Well I'll be damned. Look at that," Andrew shouted. He was staring disbelievingly, and pointing up ahead.

Whit allowed his eyes to follow Andrew's. He was just as shocked as his buddy at what he beheld. Standing right beside one of the main gates was Hoss Mitchell, and he was clean. He wore a brand new Bulldog sweatshirt, and the pants he wore were black and actually complimented the shirt. He had on his customary black cowboy hat with the ticket stubs to previous games sticking out of the red hatband, but his hair was clean underneath the hat and had actually been combed. He displayed two tickets over his head, obviously available to any taker. Not a single person in his immediate vicinity held their nose or grimaced or otherwise indicated that he smelled bad. The boys were only fifty or sixty feet away from him, and they couldn't smell a thing.

"That son of a bitch came to the game incognito," Whit fumed. "Looks like we're getting in after all."

"We've got to be careful," Andrew cautioned. "If he sees us, he might run and get lost in the crowd."

"I'll bet that's why the bastard bathed," Whit said. He was ready to extract a pound of flesh from their nemesis, along with the tickets that were rightfully theirs.

"I'll slip through the crowd and come at him from over there," Andrew said, gesturing to a spot to Hoss's far left. "You stay right here and wait until I get in position. When I give the sign, we'll rush him from either side. That way he won't be able to get away."

"OK," Whit agreed. "But after we get the tickets, I'm gonna kick his fat ass."

Before the boys could put their plan into action, an athletic looking man, dressed in a brown suede blazer and dark slacks approached Hoss. "Oh,no," Andrew exclaimed. "He's fixin' to sell the tickets. And I'll bet that's a Notre Dame fan, too."

The boys watched in horror as Hoss held out the tickets for the man to study. To their utter dismay, the man reached into his pants pocket and pulled out three one-hundred dollar bills. A big smile lit up Hoss's face as he reached for the cash. His smile turned to a puzzled frown as the man pulled the money back out of his reach. Then another man came from out of nowhere and spun Hoss around. The second man slapped handcuffs on Hoss Mitchell's fat wrists as the first man produced a gold badge and started reading to Hoss from a typewritten card.

Whit and Andrew stared in disbelief as the two men led Hoss— and the two tickets—to a waiting paddy wagon.

"We'll never get a ticket!" Whit was so frustrated that he was close to tears. "Damn, I want to see this game," he screamed. His frustration grew with each "How Bout Them Dawgs." The battle cry was becoming as commonplace as it had been the night before. Hordes of Georgia fans rushed past them, eager to find their seats and prepare to watch their team do battle.

Andrew, too, was beginning to lose hope. "If we don't get a ticket," he said, "one of us will go in and the other one will fall down and act sick, like Terri Lynn did at the Gator Bowl."

"I don't think it will work," Whit answered. "From what I've seen down here this week, they'd let us lay on the ground 'til the cows came home."

People were now everywhere. Screaming and shouting and barking like dogs. Suddenly, the sound of intense sirens split the air. "You reckon that's the cops hauling Hoss off to jail?" Whit asked hopefully.

Before Andrew could answer, someone in the crowd began shouting, "Here they come! Here they come! Here come the Dawgs! Here they come!"

Every person in the vicinity rushed toward the large stadium concourse where two great silver buses, escorted by six police motorcycles, had pulled right up to the gate. Andrew and Whit followed along, jostling and pushing good-naturedly, determined to see their heroes. The police had cordoned off a narrow passageway for the players to walk through, and Whit and Andrew somehow managed to press themselves right up against the yellow nylon rope. The players emerged two-by-two. They wore identical gray slacks, black blazers, white shirts and red and black ties. They were stone faced and looked straight ahead. They looked exactly like they were marching to war, which in fact, they were.

Thunderous cheers greeted even the most obscure player. When Scott Woerner and Buck Belue walked by, shoulder to shoulder, the crowd exploded. When Herschel Walker disembarked from the bus the noise was so loud that the sky almost fell. Herschel tried to remain stone faced, but a slight smile played at the corners of his mouth as he walked through the admiring throng.

Whit and Andrew had forgotten their predicament for the moment and cheered as loudly as the rest for the young gladiators that they might or might not get to see play. As the last of the young stalwarts walked past, Andrew looked back toward the bus to see if there was anyone else. Just as he did, perhaps the largest shout of the day went up. Chill bumps broke out on Andrew's arms and the hair on the back of his neck stood up. Not six feet away and heading straight toward him was the great Erk Russell. Andrew grabbed Whit's arm and pointed. They both were in absolute awe of the legendary defensive coach.

The boys stood slackjawed and stared at the great man with the shaved head. He looked powerful and cut the most impressive figure the boys had ever seen, even in his blazer and tie. He had an aura about him. He seemed larger than life. As he walked past the boys he was so close that they could have reached out and touched him. He passed them and then turned back, as if something had caught his attention. Something had. Out of the corner of his eye, he had seen their signs.

He looked at the boys and smiled. "Y'all need a ticket?" he asked.

They were in shock. This majestic figure of a man was about to lead his charges into battle, and he stopped to ask them if they needed a ticket. He moved closer to them, still smiling. He seemed completely unaware of the adoring crowd that was trying to press closer to him. Many were reaching across the yellow rope, trying to touch his sleeve or pat him on the back.

Neither Whit nor Andrew could comprehend the question, so startled were they by the enormity of the moment. They just stood and stared stupidly ahead.

"Y'all need a ticket?" he repeated.

An inkling of understanding began to creep into Andrew's mind, but he was still unable to speak. He just nodded dumbly, his mouth agape.

The full realization of what Erk Russell was offering hit Whit, and he began to nod his head enthusiastically. He found his voice. "Yes," he shouted. "I mean, yes sir. Yes sir, we do need a ticket. Yes sir!"

Coach Russell reached inside his jacket pocket and handed over the precious piece of pasteboard to the unbelieving Whit. "I always hold one out, just in case," he explained. Then the great man winked at the boys and hurried to catch up with the rest of the team.

Whit and Andrew stared at the ticket for what seemed like minutes, but was in reality but a few seconds. Andrew found his voice first. "Let's go to the Sugar Bowl game!" he shouted.

"If you're waiting on me, you're backing up," Whit answered with a grin.

"I knew we'd get a ticket all along," Andrew said smugly as the boys lined up at the closest gate and began shuffling toward the entrance.

"Right," Whit said sarcastically. At that moment a sharp pain cut his abdomen like a knife.

Andrew checked to make sure his bottle of whiskey was tucked securely into the waistband of his trousers, then handed the ticket he'd won in the oyster eating contest to the uniformed man at the gate. "Go Dawgs!" he said to the man, who didn't even smile in reply.

"I guess you're a Notre Dame fan," Andrew commented.

"LSU—Keep moving," was the surly reply.

Andrew watched the man tear his ticket in half and turned to look for his friend. To his surprise, he was not behind him. He turned his head in every direction, searching frantically.

"Andrew!" The cry had come from outside the stadium.

Andrew made his way against the flow of the crowd to look through

the wire mesh fence beside the turnstiles. Whit was still out on the concourse. He was holding his stomach, doubled over with pain. Tears were
welling up in his eyes.

"Come on in, man," Andrew screamed at him through the fence.
"You have a ticket. Give it to the man and come on in," he demanded.

Whit was in too much pain to reply. He dropped to his knees, still
holding his stomach. He felt like his insides were about to burst. Tears
which he could no longer contain began to flow down his cheeks.

Andrew grabbed the sleeve of the surly ticket taker. "My buddy is
sick out there. I got to get him in to the first aid station."

"You can do better than that," the man replied. "Five people already tried that at this gate today."

"No, I'm serious," Andrew insisted. "He has a ticket, but he's sick.
I've got to get him in here."

"No passes out," the man said. "If you go out, you'll need a ticket to
come back in."

"Are you crazy?" Andrew screamed. "He's sick. He needs help."

"Then go help him," the ticket taker said, "but get out of the way.
This is a big game. People are trying to get in."

Andrew ran back over to the section of fence. Whit was now almost
prostrate. Andrew tried to get the attention of somebody, anybody, still outside the stadium who could help get Whit up and through the gate. The
fans had seen so many drunks passed out on the streets of the French Quarter that they thought Whit was just another college student who had had
too much to drink. To Andrew's amazement, person after person passed
him by. Whit was in so much pain that he had quit groaning. His body had
gone into a state of semishock as a defense mechanism against the excruciating pain in his abdomen. This made him look even more like he was merely

drunk. He didn't respond at all to Andrew's shouts.

Andrew tried once more to reason with the ticket takers. This time he approached a uniformed black woman. "My buddy is outside," he explained. "He's sick and I need to get him to the first aid tent."

"Get lost, Dog Boy," was her surly reply.

Andrew took a long look at all the Georgia and Notre Dame fans who were hurrying up the stadium's wide ramps to find their seats, eagerly anticipating the arrival of the teams on the playing field for the pregame warmups. With a deep sigh, he turned and fought his way back through the flood of people who were still flowing into the building, and went to attend his stricken friend.

# Chapter Twenty-eight

Andrew couldn't believe what had transpired over the past ten minutes. Thousands of normal, decent, hard working, go-to-church-on-Sunday citizens had walked over and around his friend as he lay on the concrete, obviously in pain. At least half of them had been Georgia people. Andrew had almost as much trouble getting out of the Superdome as they had had getting in. He had felt like a salmon swimming upstream. Even when he had reached Whit's side and started screaming at people to stop and help it had done no good. The multitude was as relentless as ancient Romans must have been, fighting their way into the Coliseum to see another Christian thrown to the lions.

Andrew couldn't even get a policeman to listen to his plea. They had seen so many drunks in the past twenty-four hours that they were immune to worrying about one more. Whit was in so much pain that he couldn't speak coherently. All he could do was moan and hold his stomach. Andrew had finally remembered that they had parked in the parking lot of a big hospital. In desperation, he picked his friend up and threw him over his shoulders in the same fireman's carry Frank Reynolds had taught him in the Boy Scouts, many years earlier. As he bent over to hoist Whit up on his shoulders, the bottle of Jack Daniel's whiskey he had tucked away in his pants slipped out and crashed against the hard surface below, shattering the bottle.

"Shit," Andrew said. "Looks like our luck has made a turn for the worst, buddy boy. Hang on pal, you're going for a ride."

Andrew headed around the concourse in what he hoped was the

right direction. Soon he saw the huge hospital in the distance. He dodged people and cars and made his way back across four lanes of traffic, back underneath the expressway viaduct, and onto the steps at the front door of the emergency entrance of the Hotel Dieu, a Catholic hospital.

"Great," Andrew thought, as he paused to catch his breath. Looking through the glass door, he could see a group of nuns crowded around the television in the emergency room lobby. "We're playing Notre Dame across the street and now I show up at a Catholic hospital with my best friend across my shoulders. Everybody in this place is sending up prayers for the other guys." He had a sudden flashback to three weeks earlier and the emergency room of Leesdale General. He shuddered at the thought of running into a Cajun version of Nurse Bahlraccker. He took a deep breath and pushed the door open with his knee and stumbled into the room.

Andrew hadn't gone one step into the room before a nurse came running up to him, pushing a wheelchair. She helped him get Whit into the chair and began asking Andrew what was wrong.

Andrew couldn't help but stare at the woman. She was absolutely stunning. She was as tall as Andrew and as large, but there wasn't an ounce of fat on her body. She had blonde hair and gray eyes. She must have been about thirty years old. She looked like Andrew's idea of an Amazon queen. She was dressed in a traditional nurse's uniform from the soles of her white shoes to the top of her old-fashioned nurse's cap, and Andrew had never seen anyone look more beautiful in a uniform of servitude.

A sudden twinge of guilt overcame him as he remembered the circumstances in which he had come in contact with this gorgeous creature. He realized that she had asked him a question for the second time, and stammered as he tried to reply. "I. . . We . . . I mean . . ."

Nurse Amazon interrupted him. "Take it easy," she said, "and catch your breath. Now, there are some things we need to know so we can help your friend. Follow me." She was already pushing Whit past the front desk and through a set of double doors. Andrew followed close behind.

"He's got insurance," Andrew assured the nurse as he hurried to catch up with them. "And I know his address. At least it's on his drivers license in his wallet."

"We're not worried about that right now. Those weren't the kinds of things I was talking about," Nurse Amazon said over her shoulder. They were in a small room and two orderlies were lifting Whit out of the wheelchair. They lay him on his back and a second, more normal looking nurse, joined Nurse Amazon. She made herself busy taking Whit's pulse and blood pressure. Nurse Amazon turned her attention to Andrew.

"Has he taken any drugs?"

"None that I know of," Andrew answered. Then he realized what the nurse was really asking. "You mean illegal drugs? No way. This guy doesn't even drink. He was probably the only sober person in this city last night. Well, I mean I was too. But I didn't want to be; he did."

"Where does it hurt?" she asked, turning her attention back to Whit. He could only moan. He shook his head back and forth and rubbed his lower abdomen.

"His pulse and blood pressure are normal," said Nurse Number Two. "But he has a fever. Should I call for Dr. Boggus?"

Nurse Amazon nodded and turned again to Andrew. "How long has he complained about his stomach?" She had loosened Whit's belt and was probing at his stomach, causing Whit to wince sharply each time she put pressure on the wrong place. "My word," she said. "He's tight as a drum."

"He's been complaining off and on all week," Andrew offered. "Three weeks ago he had a bad spell, and I had to take him to the emergency room back home. They said it was just gas."

"Has he been throwing up?"

Andrew thought. "He might have yesterday, I can't remember. But I don't know if that would count. Hoss Mitchell was around and there were all those oysters and everything."

"Damn," Andrew thought to himself. "I sound like Bonnie Faith."

The nurse looked at him, a bit of bewilderment showing on her beautiful face, and went on to the next question.

"Has your friend ever had surgery before? I don't mean like a knee operation or his tonsils out. I mean where they would have made an incision on his stomach area. Well, here's a nice long scar." The nurse had pulled back Whit's shirt and answered her own question.

"That must be from when he was in a car wreck in the tenth grade," Andrew offered. "I don't know what they did, but he got to miss two weeks of school."

"Damn," Andrew said to himself again. "Now I'm talking like a stupid teenager. Ninety minutes from now and less than a thousand yards away Georgia's playing for the National Championship. I'm standing beside the most gorgeous woman I've ever seen. My best buddy could be dying for all I know, and all I can do is make comments that would make Bonnie Faith look like a rocket scientist next to me."

"Hello, Deena. What are we looking at?" Andrew turned toward the voice and saw a distinguished looking older man in a shirt and tie and white lab coat. He had a stethoscope around his neck, and Andrew assumed he was a doctor.

"Hi, Dr. Boggus." Nurse Amazon, who now had a first name, confirmed Andrew's assumption. "He has the classic symptoms of a bowel obstruction. Extreme tenderness in the lower abdomen. Very, very tight. Symptoms have come and gone over the past week. Had a severe attack three weeks ago. Small town emergency unit diagnosed it as gas. May have vomited at least once in the past twenty-four hours and now has a fever."

The doctor had been pressing and probing on Whit's stomach the entire time Nurse Deena was talking. Andrew looked at the clock on the wall above the examination table. "My word," he thought, "its only 12:15." It seemed like hours had passed since Erk Russell had given them the ticket. In reality it had only been a little more than thirty minutes. Thinking about the ticket, Andrew looked at Whit, trying to determine if the ticket Erk Russell had given him was still in his pocket. "Stupid jerk," he admonished himself. "You don't need to be thinking about a football game at a time like this." The doctor's voice brought him back to reality.

"Send for an NG tube," he instructed the nurse. Deena had already anticipated this order, and Nurse Number Two was back with the needed piece of equipment before Dr. Boggus had gotten the instructions out of his mouth. He smiled his thanks and then skillfully guided the rubber hose down Whit's throat, past his larynx, through his esophagus, and into his stomach. A fountain of green slime exploded from the tube, spraying both nurses and the doctor. After the initial eruption the nasty green colored gism continued to flow  until Nurse Deena had filled up two canisters and started on a third. Finally the stream slowed to a trickle and then stopped.

Andrew had turned ghost white when he saw the eruption and quickly sat down on a stool in the corner of the room and struggled to keep from throwing up himself.

The three medical professionals turned in unison to look at him. Then they looked at one another and laughed. They had forgotten he was even in the room. The doctor spoke to him first, genuine concern in his voice. "Were you at the game?" the doctor asked, nodding in the direction of Andrew's midsection.

Andrew followed the doctor's gaze and was mortified to see that he still had Terri Lynn's sign around his neck. He self-consciously took it off and slid it under the stool before answering. "Yes, sir," Andrew said. "I was actually in the stadium and then I couldn't find Whit and then I saw him outside on the ground. I tried to get help, but everyone just ignored us. I didn't know what to do, so I brought him over here."

"In a cab?" the doctor asked.

"On my back," was the matter of fact reply.

"Well, thanks to your being so responsible, your friend will be all right. Another twenty or thirty minutes, though, and it would have been a different story. He's lucky to have a friend like you looking out for him."

"What are you saying, Doc? Is something really bad wrong with him?" Like most young people, Andrew felt immortal, and figured his friends were, too.

"We'll have to run several tests to be sure, but I am fairly certain that your friend has a very serious condition known as a bowel obstruction. They are caused by scar tissue left from previous surgery. I believe your friend is suffering from two obstructions, one complete and one partial. The food keeps being digested, but has no place to go. The partial obstruction in the upper end has prevented him from vomiting all that stuff out. His intestines were stretched so thin that they were at the point of rupturing."

"What would have happened then?" Andrew asked.

"He would have probably bled to death before anyone could have gotten him medical treatment." The doctor made the statement as if he were describing the effect of an ingrown toenail.

Andrew shuddered and took a deep breath. "What now?" he asked the doctor.

"Well, there is no immediate danger now, because we have drained his stomach. The nurses will get him stabilized, and the lab will take about a million X-rays and and do a million and a half other tests. A female associate of mine will put on a rubber glove and place her finger up his rectum. In short, he's going to have a miserable time. It will take about three hours, but when the tests are all done, we'll know how to proceed. But don't worry about him. He couldn't be in better hands. And I happen to know that one of the nuns just loves Herschel Walker and is secretly pulling for Georgia. I'll get her to say a special prayer for your buddy.

"Meanwhile, I believe the front desk would appreciate some help from you in filling out your friend's admission papers. I need to write some orders and clean up this green mess your buddy spewed all over me. I believe we'll be done at about the same time, and you and I can walk across the highway and watch a football game. We ought to just about make kickoff."

Andrew's head was spinning. He was having a hard time comprehending all he was hearing. He fumbled around in his mind for words that wouldn't come. Finally he spoke. "I couldn't go to the game and leave Whit here like this."

"Nonsense," the doctor said. "He's better off than you. Wouldn't you like to have Deena take care of you for three or four hours?" He smiled at the very capable RN who was busy putting a hospital gown on Whit. The injection she had given him earlier had rendered him practically unconscious. "There's nothing you can do for him right now. You've saved his life today. You don't need to miss the game, too. And I'm not a Notre Dame fan, if that's what you're worried about. I graduated from Tulane. I hate the damn Yankees. Of course I can't let the good sisters know that."

Andrew took a deep breath, then thought of something else. "Well, unless there is still a ticket in Whit's shirt, I can't get in the game. I had already given them my ticket and gone in the dome."

"No ticket in his clothes," answered Nurse Deena. "Just these," she added, handing Andrew Whit's wallet and the keys to Terri Lynn's car as she rolled Whit out of the room and down the hall to begin his tests.

"No problem," said Dr. Boggus. "I have two tickets. I'd be honored to watch the game with such a responsible young man as yourself."

Andrew had never had the word responsible used to describe him in his entire life, and now this man had used it twice in one conversation. A thought hit him. "Why do you have an extra ticket? Everybody in town wants to go to this game."

The doctor let his gaze fall to the floor and a pained expression came over his face. "One of the tickets belonged to my dear wife, and she passed away; God rest her soul."

Andrew didn't know what to say. "I'm sorry," he finally responded, then another thought hit him. "No disrespect," he began, "but why didn't you invite one of your friends to go and use the ticket?"

"Couldn't," explained Dr. Boggus. "They're all at the funeral."

"No," Andrew said in disbelief. "You're not serious!"

"No," agreed Dr. Boggus, " but its a great line and I've waited years to use it. I never invite friends to the game when I'm on call. I never know if I'll get to go or not. Go fill out those forms and let's go watch Herschel."

Andrew didn't wait to be told again.

# Chapter Twenty-nine

After risking his life crossing Claiborne Avenue for the third time that day, Andrew entered the Superdome for the second time that day and followed Dr. Boggus to the best seats he'd had for a sporting event since he was fifteen and had sat alone in the press box of the Leesdale Little League field with Linda Lou Humphries on his lap. He couldn't believe his eyes. He was dead center on the fifty yard line. He looked at his ticket stub. Aisle 142: Row 34: Seat 34. "Thirty-four. Herschel's number. Its a sign," he said to the heavens. "Its got to be a sign."

Andrew and the good doctor settled into their seats just as a lady with a beautiful tenor voice finished singing the National Anthem. For once, Andrew was thankful for something Jimmy Carter had done. His presence had delayed the game long enough for Andrew to see the kickoff.

Andrew was in a daze. He couldn't believe that he was finally at the game. It had been years since he'd watched a Georgia game without benefit of alcohol. His mind kept drifting across Claiborne Avenue to the Hotel Dieu Hospital and his best friend. He felt like he wasn't a part of the crowd in the stadium. He saw the game through a fog, as if he were detached, somehow, from all those around him.

But he sat in the crowd of nearly eighty-thousand people, and he saw the game. He saw it all. He absorbed it. He let it soak into his psyche. He stored it away in his memory so he could call it up, in bits and pieces, time after time, for the rest of his life.

He saw Rex Robinson move forward for the opening kickoff and send a high, floating ball all the way to the Notre Dame end zone. He saw it hit the ground right between the two Notre Dame return men, and he saw one of them hurriedly down it for a touchback. He then saw the hated Irish drive to the Georgia thirty-three and kick a fifty yard field goal to take a 3-0 lead.

He saw Scott Woerner return the Notre Dame kickoff to the Georgia twenty-two. He saw Buck Belue give the ball to Herschel on the first play of the game for a two yard gain. Then he saw Herschel run around end for seven yards and get rolled out of bounds near the Georgia bench. To his horror, he saw Mike Cavan, a Georgia coach, and Warren Morris, the Georgia trainer, huddle around Herschel on the sideline as Carnie Norris ran onto the field to play tailback.

"My God," thought Andrew. "Our very first possession and Herschel's hurt."

He didn't take his eyes off the big back as the trainer led him over to the bench and removed his jersey and shoulder pads. Andrew longed for a radio so he could find out what was wrong. He caught himself wondering if Larry Munson were broadcasting the game. He saw the doctor working with Herschel's shoulder and once again his mind drifted across the street. He wondered what the medical staff there was doing to Whit, and he wondered if a Catholic nun would really say a prayer for a Bulldog fan.

To his great relief, Andrew saw Herschel run back onto the field the next time Georgia got the ball. He wouldn't know until the next day that Herschel played against Notre Dame and gained 150 yards after having separated his shoulder on his first carry of the day.

Andrew was hardly even aware of the people around him. He could have been the only person in the stadium, or he could have been somewhere watching on a giant three dimensional television set; he was that far removed from his surroundings. But he saw it all. He saw Notre Dame drive to the Georgia twenty-four and then line up to attempt another field goal. And he saw a freshman roverback named Terry Hoage, who would grow up to be an All American, rush through the center of the Notre Dame line to block the kick.

He saw Buck Belue give the ball to Herschel for seven, for seven again, for eight, for seven, for one and for one. Then he saw Buck Belue sacked for an eleven yard loss and Rex Robinson tie the game with a 46 yard field goal. It was still the first quarter. The giant clock read 3:33.

Andrew couldn't believe what he saw next. For the second time he saw two Notre Dame players watch Rex Robinson's kickoff float to the ground untouched. But this time Bob Kelly fell on the ball at the Notre Dame one, and two plays later Andrew saw Herschel Walker go up, up, up and over. He saw him land on his dislocated shoulder in the end zone to give Georgia the lead. Andrew saw it all.

He saw Chris Welton recover a fumble two minutes later, on the Notre Dame twenty-two. He then saw Herschel gain twelve yards, Buck seven, and Herschel three more for another touchdown.

At halftime he allowed himself to breathe. Georgia led 17-3. Buck Belue hadn't completed a pass. Georgia had scored all 17 of their points in a three minute spurt. Except for Herschel, Georgia had been held to minus yardage. Notre Dame had outgained the Dogs two to one. But the score was 17-3, and those were the only numbers that mattered.

As the two bands played during halftime, Andrew stretched and looked around him. He was surprised to learn that he was sitting right in front of two Notre Dame fans. They were a nicely dressed couple from the Midwest. The lady wore an expensive wool skirt and sweater combination, and the man wore a Notre Dame tie beneath his blue blazer. Andrew hadn't heard them cheer one time. Neither did he remember cheering, or talking to Dr. Boggus. He just remembered watching. He had never been so intense in his entire life. His stomach churned and his palms sweated; he could hardly stand the tension as the teams returned to the field after halftime.

The second half was more of the same, only worse. Notre Dame was driving relentlessly toward the Georgia goal line, but on fourth and one, from the Georgia thirteen, the Irish quarterback threw a pass into the end zone, which Scott Woerner intercepted.

Later in the quarter, the Irish did score. Mixing the run and the pass, they drove the ball fifty-seven yards and scored on a one yard plunge. The extra point made the score 17-10, and Andrew could hardly breathe.

But he continued to watch, and he saw it all.

He saw Greg Battle break through the line and barely get enough of his hand on a Notre Dame field goal attempt to make it go wide of the mark.

He saw Mike Fisher intercept a pass at the Notre Dame thirty-seven, to end an Irish drive before it could get started.

He saw Rex Robinson just miss a forty-eight yard field goal that could have given Georgia some sweet insurance.

He saw Buck Belue throw eleven straight incomplete passes, and he saw the Georgia quarterback being battered time after time by the Notre Dame defense. But he didn't see him throw an interception, or fumble, or make a bad hand off.

He saw Notre Dame take over at their own forty-three yard line with 5:10 left in the game and begin driving toward what could be the winning score. The Georgia crowd was as silent as death, or at least it seemed that way to Andrew. He watched the enemy pick up seven yards on the very

first play, and his heart was in his throat. He looked on the Georgia sideline. Vince Dooley was standing with his arms folded, watching. His head-
set had been discarded for the time being. Herschel Walker and Buck Belue
stood shoulder to shoulder on the sideline, helmets under their arms. Erk
Russell was kneeling. He looked like he might be praying.

For the first time that day, Andrew heard the Notre Dame fans
behind him. The man said, "Let's go Irish, we need a score."

Andrew turned and looked the distinguished looking man squarely
in the eye. "Go to hell Notre Dame, and go to hell Yankees," he said.

The man looked into Andrew's eyes and saw a look he had never
seen before. Without saying a word, he and his wife left their seats and
disappeared up the aisle.

Andrew turned his attention back to the field in time to see Eddie
Weaver sack the Notre Dame quarterback on second down. The Irish com-
pleted a six yard pass on third down, which made it fourth and one at the
Georgia 46.

Andrew's heart started pounding, and sweat began pouring from
his face. He looked toward the heavens, but all he saw was the expansive
ceiling of the Superdome. He thought about Whit and wondered what his
buddy was going through across the street. Strangely enough, he thought
of his father and wondered where he might be watching the game. He
thought about Larry Munson and wondered what he might be saying, if he
were saying anything at all. Then he looked back toward the field to see
what he must see.

What he saw was Scott Woerner intercepting a pass at the Georgia
thirty-four with 2:56 left between the Dogs and destiny. Andrew looked at
the sideline again. Erk Russell was still on one knee. Vince Dooley looked
as calm as ever. "Give the ball to Herschel," Andrew said, to no one in par-

ticular.

Buck Belue rolled to his right for six yards and ran out of bounds. "Stay in bounds, Buck," thought Andrew.

Buck handed the ball to Herschel, and Notre Dame pounded him. He might have gained a yard. Notre Dame called time out with 2:42 left.

"Give the ball to Herschel," Andrew said again.

Buck Belue kept it for a first down

Herschel carried twice for a total of three yards, and it was third and seven. Again Buck Belue rolled out. "Don't pass it," Andrew thought. But pass it Buck did, and Amp Arnold caught it for seven yards and a first down and Georgia had the ball and the lead and the clock and Notre Dame had only one time out.

The rest of the game was a blur to Andrew. There were too many emotions running through his mind and his heart to know exactly what happened. But he knew that Georgia kept the ball, and he knew that Notre Dame called their last time out with :37 showing on the clock, and he knew that when Buck Belue fell on the ball with fourteen seconds left that the Irish couldn't stop the clock again.

Andrew stood in a trance as the players lifted Vince Dooley to their shoulders and carried him to the center of the field. The floor of the Superdome was engulfed in a red sea as Georgia fans poured onto the playing surface in wave after wave. They screamed. They shouted. They pointed fingers toward the sky. They laughed. They cried. Total strangers hugged one another. They tore down both goalposts. They got down on all fours and barked like dogs. They would never forget this moment. Never.

Andrew stood at his seat and watched it all.

After a few moments, Dr. Boggus touched his arm. "Don't you want to go down there and celebrate?" he asked. He had to practically scream to be heard above the roar of the crowd.

The doctor's voice brought Andrew back to reality. "No sir," he said solemnly. "I want to go and see about Whit."

The doctor and the young man made their way out of the domed stadium and, yet again, Andrew made his way across four lanes of traffic on Claiborne Avenue and underneath the expressway viaduct.

# Chapter Thirty

Andrew's head was spinning as he sat in the second floor waiting room at the Hotel Dieu Hospital. Too much had happened in too short a time. He kept playing the events over and over in his head, trying to make sense of it all. In the space of five hours he had been given a ticket to the Sugar Bowl by Erk Russell, watched his best friend collapse on the pavement outside the Superdome, been refused help by literally thousands of people, carried his friend across four lanes of heavy traffic, and sat in a seat on the fifty yard line, with a total stranger, and watched Georgia win the National Championship of college football. "What next?" he thought.

While Andrew and Dr. Boggus were at the game the hospital staff had completed the long series of tests on Whit and assigned him to a room on the surgery floor. The nurses had instructed Andrew to wait while the doctor went over the results of the tests. He was more than happy to have a few moments of solitude to try and figure out exactly what had happened. He hadn't a clue what he should be doing.

"Andrew, Dr. Boggus is with your friend and would like to see you."

Andrew was startled by the voice and looked up to see Nurse Deena standing beside him. She looked as wonderful as she had the first time he saw her, several hours earlier.

"How is he?" Andrew asked, unable to turn away from the nurse's beautiful gray eyes. "Whit, I mean," Andrew added, wishing instantly that he hadn't.

Deena smiled at him. "He's coming around a little. We've had him pretty drugged up. He wants to know all about the game. We tried to tell him that Georgia won, but he says he won't believe it until he hears it from you. He's in 226. Come on down and see him."

Andrew followed the nurse down the hall. He couldn't get over her size. He couldn't understand how a woman could be as big as he was and yet look as good as she did. Midway down the hall, Nurse Deena made a right turn into the room, with Andrew practically on her heels. He was not prepared for what he saw.

Whit looked terrible. He was pale and had dark circles under his eyes. A clear plastic tube ran from his nose into some sort of bag, and ugly green slime was draining through the tube sporadically. He had an IV needle stuck in his arm, held in place by white tape. It was attached to another tube which was in turn attached to a bag of fluid, which was hanging from a metal post beside the bed.

Whit's eyes were glazed over, but they showed a little sign of a spark when Andrew walked into the room. He tried to speak, but the tube in his nose ran all the way down his throat, making it impossible for him to be understood.

Andrew pretended he knew exactly what Whit had said. He walked across the room to stand by Whit's bed and clapped him softly on the shoulder. "Yeah. How 'bout them Dawgs," he said. "We did it. We really did it. Herschel was incredible, and the defense kept bending and bending, but they never broke."

Whit tried valiantly to smile.

Finally, Dr. Boggus spoke. "Andrew," he said. "Whit's condition is just as I thought. The X-rays show that his bowel is completely obstructed in not one but two places. I can't emphasize how lucky he was that you got him here when you did. It's a miracle that his intestinal wall hadn't already ruptured."

Andrew looked at the doctor. He didn't think he had ever met a more genuine person and felt instinctively that he could trust anything that he had to say. "So what happens now?" Andrew asked.

"He needs surgery to clear the obstruction. The sooner the better. Two of my associates have examined him and looked at all the test results, and we all concur. He needs an operation."

Whit was still under the influence of very strong painkillers, but he was lucid enough to understand the implications of what the doctor was saying. He began making noises and shaking his head from side to side.

Andrew thought for a few minutes, not sure what questions to ask. "How long would he be laid up?" he finally asked.

"Eight days. Maybe ten," was the doctor's frank reply.

Whit began making guttural sounds, and Andrew let out a sharp breath. His eye's met Whit's, and he immediately understood the pleading he saw there. He tried to select his words as carefully as possible. "What about if I took him home?" Andrew asked. "Wouldn't he be all right until we got back to Georgia? I can make it in ten hours, easy."

The doctor's expression was kind, but his words were firm. "No chance, Andrew. It's too risky. Too many things could happen. I don't think you realize just how sick your friend is."

"Yes sir," Andrew answered. "I understand. I just don't think you understand how stubborn Whit is. He's a Linthead, you know. That's somebody who was raised up in a cotton mill village. His mama lives by herself in Leesdale, and she'd worry herself to death if Whit was to be out here in the hospital for a week or more. Does he have to give you his consent before you can operate?"

Now it was Dr. Boggus's turn to measure his words carefully. "That's a little bit of a gray area in this case. Since he is conscious and aware of the circumstances, I'd have to say that he probably does."

Andrew took another look at Whit. His eyes met Andrew's with a hard glare. Andrew had seen that look before. "Well, Doc," he said. "I'd say we'd better go to Plan B, 'cause I think we'd have a better chance of taking the Sugar Bowl trophy away from Freddie Gilbert than we have of getting Whit to agree to be operated on out here."

"Well, he can't drive to Georgia in his condition. The only other alternative I can think of is to put him on a flight to Atlanta and have an ambulance meet him there to take him to your local hospital. If you can give me the name of a good surgeon in your home town, I can call him and fill him in on Whit's condition and send our test results along with you. You will have to be responsible for getting him on a plane."

"There's that word," Andrew thought. It didn't seem nearly so repulsive anymore.

"Andrew," Dr. Boggus said. "There is one problem you might encounter. I can write you a release that will help get him on a flight, and we can give him a shot of morphine just before you leave the hospital. But we'll have to leave the drainage tube and the IV in. The airlines will require you to have an RN on board with him or they won't let him fly. I don't know where you'll find a nurse who wants to make a round trip flight to Atlanta on New Year's. My best advice is to talk Whit into having the operation here."

The wheels were spinning in Andrew's head. "I'll handle it," he told the doctor. "If you'll call Leesdale General Hospital in Leesdale, Georgia and ask them to put you in touch with Dr. Palmer, he'll know what needs to be done. I'll take care of everything else."

Andrew turned toward Nurse Deena and gave her his most charming smile. "May I talk to you for a moment— outside?" he asked.

The nurse returned his smile but immediately began to shake her head. "I'd love to help you," she said, "but I have a husband and a three year old at home. I work seven to seven, and they are both home waiting for my shift to end. They just wouldn't understand."

Andrew smiled even bigger. His teeth gleamed under his thick black mustache. "Just hear me out," Andrew asked politely.

Nurse Deena followed him into the hall as if drawn by a magnet.

Fifty minutes later, Andrew and Nurse Deena were pushing a very groggy Whit through the airport lobby in a wheelchair. Before they had shot Whit full of morphine, he had made Andrew know that under no circumstances was he to let Mary Johnson know what was happening until they were safely back in Leesdale.

Dr. Boggus had made all the arrangements with Dr. Palmer. The New Orleans physician had been surprised at how agreeable the Leesdale doctor was to having Andrew bring Whit back home. Dr. Boggus thought it was a bad plan, but he just didn't understand what being close to his loved ones would mean to Whit's recovery. Dr. Palmer did.

Andrew had called the airlines and found out that with a letter from the hospital certifying the medical emergency, he could get two one way fares for $320. By using Calvin's share of the trip money, he could buy two tickets and have five dollars left over. The airlines insisted that a nurse accompany the patient, but agreed to allow her to return to New Orleans for free.

The hardest thing he had done was call Terri Lynn and explain what had happened. He felt that someone at home needed to know. He just had to trust that his sister would be able to come up with an excuse for being out of the house that night, and that she could keep her mouth shut until everything was under control. Luckily, she had answered the phone when he called. Andrew didn't know what he would have done if his father had answered.

Andrew left all their luggage in the trunk of the Camaro. The only thing he carried was a small leather pouch that he had taken from the trunk. He still wore the same clothes he had put on that morning. It had turned colder as the sun went down, and the wind was blowing briskly. Andrew dug around in the trunk of the car until he found an old baseball cap to wear. He noticed that Deena had tied a scarf over her blonde hair. Whit was full of morphine and didn't notice anything.

The trio made their way through the crowded airport and found their gate just as the flight was beginning to board. Andrew stood behind the wheelchair and talked to Whit while Nurse Deena presented the two tickets and all the medical certifications that were necessary. Whit could have been on another planet and wouldn't have known it.

Finally, the gate attendant was satisfied that the paperwork was in order and motioned for the nurse to bring her patient onto the plane. Andrew flashed the lady at the gate a big smile. "My brother," he said. "Is it all right if I help get him situated?"

The tired gate attendant nodded, and Andrew pushed his buddy down the long corridor and onto the plane. He helped Whit's personal nurse make sure he was well situated and comfortable in his aisle seat. They fastened his seat belt, made sure the tube in his nose was draining properly, and propped him up with pillows.

Andrew turned to the stunning blonde and put one hand on her arm. "You're a real champ," he said to her.

She shocked him by giving his arm a squeeze and kissing him, squarely on the lips. It wasn't much of a kiss, but it was a kiss.

Andrew leaned forward, lifted up the scarf she had put on to keep her hair from being blown, and whispered something in her ear. She hesitated, then nodded. Andrew walked hurriedly to the bathroom in the rear of the plane. Deena stood and fussed over Whit for a couple of minutes and then walked quickly to the back of the plane as well. She looked around to make sure she was not noticed, then went into the same bathroom Andrew had gone into.

Three minutes later the flight attendants were making their way down the aisle of the plane, checking boarding passes before giving the word for the pilot to taxi away from the gate. They barely noticed the tall person in the khaki pants, red sweater, and baseball cap who walked hurriedly up the aisle and exited the plane. When they reached Whit's seat he was sound asleep, because of all the painkiller in his system. They assumed his caretaker was in the restroom and wished she would hurry up and take her place in the seat beside him. All the paraphernalia sticking in and out of the unfortunate young man made them nervous.

As the pilot backed the large jet away from the gate and prepared to taxi down the runway to takeoff position, the stewardesses made themselves busy preparing to give takeoff instructions. They were relieved to notice the nurse hurry up the aisle and step over her patient to take her seat beside the window. They were a little miffed when she covered her head with a pillow and seemed to go to sleep before the plane was even airborne. "So what?" they asked themselves, "as long as the patient stays knocked out."

Forty minutes later, after the Seat Belt signs had been extinguished and after the passengers no longer had to keep their trays and seats in an upright position, the flight attendants began serving the in-flight meal. Whit was still out cold, but the young girl who was having to work the holiday flight to Atlanta wondered if she should waken his nurse and ask if she were hungry. She leaned over the seat and was about to tap the nurse on her shoulder, but decided not to.

Sticking out from under the tight white skirt of the nurse's uniform and covered by sheer white hose were the two hairiest legs the young girl had ever seen on a woman.

# Chapter Thirty-one

The big plane glided to a smooth stop at Hartsfield International Airport in Atlanta, and the skillful pilot slowly maneuvered it up to the gate. It was nine o'clock in the evening and had been dark for hours. Most of the passengers ignored the requests of the flight attendants and began standing up in the aisle and removing carry-on bags from the overhead compartments while the plane was still moving. A few were Georgia fans, returning triumphantly from the Sugar Bowl. Most were weary travelers who had been spending the holiday with relatives and were eager to get home and get a good night's sleep.

A stewardess had leaned over Whit, who was still heavily sedated, and explained to his nurse that they would bring a wheelchair for the patient as soon as the plane emptied. The nurse just nodded, without turning around. Once all the other passengers were off the plane, the head stewardess rolled a wheelchair down the empty aisle and stopped beside Whit.

"We're all ready for you," said the flight attendant, completely puzzled by the attitude of the nurse. Her puzzlement turned to complete shock when Andrew Hawkins, dressed in Nurse Deena Amazon's best uniform, turned to face her. He gave her his best smile. There was a curious pale spot above his upper lip, as if the skin there had not been exposed to sunlight in years.

"Thanks," he said. He then stepped across his buddy's legs, picked him up bodily and situated him in the wheelchair. Then he straightened his skirt and rearranged his scarf before smiling once again at the openmouthed stewardess and, with as much dignity as he could muster, pushed his best friend up the aisle of the plane, out the door, and up the long ramp into the waiting area.

He was hoping that his sister would somehow be waiting for him, to show him where to find the ambulance that Dr. Palmer had promised would be on hand. As he stepped through the gate into the airport concourse, he stopped in his tracks. He absolutely couldn't believe his eyes. Lined up before him, side by side, stood Terri Lynn and his mother and his father. Whit's mother, Mary Johnson, sat waiting in a chair beside the ticket counter. Reverend Jackson, the Methodist preacher, stood beside her with his hand on her shoulder.

Andrew stood in his tracks, speechless. He didn't even consider how ridiculous he looked in the nurse's uniform he had borrowed from an angel of mercy he didn't even know. Terri Lynn shocked him by running up and throwing her arms around Whit, holding him close to her and stroking his hair.

His father shocked him even more. He came up to Andrew, threw his arms around him and  gave him a big hug. Tears were flowing down his cheeks. "I'm proud of you, son," he said, over and over.

"Dad, the car's still out there," was the first thing he thought of to say.

"It's all right, Andrew. I'll fly out and drive it back. No, we'll fly out together and bring it back."

A sudden thought hit Andrew, and he shot an accusing glance at his sister, who had stood up to give her brother a hug. She and her father both read Andrew's mind. Before she could speak, Harry Hawkins spoke up. "She didn't tell me a thing," he said.

"Then how did you know?" Andrew asked.

"The same way everybody in this family finds out things. I eavesdropped. I'd been hoping to hear from you all week, so when the phone rang I hurried to answer it. Terri Lynn beat me to it, but I stayed on the line and I heard the whole story. I talked to a very nice doctor in New Orleans who told me how responsibly you had acted. He said you saved Whit's life.

"The ambulance is waiting at the front of the terminal. Tommy Lee Martin is out there, too. Dr. Palmer is waiting at the hospital and he'll examine Whit. If he agrees with the doctors in New Orleans, they'll operate tonight."

Andrew looked at Mary Johnson who sat helplessly, her eyes full of tears. He pushed her son's chair over to her and knelt beside her. Tears began to run down his cheeks. "I'm sorry, Mrs. Johnson. I'm truly sorry," was all he knew to say. He saw her look down at his legs protruding out from under his white skirt. She was actually smiling through her tears.

"You done good, Andrew. You done real good. I'm so thankful my boy has a friend like you."

"Andrew," said Harry Hawkins sharply, as he noticed something about his son. "Where in the hell is your mustache?"

"In the lavatory of that plane," he answered, standing to face his father. "I was afraid I'd be found out before we got airborne if I came out of the bathroom with a mustache. I figured once we got in the air that they weren't going to turn us around and go back."

"Well, grow it back. You don't look like yourself," the former pilot said gruffly. Then he smiled and softly added, "Please."

Andrew looked at Terri Lynn, who was standing beside Whit's mother. He started to speak and then stopped.

Again Terri Lynn read his mind. "We talked about lots of stuff on the way up here," she said. She didn't need to say anything else.

Reverend Jackson hadn't said a word. He finally spoke up. "I believe we have an ambulance waiting. Perhaps we'd best be on our way."

Mary Johnson looked up at him with grateful eyes.

Andrew turned and for the first time saw Bonnie Faith Dimsdale standing behind his mother. "Hey, Bonnie Faith," he said.

She grinned at him. "Andrew Hawkins. What are you thinking about wearing a white skirt without a slip? Don't you know people can see right through that thing. When Terri Lynn called me at home and told me about Whit, I told Wayne I'd better come up here because you'd probably need some help. But I didn't know you'd show up looking like a drag queen. You might want to stop by the Harrison's trailer on your way home and see if their New Year's Eve party is still going on.

"By the way, Hoss Mitchell called me at the cafe this afternoon and wanted to know if I knew how to get in touch with y'all out there in New Orleans. He said something about not getting to make another phone call, but I didn't figure y'all would be studying Hoss, so I hung up."

The preacher held up a hand to stop Bonnie Faith's soliloquy. "I think we need to go," he said kindly.

Whit was slowly coming out of his stupor and had no idea where he was. He couldn't imagine why all these people were standing around, staring at him. His eyes finally focused enough to recognize his mother's face. He motioned for her to lean over, so he could tell her something.

Mary Johnson leaned over and held her ear close to her son's parched lips.

"How 'bout them Dawgs, Mama," he whispered.

# E p i l o g u e

March 10, 1981

Whit Johnson had had a wonderful twenty-second birthday. Harry and Ellen Hawkins had treated him and Terri Lynn to a steak dinner at the local country club. Afterward, they had stopped by his mother's house for coffee and birthday cake. His mother's fiance, Reverend Jackson of the Leesdale Methodist church was there, and the happy couple couldn't have been more excited about their upcoming wedding.

After the celebration at Mary Johnson's house, Terri Lynn had called her parents to let them know that she was going to Whit's trailer to watch *Saturday Night Live* and would be home a little later than usual.

Whit's operation had gone smoothly. He had indeed been confined to the hospital for ten days and then spent three weeks recuperating at his mother's house in the mill village. He wouldn't admit it, but it felt good to be back in his old room with his mother taking care of him and making a fuss over him. It did Mary Johnson a world of good, too.

The Methodist minister had been a regular visitor. He felt it his sacred duty to offer spiritual strength to the ill and downtrodden. He seemed to feel that they especially needed spiritual uplifting around supper time. By the time Whit had recovered enough to return home, the good Reverend was already in the habit of calling at supper time, so he just continued the practice. On Valentines Day he had proposed marriage to Mary, but she made him ask Whit for his blessings before she would say yes.

The Harrisons got back together and canceled their divorce proceedings. They moved to Waco, Texas along with Billy and Jennifer Jacobs. Rumor had it that they were living in some sort of commune, but Whit didn't believe it.

Wayne Dimsdale's back finally got well around the middle of February. Leon gave Bonnie Faith a week off and they drove to Gatlinburg. According to Bonnie Faith they didn't leave their cabin for the entire seven days. When they got back in town, Wayne had to ask for another week off from the saw mill to rest up.

Earl Dobbs left the Leesdale community and moved to Charlotte, North Carolina. He heard there was a great need for televangelism in that area. He also heard that it paid big bucks.

Calvin Clarke was very understanding about his money and had his uncle send Whit a football autographed by the entire Notre Dame football team. It was a nice gesture, anyway.

Hoss Mitchell had not been heard from since he called Bonnie Faith at the diner on New Year's Day. His parents thought about calling the New Orleans Police Department, but were afraid that they might help them locate Hoss, so they didn't.


Whit was sitting on the couch in the living room of his trailer. He had fallen asleep during a sketch with Steve Martin and Chevy Chase. Terri Lynn had also fallen asleep. She was stretched out on the couch with her head in Whit's lap. Suddenly the telephone woke them both up. Even the ring sounded drunk.

Whit reached over and picked up the receiver. "Is that you, Andrew?"

"Whit," came the voice on the other end. "We got to go."

Whit yawned. "Go where, Andrew?"

"Go where? To spring training of course. Hey, the Braves might be pretty good this year. That Dale Murphy is going to be a hot player. Think about it, Whit. We could be stretched out in the sun on West Palm Beach, with girls in tiny bikinis everywhere you look. We could drive over to Ft. Lauderdale for the wet T-shirt contest at the Candy Store. We can even take in a ballgame or two. The Braves play the New York Yankees three times this week."

Whit softly replaced the receiver in its cradle.

"Who was that?" Terri Lynn asked.

"Nobody," Whit answered. "Nobody at all."